W9-AFJ-041

05/24
STAND PRICE
$ 5.00

The Teller
of Tales

By the same author

Here We Go, Round The Mulberry Bush
The Other Half
The New London Spy
The Beatles
The Rise and Fall of Jake Sullivan
I Knew Daisy Smuten
A Very Loving Couple
Body Charge
The Glory Game
A Walk Along the Wall
George Stephenson
The Creighton Report
A Walk Around the Lakes
William Wordsworth
The Grades
Father's Day
A Walk Along the Tracks
Great Britain: A Celebration
Flossie Teacake's Fur Coat
A Walk Round London's Parks
The Good Guide to the Lakes
The Joy of Stamps
Back in the U.S.S.R.
Beatrix Potter's Lakeland
In Search of Columbus
Striker
Hunting People

THE TELLER OF TALES

In search of Robert Louis Stevenson

HUNTER DAVIES

*To Pucky and Tommy
with Literary Love —
Hunter Davies*

SINCLAIR-STEVENSON

For
Annabelle and Marion,
my Scottish sisters

First published in Great Britain in 1994
by Sinclair-Stevenson
an imprint of Reed Consumer Books Ltd
Michelin House, 81 Fulham Road, London SW3 6RB
and Auckland, Melbourne, Singapore and Toronto

Copyright © 1994 by Hunter Davies

The right of Hunter Davies to be identified as author
of this work has been asserted by him in accordance with the
Copyright, Designs and Patents Act 1988.

A CIP catalogue record for this book
is available at the British Library
ISBN 1 85619 263 6

Typeset by Falcon Graphic Art Ltd
Wallington, Surrey
Printed and bound in Great Britain
by Mackays of Chatham PLC

Contents

Acknowledgements

I would like to thank all the RLS enthusiasts, lay and professional, in Scotland, England, France, California, Hawaii, Fiji and Western Samoa, who have helped me so much over the last four years by making free their knowledge and material, and all those along the way who offered hospitality and comfort.

In particular: Lady Dunpark, Jenni Calder, John Mirylees, the Very Reverend Dr W.B. Johnston, Alistair Ferguson, Allen Rogers, Jim and Aurore Sibbet, Lady Stair's House Museum, Helen Lawson and Dr Iain Brown of the National Library of Scotland, Edinburgh; Ruth Popham of the Bournemouth Reference Library, Lawrence Popplewell, Garnet Langton; Ernest Mehew; Barbara Catchpole of Elegant Resorts, Chester; Peter Crangle in Monastier, André du Lac, Michel Eudes of Langogne, Abbaye Notre Dame des Neiges; Claude Gibelin of Hyères; Dr John Davies of San José, Jonathan Williams of Monterey State History Park, Rosemary Smith, Beth Atherton of the Silverado Museum, Dr Jack and Carolyn Fleming of Florida, Robert E. Van Dyke of Honolulu, Ellen Shaffer, Rex Maughan, Dan Wakefield and Jim Winegar; Martin Livingston of Vatulele; Western Samoa Visitors' Bureau, Chief Mataafa, Fuimaono Feretoi Tupua, Robert Barlow, Honorary British Consul, Apia, and Mataina Teo, Chief Librarian, Apia.

Introduction

It is hard to think of a writer more loved in his life-time and since his death than Robert Louis Stevenson, for both his prose and his personality. Then and now, people catch one sniff of him, the style of his writing, the romance of his life, and off they go, fans for ever. J.M. Barrie said that RLS were the best-beloved initials in recent literature. Inevitably, there have been a great many books about him. Why should I add another?

To celebrate, that's one reason: 1994 is the centenary of his death, so there will be many exhibitions and events marking his life and works and importance. We also know more about him today than when he died in 1894, about his relationship with his wife, and the woman he did not marry. His story is so rich that each decade we can dig into it anew, identify or wonder, seeing it from our own perspective. What I have also done is follow his trail, trying to catch glimpses of him by visiting places associated with him in the past.

This is hardly a new idea. Here, on my shelf of nearly 200 RLS-related books I have borrowed or bought in the last four years, is one by a certain Laura Stubbs called *Stevenson's Shrine*, published by De La More Press of Regent Street, London, in 1903. Slightly foxed, only fifty-eight pages, but some good photos – a snip, I thought, at £14. Laura Stubbs describes her RLS pilgrimage to Samoa, just eight years after his death. So, I am ninety years late in thinking of that angle, though she did only go to Samoa, not to the other sites. But here is a 1915 volume called *On the*

Trail of Stevenson, by an American, Clayton Hamilton, published in London and New York. Much bigger format, 145 pages, boring illustrations, can't see what I paid for it, as I've rubbed out the price to hide it from my wife, so probably too much. Hamilton did visit the sites in Edinburgh, England, Belgium and France – but not Samoa.

Since 1915, many other people have followed the same trail, taking in Samoa, the latest being Nicholas Rankin with *Dead Man's Chest* in 1987. Where my book is different, or so I like to think, is that I have not mixed the past and present together. To do so would have made the story complicated for readers who knew nothing about Stevenson as there is always a tendency to anticipate events which have not happened or books not yet written. I have strictly divided the past and present chapters, and tried never to jump ahead in either.

I have also, which I think is new, written the present-day chapters more informally – as 'Letters to Louis'. His own letters are so enticing, so intimate, so entertaining, so full of jokes, that when reading them you become convinced you are his special friend. So I decided to answer back, sending him little letters, telling him what had happened to the places he once knew. I cannot claim that the biographical chapters contain anything dramatically new, as I have tried to tell the story as simply as possible, though bringing it up to date as far as academic research goes, but in the present-day chapters there have been many developments, especially in Samoa, as you will discover.

A new collected edition of Stevenson's letters is due to begin publication in 1994. The editor is Ernest Mehew, a retired civil servant, living in Stanmore, Middlesex, who took over the job in 1969. He must have created some sort of record for delayed delivery, for it is only now, twenty-five years later, that the first volumes will appear. It has been a huge job. There will be eight volumes in all, coming out in the next few years, containing twice as many letters as Sidney Colvin's five-volume collection of 1924.

Once these are available, you can guess what will happen. There will be another rash of RLS books, with authors scurrying to produce the definitive life, containing all the known material, major and minor. My shelf will have to be enlarged, something I will undertake with pleasure. The life of Robert Louis Stevenson is one of endless fascination, however it is treated.

Hunter Davies
Loweswater, 1994

I

Childhood

1850–67

Robert Louis Stevenson was born Robert Lewis Balfour Stevenson on 13 November 1850 at 8 Howard Place, Edinburgh, Scotland. Note the spelling of his second Christian name. Only later did he style himself Louis, with its hint of bohemia, foreign parts, exotic connections – which is not to suggest he was trying to escape his family name, or names, for there are two families lurking there, both of which made him feel proud, made him feel grateful, even when he had distanced himself from everything they stood for.

Robert Stevenson – that part came from his grandfather, one of Scotland's most eminent engineers, a member of a dynasty which spanned five generations of lighthouse- and harbour-builders. In the middle sits Lewis Balfour, his grandfather on the other side, the Reverend Dr Balfour, Minister of the Church of Scotland. Distinguished men, on both sides, very Scottish, very Victorian, very worthy.

The Stevensons had originally been humble farmers, millers and maltsters, not in the Highlands, as RLS would have preferred, to give an extra romantic stir to the family pot, but in the more mundane Lowlands, in Renfrewshire, near Glasgow. Robert, his grandfather, born 1772, died 1850, just two months before the birth of RLS, built the Bell Rock lighthouse and many other lighthouses and beacons around the coast of Scotland. In 1814 he was accompanied on his annual tour of the Northern Lights by

Sir Walter Scott, collecting material for what became *The Pirate* and *The Lord of the Isles*. It is a nice literary connection. Scott found Robert Stevenson an agreeable companion and praised his scientific skills.

Thomas Stevenson, father of RLS, appears to have had some creative interests as a boy, writing and telling stories, but he quickly subjugated them, doing what his father Robert desired, nay commanded, and joined the family business, along with two of his brothers. He in turn became a consultant to the Commissioners of Northern Lights, built lighthouses and harbours, and is credited with developing the first revolving lights. He also produced several solid scientific works on various aspects of lighthouse construction and was interested in currents and stress.

A strange background for a writer, to be born into a family of engineers? Not really. Most authors have non-literary backgrounds. Thackeray's was military, the Brontës' clerical, Scott's legal, Hardy's agricultural, Dickens' menial. Engineers tend to be disciplined and hard-working. They make plans, fashion landscapes, create structures, not to mention all that worry about currents and stress and illumination.

The Balfours can be traced even further than the Stevensons, back to the fifteenth century, gentry almost all the way, producing many notable clerics, doctors and philosophers. They called themselves the Balfours of Pilrig – Balfour, like Stevenson, being a common Scottish name, not all who bear it being connected – after a mansion called Pilrig, set in its own estate between Leith and Edinburgh, which they bought in 1718. Margaret Isabella Balfour, RLS's mother, was the daughter of the Reverend Dr Balfour, Minister at Colinton, on the south side of Edinburgh. Her brother George became Physician in Ordinary to the Queen in Scotland; brother John was a doctor in the service of the East India Company and the last man out of Delhi when the Mutiny started; brother James went to New Zealand and became engineer to the Crown Colony. How pleasing, how interesting, to have so many distinguished relatives on both sides, but it means that a child born into such a formidable, enterprising family can hardly call himself a self-made man, rising from nowhere, unless of course he pursues a career where none of his kin has gone before.

Thomas Stevenson met Margaret Balfour on a train, so a family story runs, on a journey to Glasgow; they married in 1848 when he was thirty and she was nineteen. Just as well they genuflected to their own parents, and gave the paternal grandfathers their due and proper mentions in their first child's name, because they never went on to have another. Yet Thomas was one of thirteen children – eight of whom died young – and so was Margaret. They had a baby quickly enough, so why were there no more? Was it a bad birth, with a helpful doctor advising Stevenson to lay off and give his wife's health a chance? During her son's childhood, Margaret was always poorly, complaining of being weak and chesty, usually staying in bed till midday. Hard to believe it was a deliberate decision to have only one child, given the state of Victorian contraception, and those fecund Balfours and Stevensons, watching and waiting for another little engineer or doctor to prepare himself to run the Empire.

In the family legends, both oral and written, to which Maggie and her son both later contributed copiously, this subject is not mentioned, but then it would not have been in the late nineteenth century. We can only guess at the reasons, but the fact did have an important effect on RLS. He felt it, being an only child, imagining himself an intruder in his parents' life. 'The children of lovers are orphans,' he wrote later. He believed it contributed to his loneliness as a child, but then lonely children like to clutch at patterns on the wall and explanations on their counterpanes. People usually presume that an only child will be spoiled and cosseted, every little whim indulged. On the other hand, they can be so desperate to break free that they will try to escape emotionally and geographically at the first available opportunity. We shall see. We are all very clever these days at discovering in most childhoods suitable explanations for what happened afterwards. Especially when we know what happened afterwards.

Thomas, once a dreamer and low achiever at school, a practical joker as a young man, turned out a solid, God-fearing middle-aged man, a pillar of his profession, rising slowly but surely, but bothered with periods of deep depression. His son always tried hard to be fair to the two sides of his father's nature. 'He blended sternness and softness that was wholly Scottish and at first somewhat bewildering; with a profound essential melancholy of disposition and the most humorous geniality in company; shrewd and childish, passionately prejudiced, a man of many extremes, yet he was a wise adviser, had excellent taste, though whimsical and partial.'

He was traditional and unbending in his politics – which were staunchly Conservative – and in his religion, yet he deviated in many ways from the image of a stern Victorian father. He loved intellectual argument, on any subject, even religion, and encouraged it in his home and round his table. He thought dogs had souls, did not care for schoolteachers or formal education, believing you learned from life. He favoured a marriage law which would enable any woman to have a divorce for the asking, but not the man, on any grounds whatsoever: not exactly normal Victorian, or even modern, belief. He was a staunch churchgoer and published works in defence of Christianity, yet he refused to be an elder in the church, maintaining he was not worthy enough – without explaining why – though he served on several Church of Scotland committees. In his will, he left money to help fallen women. When Gladstone did something similar, tongues wagged. No such scandal ever touched Thomas Stevenson.

He was unlike his son in both physique and temperament. Louis – as he always called himself – had quite chubby cheeks in the early baby photographs, dressed in girls' clothes, but you can quickly see his arms and legs growing thin and weedy. Very soon his face appears to cave in, his chest and hips to disappear, leaving hardly any flesh on his bones. Thomas by comparison was broad-shouldered and heavy-chested. He spoke solemnly, slowly, gravely, whereas little Louis verged on the hysterical, words flooding from him as he danced around, getting over-excited and over-animated, full of nervous energy. Hyperactive, we would call him today, and no doubt very exhausting. Yet, during his childhood, Louis had a strong and loving relationship with his father. Louis would bound down the stairs when he heard Thomas coming home from work and loved listening to his stories, told solemnly and seriously, but usually with a droll punchline, easily missed. Louis once locked himself in a room, when very little, and began to panic. His father talked to him through the keyhole, calming him down with little stories, till

Louis became so taken with the stories he did not want the door to be unlocked.

Maggie, as she was always known, was an optimist, ever cheerful despite ill-health, just like her son. She was thin, but not as spidery as Louis became, well-dressed, with a good complexion, and considered very attractive. Louis was proud of her looks, compared with other mothers', when she picked him up from school. She was not quite as fragile as she often made out, and her health did surprisingly improve with age. Her father, when young, had also suffered from a 'weak chest and nerves' which necessitated long intervals in the Isle of Wight, but he lived to the grand old age of eighty-three. Maggie, when her son was young, usually managed to be up and about in the fore-noon, dropping in her card at the houses of other ladies of Edinburgh's New Town, arranging dinner parties, entertaining visitors, doing gentle charity work, lightly putting in her day. She kept a diary during her son's early years, in which she called him Smout, a Scottish term for a baby salmon. This was the name given to him by his father, who, on first seeing his son, remarked that 'he had never seen such a wee thing – he's just a smout'. In her diary, Louis's mother displays a nice turn of phrase and keen sense of humour; which was just as well since Louis was a worry, almost from the beginning. They feared for his life when he was two, running a fever and apparently wasting away. When he was three, he came to his mother and enquired anxiously, 'Do you think I'm looking very ill?' His mother also records his concern for horses and sheep because they did not know about God. He suggested they should have the Bible read to them. Another time he told her, 'Mamma, I have drawed a man. Shall I draw his soul now?'

These latter remarks would suggest the early influence of the dreaded Cummy, or the marvellous and wonderful Cummy, which was the accepted image of her. In old age, she turned into something of a legend, written about in books and memoirs, her diary later published, her face appearing on postcards, the saintly servant who saved a literary genius for the nation, all thanks to loving care, plus a generous dosage of God.

Alison Cunningham was twenty-nine when she took charge of the eighteen-month-old Louis at Howard Place, after a sequence of nurses who were less than suitable. Two left for no known reason; the third was found drinking in a pub with Louis, wrapped in a shawl, sleeping on the bar. This was not the sort of disgusting behaviour one would ever associate with Cummy. She came from a fishing village in Fife, the daughter of a weaver, well educated for her class, but then Scottish education was noted for providing for all, regardless of social background. She was experienced as a nanny and had previously worked with one of the family's Balfour relations. She was strong in limb and personality and devoted herself totally to little Louis's health and well-being, spending sleepless nights by his bedside when he was ill, cradling and cuddling him, singing and praying for him, reading him tales from the Bible or Bunyan. When she had saved him once again from the edge of darkness, she took him on long healthy walks, his body well wrapped up for fear of fevers and his head muffled to ease the earache from which he always seemed to suffer. She liked to take him to the Botanical Gardens, very near their Howard Place home, or to local cemeteries, such as Wariston, not perhaps the jolliest of excursions for a child with an over-rich imagination. 'My parents and Cummy brought me up on the Shorter Catechism, porridge and the Covenanters.'

The Catechisms meant rote learning, religious responses, which all good Scottish Presbyterians were taught. Cummy had read him the Bible, from start to finish, three times before he himself could read, according to her own memories, and he had his favourite bits which he insisted on hearing again. One of his favourite games was to play at being a minister, putting a paper collar round his neck and addressing an imaginary audience from an imaginary pulpit. Now and again he was allowed a break from a biblical diet. 'Why Cummy, it's daylight now; put away the Bible and reach for that new book of Ballantyne's.'

Cummy was strict and rigid in her religious beliefs, bigoted against Catholics, disliking all card games and theatres, considering it a sin to work or enjoy oneself on the Sabbath, yet she also had a taste for stirring adventure stories, especially about pirates, or smuggling on the coast of her home in Fife, or historical sagas about the Highlanders and the Covenanters. On Saturdays she would buy penny magazines, aimed at servant girls, about wicked baronets and true love, which she and Louis would enjoy together.

Lord Guthrie, who later wrote a memoir of Cummy, maintained that she did have a vivacious side, grabbing your arm to tell a good story, and even gesticulating – 'as the Scotch seldom do'. He was brave enough to ask her in old age why she had never married, mentioning a certain man to whom she was said to have been devotedly attached, turning him down because she had resolved not to leave Louis. 'Devoted to that man! Fiddlesticks.'

Cummy did not care for the pet name Smout, considering it more suitable for a dog. She preferred to call him Lou or My Laddie. When people approached them out walking and asked the little boy's name, Louis would often reply 'Smoutie', just to annoy. From around the age of three, before he could write, he was requesting her to sit down and take dictation. ' "I've got a story to tell, Cummy – you write it," he'd say. But he just havered.'

They obviously were good friends, and there is no doubt she nursed him through some terrible illnesses, when his own mother was unable or unwilling to stay up all night, or his father was away inspecting lighthouses. But Cummy also put the fear of the Devil into young Louis, not to mention Sin and other assorted evils. As he and Cummy listened down the stairs to his parents entertaining below, drinking and chatting or, oh horrors, playing cards, he did believe they would go to Hell, giving himself the sort of nightmares which he remembered for the rest of his life. 'I would not only lie awake to weep for Jesus, but I would fear to trust myself to slumber lest I was not accepted and should slip, ere I awoke, into eternal ruin.'

The strange thing about these nightmares, induced by Cummy and her religious rantings, fairly typical of the times though today we might consider them to be the result of indoctrination, was that Louis remembered them vividly – yet he never blamed Cummy. All his life, he was faithful in his affection, writing and remembering and thanking her for what she did. He later dedicated a book, *A Child's Garden of Verses*, to her: 'My second mother, my first wife/the angel of my infant life.' She did act like a mother, so that is understandable, but the 'first wife' phrase is intriguing. How could a little boy think of his nurse as a wife? Did any sort of intimacy take place? Is it an indication of the sort of wife he was looking for in life, to boss him around, but nurse him when he was ill?

Lord Guthrie's little memoir about Cummy, published thirty years after those children's poems appeared, offers a simpler explanation. It goes back to an incident on Edinburgh's Waverley Station when Louis was very young. He was waiting with Cummy to meet his parents arriving from London. 'On the platform was the auld minister of the Tron Kirk,' so Cummy remembered. 'He kent Lou and he says to him "Ye'll be thinking of marrying soon, Louis?" Says Lou with a very grave face, "I'm married already." "Oh," says the Minister, "who is the leddy?" "This is her," says Lou, pointing to me! Ever after that, the auld Minister used to ask Lou how he was gettin' on wi' his wife . . .'

So, the dedication was perhaps no more than a private joke, an old memory between them.

Louis's first known literary creation was religious, a biography of Moses, done when he was six. It was dictated, not to Cummy this time but to his mother, and was inspired by his Uncle David – his father's brother, one of the lighthouse engineers – who had offered a prize for the best essay on Moses written by any junior member of the family. Not so easy to win, when you think how broad the field was, with around twenty first cousins liable to compete. His mother insisted that every word had to be his own. She would simply write it all down. He told the story by acting, playing all the parts, and, when it was finished, he illustrated it with his own drawings. They showed the Israelites crossing the Red Sea carrying large portmanteaus and smoking enormous cigars. He did not win first prize, according to Lord Guthrie, but did get a consolation prize of a pound and a Bible picture book, according to his mother's memory.

In 1853, the family had moved from Howard Place to the nearby Inverleithen Road, to another dampish house, on the edges of the New Town. Four years later, when Louis was seven and Thomas was by now going up in the world, they moved to 17 Heriot Row, a much bigger, handsomer house, right in the heart of the New Town. That became the Stevenson family home from then on.

The New Town was not particularly new, even in those days,

the first broad Georgian squares and imposing crescents having been built towards the end of the eighteenth century. This was when the middle classes began to come down the hill from the Old Town clustered round the castle with its medieval wynds and closes and its ten-storey-high crowded tenements (the world's first skyscrapers, built long before New York was heard of, and for similar reasons – because space was limited). There had once been a loch where Princes Street gardens now stand, but this was filled and the flat lands behind laid out for the New Town, giving the professional classes proper air and space and modern amenities. It coincided with the end of the Old Town's golden age, which had been at its height in the eighteenth century, when Smollett lived on the Royal Mile, Oliver Goldsmith studied medicine at the University, Robert Burns arrived to become an idol of Scottish society, Sir Henry Raeburn was painting, Robert Adam and his brother were leading architects, David Hume was philosophising and Adam Smith being economical with his new truths.

After the creation of the New Town, the Old Town was neglected, allowed to become a slum, smelly, smoky (hence 'Old Reekie'), the haunt of criminals and prostitutes, though it did still have its professional elements, thanks to the law courts and the University. Nice people from the New Town, such as the Stevensons, did not go there after dark, unless they were up to no good, looking for drinking dens or fallen women. Everyone knew the gruesome Old Town tales, about people like Deacon Brodie, a respectable cabinet-maker by day but a burglar by night, or Burke and Hare, the body-snatchers, who stole corpses to be used for medical experiments.

By the time of Louis's birth in 1850, the New Town was solid and professional, the home of lawyers and bankers, not so rich in artists or scientists, though Sir James Simpson, the pioneer of chloroform, was still living round the corner from the Stevensons' new house in Heriot Row. Edinburgh's great names of the mid-nineteenth century, unlike their eighteenth-century predecessors, moved out just as quickly as they could. Alexander Graham Bell, born in Edinburgh a couple of years before RLS, attended Edinburgh University, but he had emigrated to Canada by the time he invented the telephone. The writers did much the same. A generation earlier, Walter Scott had stayed, yet still managed to turn himself into Britain's most popular author. Thomas Carlyle left the city in 1828 to make his name in London, returning temporarily in 1866 when he was made Lord Rector of the University. Then there were three writers, near-contemporaries of RLS, all born in 1859, who got out of Edinburgh so quickly that we never even think of them as Scottish. Kenneth Grahame, author of *The Wind in the Willows*, left Edinburgh in his infancy, so it is perhaps unfair to count him, but Arthur Conan Doyle, also born in Edinburgh, remained in his New Town home till he had qualified as a doctor, then fled south, complaining of the cold. He settled instead in Portsmouth. Annie S. Swan went to school and spent her early life in Edinburgh, then moved to London to write her immensely popular heart-rending novels.

Thanks to his bad health and possibly his father's rather cynical views on education, Louis did not start school till he was around six. He attended a couple of little local schools, one in Canonmills and one in India Street, before going to Edinburgh Academy, one of Edinburgh's leading schools, when he was eleven, enrolling with a couple of his cousins. He appears to have been an odd boy out at all these schools, picked on for his funny ways, his affected voice, his nervous, over-excited mannerisms, but then it must have been tough for an only child suddenly to be thrown in amongst the rough lads. His weak chest did not help. He was unable to take part in playground games or compete in team sports. In later life, when he had a bit of health, he preferred solo activities, like walking or canoeing.

The best times were in the long summer holidays, playing with his Balfour cousins, amongst people who knew him, at his grandfather's manse at Colinton. There he took the lead in inventing games in the overgrown garden, beside the mill or down by the river, the Water of Leith. His favourite cousin was Bob Stevenson, three years older, bright and clever, with whom he played complicated word games set in imaginary countries. The Colinton summers came to an end when Louis was ten, on the death of his grandfather. A new minister took over the manse and Louis's unmarried aunt moved away.

A few years later, his father took on the lease of a cottage at

Swanston, just south of Edinburgh, in the Pentland hills, which became their holiday home for many years. They also made excursions elsewhere in Scotland, and to England and Europe. Many of these trips were ostensibly for the sake of Mrs Stevenson's health – not Louis's – but it is remarkable how often, and for how long, Mr Stevenson himself managed to get away. It was a clear indication business was doing well that he could take such long vacations.

In 1863, they set off on 2 January, always a good time to leave Edinburgh, and did not return for five months, more a Grand Tour of the Continent than a mere family holiday. There were five in the party – Louis, his mother, his father, a girl cousin and Cummy. Her diary of the tour shows her continually being affronted by the behaviour of the natives. The first shock was in London where she witnessed vessels plying up and down the Thames – on a Sunday: 'How sad it is to see such things. How God's Holy name is dishonoured.' On the Continent, she was outraged by the sight of fat Roman Catholic clerics, eating and drinking, and, on one occasion, playing cards for money.

They travelled across France by a combination of trains and coaches and arrived in Menton, where they spent two months, then returned slowly through Italy, visiting Pisa, Naples, Rome and Florence. They crossed the Brenner Pass to Switzerland, followed the Rhine to Cologne, through Belgium and home. By this time, Cummy was desperate for a decent cup of tea. She did manage a few glasses of wine along the way, finding it quite acceptable, and helped to distribute some anti-Papal tracts. Louis left no diaries or letters of this long trip, but then he was only twelve, so we have to rely on Cummy's account, which is extremely boring, listing towns visited, churches inspected and mainly found wanting. She had to eat alone in hotels in the evening, sometimes with other servants, sometimes having to brush off unwelcome approaches from men. Louis added little drawings on some of her letters, but no words.

One of Louis's first known letters was written the following winter, in November 1863, from a little boarding school in London, kept by a Mr Wyatt at Spring Grove, Isleworth. It is quite a surprise, to find Louis at a boarding school, and in England, when his parents appeared to love him so dearly, but Mr Stevenson had taken his wife to Menton once again for the winter.

Perhaps they had decided not to upset Louis's education any more. There was another reason for taking him away from the Academy in Edinburgh, after only eighteen months. His Aunt Jane was by now living near the London school, having left Colinton, so he could board with her. Two of his cousins were already at the school.

This early letter, written from Spring Grove School on 12 November 1863, is in franglais, and must have amused his parents, except for its ending. 'Jai recu votre lettre Aujourdhui et comme le jour prochaine est mon jour de naisance je vous écrit ce letter. Je suis presque driven mad par une bruit terrible tous les garcons kik up comme grand un bruit qu'il possible. I hope you will find your house at Mentone nice. My dear papa, you told me to tell you whenever I was miserable. I do not feel well and I wish to get home. Do take me with you.'

So his father picked him up. Louis had only lasted one term at the London school, then it was back to Edinburgh. This time he was enrolled at what sounds like some sort of special school run by a Mr Thomson in Frederick Street, catering for lame ducks of the middle classes, for boys who had not managed to fit in elsewhere, either through ill-health or for other reasons. There was no homework and no nasty boys to annoy or tease him.

He still enjoyed long holidays away, going with his mother to Torquay in 1865 and 1866, and began to fantasise about travelling one day further afield. While he was on holiday in the Highlands, a drunken old woman read his fortune and told him he would be very happy, would visit America and 'be much upon the sea'. A few years later, a New Zealand friend of his father's came to the house and predicted that, with his weak chest, the place for him was not America but the South Seas. 'A certain Mr Seed, a prime minister or something in New Zealand; he spotted what my complaint was, told me that I had no business to stay in Europe, that I should find all I cared for in the Navigator Isles; sat up till four in the morning persuading me, demolishing my scruples. And I resisted. I refused to go so far from my father and mother . . .'

In 1866, Louis's first published work appeared. *The Pentland Rising* was a slim, sixteen-page pamphlet about a military engagement in Covenanting history which had occurred in 1666 near the

Stevensons' Swanston cottage. His father had encouraged Louis's historical research and paid for a hundred copies of the pamphlet to be printed. When it was finished, Thomas Stevenson decided he did not like the way Louis had written it and withdrew all copies from public sale, hence its rarity value.

All the same, the printing of the pamphlet is yet another example of the devotion and attention, love and money, which his parents lavished upon Louis, protecting him from some of the harsher facts of life. He had had expensive and exotic holidays, a change of schools when they didn't suit, a change of air when his health was bad, most of his passing interests indulged. No wonder so many fellow-pupils thought him spoiled and affected while his schoolmasters found it 'pleasanter to talk to him than to teach him', as his mother shrewdly observed.

In 1867, Louis enrolled at Edinburgh University, much to his parents' pleasure. It was probably partly due to their contacts, as Louis at seventeen does not appear to have passed many examinations. He intended to read Engineering.

2

Edinburgh Today

Dear Louis,

If I may be so bold. That was your name from university onwards, so I might as well use it now. The only thing wrong with Louis is that in my head I pronounce it the French way, forgetting you stressed the s on the end, as if it still were Lewis. I don't believe, by the way, that story some of your old friends put around that you changed it to please your father, who had a hatred for a nasty Edinburgh radical called Lewis and was worried people might think you were somehow related. I suspect it was one of the first things you did when you started university, trying Louis on for size along with your first velvet jacket.

Many books about you have called you 'RLS' all the way through, which is short and neat, but it does seem a bit impersonal, a bit abbreviated, as if we'd never met. Of course we haven't, but after these years on your trail one starts to presume a certain intimacy. All biographers suffer from this delusion, fooling themselves that they have acquired inside knowledge, if not a personal relationship. You must know the feeling. You did some biographical work. Like you, I never use my first Christian name, so I know how you must have felt when new teachers, at those endless schools, picked up your forms and said come out here, Robert, and you'd turn and look, wondering who this new boy was. I did like your franglais, by the way, and can't wait to start using your letters properly.

I'm writing these present-day letters because I thought it might interest and amuse you to hear what's been happening to some of the places you once knew so well. In your own witty, marvellous personal letters, you always gave such good descriptions to your friends back home of the places you'd seen. I won't try your more complicated jokes, such as having pretend characters as the authors of the letters, or reverting into Scottish dialect, but will simply attempt to pass on the atmosphere and flavour, plus a few facts, about familiar places and unfamiliar people. I'm sure you'll approve. Remember that time you were going to swap consciences with your friends? What a lark. Well, I'm swapping letters. I've read yours. Now here are some of mine.

Right, so off I went to Edinburgh, first stop Heriot Row. Yes, I know I should have taken it chronologically and gone first to Howard Place, but Heriot Row is the prime pilgrimage spot for all Stevensonians. As you know. Even in your life-time, the tourists were flocking there. I'd been told it was inhabited by Lord and Lady Dunpark, which I'm sure will please you, having not just the quality but the legal quality. From *Who's Who*, I gathered he was a Scottish Law Lord and she was Irish, formerly Kathleen Macfie, at one time a member of Edinburgh District Council. That would have pleased your father. I'd been told a story about Lady Dunpark waking up one morning, looking out of the window and seeing a group of people. Presuming it was yet more Stevensonians, come to worship outside her lovely house, she brought out some tea. Much to their amazement. They turned out to be left-wing demonstrators who just by chance had gathered outside, all ready to join an anti-poll tax march on Princes Street.

I'd rung her, out of the blue, which was bad form, as I should have written first, and she was frantically busy, house full of people, just got back from Ireland, not possible today, but she said she'd see me tomorrow. I went round all the same, to have a gape from the outside.

Heriot Row is very imposing, still the grandest terrace in the New Town, still with houses on one side only. Opposite is Queen Street Gardens, which are private, though a key can be rented. Several of the houses are now prestige offices, mainly legal, by the look of the name plates. At number 9, a brass plaque announces, 'Please do not ring unless an answer is required.' A hand-tooled command, not the sort you buy over the counter in Woolworths. It seems to set the tone for the whole row. Do please keep off, we are awfully superior.

Number 17 has a black front door and a couple of very tasteful, highly polished brass plaques. The one beside the front door says, 'This is a private house, not a museum.' At the foot of the steps, beside the iron railings, there is another gate, with a verse from your very own *The Lamplighter*: 'For we are very lucky with a lamp before the door. . . .' And there it is, a reproduction of the actual lamp which you could see being lit as a little boy, lying in bed. Shaped rather like a globe, painted black. You must remember it. Every house in the row has an identical lamp.

I arose bright and early next morning at my hotel nearby in Northumberland Street. Well, not quite a hotel, but high-class lodgings, very desirable, which you have to book up about a year ahead, very popular with Americans, and not just because the landlord, Jim Sibbett, plays the bagpipes at breakfast. Alas, just as I was about to leave for Heriot Row, I got a message from Lady Dunpark. Lord Dunpark was not well. She couldn't see me today. Some other time. Very sorry. Bad start. This could be a rather thin letter, my dear Louis.

I decided to try Howard Place instead, and an English voice this time, not Irish, gave me an appointment.

Your birthplace, Louis, is on a busy main road today, Inverleith Row, of which Howard Place is a part. The traffic roars past and, from the outside, number 8 looks rather humble and undistin-guished, just two storeys high, perhaps a labourer's cottage at one time, or a gardener's, provided for one of those working across the road in the Botanic Gardens. I was early, so I had a quick look round, and they are magnificent gardens – no wonder Cummy took you there so often – and, best of all, they are free. You don't pay a penny to explore the twenty-seven acres of beautifully tended grounds, or the vast Victorian hothouses.

The door at number 8 was opened by John Mirylees, a brisk, military gentleman, who led me into a surprisingly large entrance hall, decorated with an elaborate plaster of *The Massacre of the Innocents*, and thence into the main hall and the bottom of a stone staircase with black-and-gold-painted iron banisters, topped in mahogany. In fact the whole interior of the house was impressive, giving the lie to its unremarkable front. Your parents, Louis, had done quite well to have had this house as their first married home. Although it had appeared to possess only two storeys from the outside, there is a basement level, hardly seen from the road, leading out to the back garden, which gives the house three proper floors and a total of ten rooms. Two maids, plus Cummy, could easily sleep and work in the basement, leaving the family with ample space in the two floors above.

John's mother, Muriel Mirylees, who was English, moved into the house in 1926 as curator for the Robert Louis Stevenson Club, which had bought the house to use as a museum. She and her family lived in the basement, and upstairs was the museum. John remembers as a boy showing people round, one and sixpence a time, when his mother was busy. The house was filled with RLS furniture and mementoes, all of which later went to the Lady Stair Museum.

People at his school, Melville College, used to ask him if he was scared, living in a house that was a museum. 'They thought I must be seeing ghosts all the time. I explained it was RLS's birth house, not death house, and that I saw him as a kindly presence, a lovable spirit.' In 1963, when the collection moved, the house was put up for auction and his mother bought it for £4,000. 'At the time, it was worth half that, which is what the next door went for, but there was a Pole bidding against my mother who put the price up. He wanted to turn it into a gentlemen's club.'

His mother died in 1986, aged ninety-three, and John moved back into the house with his English wife, Jean. He is now retired, after twenty-one years in the army, ending as a major in the Royal Leicesters, then twenty-one years as a businessman, working for Metal Box. He has a keen interest in RLS, naturally enough, but his main passion in life is Roman Britain. What he really wanted to talk about was a book I once wrote about Hadrian's Wall. I could hardly remember any of it.

I'm sure you know the feeling, Louis. Writing any work of non-fiction is like an examination, only it lasts longer. You learn it all, over two years, or four years, live and breathe it, bore your nearest and dearest over every meal, then once it's safely between hard covers, offered to the public to give it a high mark, alpha plus, well done, or delta, must try harder, it goes completely from your mind.

There are no RLS objects left in the house, except for a drawing, signed Alex Wilson, which I did not recognise. It was given to John's mother as a present by a friend. I asked if I could see the birth room, if they knew which one it was. 'My mother told me it was this one,' said John, taking me to a first-floor room at the back of the house. Jean pointed out that it had a wooden fireplace, a sure sign of a bedroom. Living- and drawing-rooms had marble fireplaces. I looked out of the window over their neat walled garden, and beyond to a country lane, which they can enter from their own back gate. To the left were some playing fields. To the right, about a hundred yards away, hidden by houses, is the Water of Leith. They used to say that the New Town ended when you crossed the Water of Leith, so Howard Place was never socially or architecturally inside the New Town. Perhaps that was the real reason your parents did not stay long, not the alleged damp. Jean denied any hint of damp today, but then they have spent around £50,000 on the house, including rebuilding the basement, now let to students. On the open market, the house might fetch £175,000.

On the top floor is a large drawing-room, the nicest room in the house, with sanded floors, a large marble fireplace, ornate cornices and a central ceiling rose. It must have been strange, entertaining on the top floor. John thinks the room was even bigger in your day, going from front to back, but was later partitioned. No more changes can be made, as the house is now listed. I took back any remaining thoughts of this ever having been the abode of a humble gardener.

The Stevensons moved after only three years to a house just across the road, in Inverleith Terrace, a turning off Inverleith Row (number 1 at the time, but now number 9). It is slightly bigger, with an extra floor, and also higher, which John thinks must have been the main attraction. Given the choice, he would prefer it himself, as the house has better parking, being in a side road. Any day now, John expects the dreaded parking meters to arrive in Howard Place.

He took me on a little local walk, stopping on the way to point out the new front gate which Jean had got specially made when they finished the building work in the basement. It has the letters RLS intertwined, with a thistle below. I hadn't noticed it on the way in.

He led me to Canonmills, an even busier road, and stopped outside a Baptist church in a turning called Munro Place, to indicate a faded plaque on the wall. It stated that RLS had gone to a school on this site when he was aged seven in 1857. Mr Henderson's, presumably, but I didn't investigate further.

'Do you like RLS?' 'Oh yes, I think he was a really great chap, very kind,' said John, 'but he did have his vanity.' Such as? 'That painting of him by Sargent. He is rather admiring himself, don't you think.'

I was standing outside Colinton church, looking at the plaque on the wall explaining the Stevenson connections, when I heard American accents coming up the hill behind me. I looked round and saw a couple walking towards the church. The man was large and fleshy, wearing rather flashy wrap-around dark glasses, the sort which skiers use. More hick tourists, I thought, coming to peer at another Stevenson shrine. I got ready to give them the benefit of my knowledge and wisdom, plus an observation which had just come to me. This site is actually more rural now than it was a hundred years ago.

The church and manse and old heart of Colinton village are still hidden away in a dell, cut off from the main road, but the paper mills and snuff mills have long since gone, the ones which used to line the bank of the Water of Leith when Dr Balfour lived here. There are now no industrial signs at all. Everything is green and pretty, the houses neat and tidy, the little winding road over the bridge so quiet and empty that it is hard to believe that Princes Street is only five miles away.

'You've come on the Stevenson trail,' I said.

'Not really,' replied the American. 'I'm the minister.'

I looked at him in amazement. I had an appointment in an hour with Dr Johnston, Minister of Colinton, one of Scotland's most distinguished clerics. Surely this could not be he? Surely they would never let an American become Moderator of the Church of Scotland?

'Actually I'm the assistant minister,' he said, shaking my hand. 'Would you like me to show you around?'

The Reverend Terry Chapman and his wife are from Pasadena, California, over here for two years on some sort of exchange between Presbyterian churches. They find Colinton a bit quiet, compared with their Californian church, where they have to compete with scores of other churches and denominations.

He pointed out the churchyard's well-guarded gatehouse, built to keep an eye on any body-snatchers. I had been reading *The Body Snatcher* the night before, and been suitably horrified by it, but I half-believed that most of it was old Edinburgh legends, which you'd worked up into a penny-dreadful Christmas chiller.

'No, it was all true,' said Terry. 'Take a look at this.' He was pointing to what appeared to be a large metal coffin, a mort-safe, something I had never seen before, an antiquarian oddity, built to cover any freshly used grave. At one time, in the 1820s, Colinton church had six, which protected new graves for six weeks or so, till the bodies had passed their steal-by date, no longer fresh enough for medical students to practise on. I tried to move it, but failed. It was solid iron, weighing about a ton, and needed special hoists for the churchwardens to move it. They charged a rent for its use, for those who did not want their loved ones stolen, which brought in extra income for the church.

He then took me to the Balfour graves, in a special enclave, with memorials to Dr Balfour, Minister of Colinton for thirty-seven years, his wife Henrietta and their numerous children. There was Mackintosh, one of your uncles I had not heard of, who apparently became manager of the Bank of Bombay. I had heard of James, the civil engineer, the one who went to New Zealand, but I didn't know he had 'drowned by the upsetting of a boat in Timaru, New Zealand, 18th December, 1869'.

On the right-hand wall of the enclave is a new memorial to a more recent death, one of your descendants who died in a famous modern victory. 'Lt Cdr David Ian Balfour, RN, killed in action in HMS *Sheffield*, the Falklands, 1982.'

We then went into the Session House and he showed me

a photograph of Dr Balfour and some assorted memorabilia of the church, including a letter from Lord Cockburn to Dr Balfour in 1837, expressing his concern at the meagre appearance of the church tower, which he said was 'unworthy of the most beautiful site in the country'.

Dr Johnston, the minister, was waiting for me in the old manse, sitting in a pair of tracksuit trousers, as he had just returned from physiotherapy. Six months previously, he had suffered a stroke. For many weeks he was paralysed, but was now making a good recovery.

He came to Colinton in 1964 with his wife Ruth and their three children, then aged thirteen, eleven and six. Like the Balfour children, they loved the spacious lawns, the wild river-banks, the large trees and bushes for hiding in. It was in 1980 that he became Moderator, for one year only, and the following year he was appointed a Chaplain to the Queen. He has stayed at Balmoral three times, and been on picnics with the royal family.

He and Ruth graduated from Edinburgh University on the same day, but never met till years later in Germany, when he was an army chaplain and she a Wren. On the walls were mementoes of his year as Moderator, souvenirs from around the world, such as a Maori banner and an African painting. In the Balfour days, there were equally exotic items on the wall, gathered by the numerous cousins and uncles who went out to the colonies. (You mentioned somewhere that in your childhood there used to be the wing of an albatross on the wall at Colinton. I wonder what happened to that.)

The Balfours had two inside maids, a cook-housekeeper and a full-time gardener. The Johnstons have never had any help to run the ten-room house, except for a gardener who comes once a fortnight. Mrs Johnston much prefers golf to gardening.

She showed me the yew tree you wrote about. It is now so big, so extensive and so dense that it often provides ample cover for a whole church picnic, should they be forced off the lawn during a rain storm. Mrs Johnston recently filled in a survey and measured it for a Yew Tree Campaign. She then received a certificate, signed by the naturalist David Bellamy and the Archbishop of Canterbury, stating that it was 380 years old.

The Johnstons were due to retire soon, and had already bought a bungalow nearby, to make way for a new minister. Let's hope the Old Manse will soon ring to the sound of children once again. And their cousins.

Back in Edinburgh proper, I arranged a local walk with a real RLS expert, hoping to visit some of your other childhood haunts. You'd be surprised how many RLS experts there are. Jenni Calder has produced ten RLS books, including a well-reviewed biography which came out in 1980. In recent years, it has become her main writing activity, though she still has a day job, working for the National Museums of Scotland.

RLSing runs in her family, just as lighthouse engineering used to run in yours. Her father, David Daiches, the noted academic and author, wrote an RLS biography which came out in 1947. After Cambridge, Jenni did research at London University on George Orwell and Arthur Koestler, which became the subject of her first book, followed by a book on the American Wild West. She didn't want to write about RLS at first, considering it her father's preserve, but her publisher, Christopher Sinclair-Stevenson – no relation – suggested it.

'In the last ten years, interest in RLS has increased amazingly, all round the world,' she tells me. 'I have been twice to Italy to lecture on him. *Treasure Island* and *Dr Jekyll* have always been in print and always popular, but now he seems to have been rediscovered by the academics. I think one of the things which sparked it off was the fact that several European and South American writers revealed how much he had influenced them when they were young – such as Calvino and Borges. I suspect it was his style, not necessarily the content, which attracted them, but it's been enough for academics to look at RLS again, especially in Italy, Spain, France and North America. He is studied there much more than at home. I don't think he's studied to any extent in Scottish universities. Lip-service is of course paid to him as one of the three Scottish greats, but many of his books are now out of print.

'When he died, his reputation went into the doldrums, and some people dismissed his books, but his personality seemed to live on. People have always been charmed by him – the eternal, cheerful optimist. Not quite true, of course, but that's what his fans believe. People fell for him, alive or dead. They become possessive and see him as their property.'

We started off by walking up Calton Hill, right in the heart of Edinburgh, just a fifteen-minute stroll from Princes Street, a perfect distance for those who are not quite up to Arthur's Seat. So green and rural, satisfyingly steep, yet quickly climbed, with views which are immediate and spectacular, down over the city and beyond to the Firth of Forth. You used to love it, Louis. Today, it is very popular with lovers, hoping to hide away in its green dells, which have also made it very popular with muggers.

Calton Cemetery, one of the cemeteries you used to visit, is not what it was. It has been turned into a municipal parklet, the graves neat and tidy, the paths nicely gravelled, lawns well kept, no scope to frighten the life out of impressionable young minds. A notice at the entrance tells you which notables to look out for: David Hume, the philosopher, died 1776; Archibald Constable, the publisher, died 1827; William Blackwood, founder of *Blackwood's Magazine*, 1834. The first statue I came to was of Abraham Lincoln. How does he get mixed up with the Edinburgh worthies? Answer: a Scottish-American soldiers' organisation put up the money.

Then I fell over a leg, a living leg, sticking out from behind a gravestone. Attached was a body, prostrate on the ground. Nearby, another motionless being, this time draped at an awkward angle over a monument. Some of today's Edinburgh students, pulling the sort of stunt you once delighted in? No, members of a local photographic club, posing for each other.

We then set off for the Water of Leith, which runs through your childhood. The name always confused me, as I was never sure if it was a lake or a canal or what. It's a real river, which rises in the Pentland Hills and flows through Edinburgh to Leith. Hard to get at in places, so at first we had to be content with a road walk, along Warriston Road. The river below us did not look too appetising, with the usual urban effluents, nor did the buildings and little factories along Warriston Road, unless you were desperate for a B and Q supermarket or you had some urgent orders for Mackinnon and Hay, polythene bag manufacturers. Lady Haig's Poppy Factory looked a trifle more interesting.

At last, we got down to the river walk, well laid out, good surface and banks, and came to Warriston Cemetery, one of your favourite haunts. It was boarded up, with Keep Out notices, Private Property. I found a small hole at the bottom of a wire fence and said, Come on, Jenni, be brave, this is research. I know you're well known locally, with an official position, but let's chance it. I'll pay your fine.

Inside, it was totally overgrown and marvellously creepy, not just with possible ghosts, but possible security guards, ready for intruders or satanic worshippers, but we appeared to have the cemetery to ourselves, except for two pathetic supermarket trolleys. How had they been dragged in? Or were they about to be used, by some modern body-snatchers?

Most of the graves were hard to identify, as the lettering had faded and the fabric crumbled. I came across a Margaret Cunningham, died 1881, and wondered if she was related to Cummy. Why did she bring young Louis to places like this anyway?

'It suited her mentality. She did brood a lot. Louis liked cemeteries as well. It fitted his imagination, made him think about mortality.'

Jenni found a Superintendent of the Northern Lighthouses, died 1884, not a Stevenson but a James Young. Then I found something really good: the family grave and monument of Sir James Young Simpson, born 1811, died 1870, the developer of chloroform. With him, still lying there, I found his son, Walter Grindley Simpson, died 29 May 1898. Walter was one of your dearest friends from your student days. Thanks to you, he has a minor role in literature, which will last as long as you are remembered. On the death of his father in 1870, your young friend became a baronet, which amused you, judging by your jokey references in letters. Or was it showing off?

We eventually got to Leith and had lunch in a very smart waterside pub. You should see that area today, with tarted-up pubs, nicely painted old boats and twee shops. Edinburgh's Old Town has also been poshed up for the tourists, who have practically taken it over, and it is just as attractive and desirable as the New Town. But the divisions in Edinburgh are still there. The city's new housing estates, such as Pilton, have some of the worst figures for crime, drugs and Aids in all Europe. Would you, as a young man, have gone there for your amusement? Somehow I doubt it.

3

Student Days

1867–73

Louis entered Edinburgh University in 1867 to study to be an engineer. What he learned was Writing, Loving and Living, all of them self-taught. Such has been the course of many an otherwise good, well-brought-up student over the centuries.

He started with the best of intentions, aiming to please his father and qualify himself to join the family firm. He was ostensibly reading for a degree in Science, a rounded syllabus in those days, which in the first term or so included studying some Classics and Philosophy. He managed one lecture on Greek, then dropped it for Mathematics. He did some Latin, which he had always quite liked, and attended lectures for a few months, before replacing it with Civil Engineering. Most of these classes were compulsory, but he worked out various ruses to pretend he had been present, or persuaded friendly or gullible lecturers to sign the appropriate forms. He was not against Engineering as a profession at this stage. Just rather agnostic, let us say, allowing things to take their course, doing as little as possible, rolling along happily on the family conveyor belt which had been slipped underneath him so easily, so comfortably.

During the next three years, he went on several tours in his long summer vacations, getting work experience, as we would now call it, inspecting engineering works with his father, checking progress, making reports, which naturally pleased Thomas Stevenson. Louis himself greatly enjoyed these tours – at least the touring bit, sailing round the islands, going down in a diving suit, having little adventures, meeting new people, staying in hotels, all at the firm's or the nation's expense. He sailed on the yacht *Pharos*, as Walter Scott and his grandfather had done before him. Experiencing the work side was less agreeable. 'When I'm drawing, I find out something I have not measured, or having measured, have not noted, or having noted, cannot find.' On one occasion he had to write and ask his father how many pounds in a ton. So much for his Mathematics.

When stuck on his own in little hotels or lodging houses, he did a lot of reading and wrote copiously in his Engineering notebook – not on Engineering but endless verses of a very dreary poem called *Voces Fidelium* ('The Voices of the Faithful'). In lighter moods he sent funny letters back to his mother, describing people, observations, anecdotes. There is some gentle, affectionate teasing of his father, written in the knowledge that the latter would read the letters as well. 'It requires a little of the artistic temperament, of which Mr TS, CE [Tom Stevenson, Civil Engineer] possesses some, whatever he may say,' writes Louis, describing storm damage at the harbour in Wick. 'I can't look at it practically however: that will come, I suppose, like grey hairs and coffin nails.'

He met up with the well-known painter Sam Bough, had encounters with drunks and beggars, but also managed to dine and wine with the quality, such as Amy Sinclair, daughter of Sir Tollemache Sinclair, who invited him to visit her in London. 'She certainly was the simplest, most naive specimen of girlhood ever I saw.' Was this girl dragged in for his mother's sake? To keep her happy? Who knows? She is never mentioned again.

It has been suggested that he had had a passion for a country girl, daughter of some local farmer, whom he had met while staying in the country cottage at Swanston; this was supposedly the first romantic interlude in his life. His parents, so the story goes, strongly objected to the relationship. This rumour was put about later, and there are vague references in some of the poetry he was trying to write, but no details have ever emerged.

What mattered most in the early years of his university career was finding friends – male friends, soul-mates, bosom companions, kindred spirits, the sort he had never had in his schooldays.

He applied to join the Speculative Society, a student literary and debating club, very select, to which you had to be elected. There were only thirty members at any one time and they had their own premises, plus their own servant, in the middle of the old part of the university. They wore evening clothes for meetings, which were held by candlelight – one of their affectations, gas being considered rather modern and vulgar. Smoking was allowed, despite the fact that meetings took place on university premises, where it was not otherwise permitted.

Louis's family name and connections helped him to be elected, for the Spec was very much a middle- and upper-class institution for young gentlemen of good background with money behind them. Not many of those impoverished Scottish students, who came to Edinburgh from their Highland crofts with a bag of oatmeal to last them all term, ever graduated to the Spec.

The literary stuff he knew he could handle, as his reading was wide, his conversation rich and he had already written some poetry and other jottings, but, when it came to debating, he was a disaster. His maiden speech was greeted with silence, members snubbed him or sloped off to the pub, and he had to walk home on his own, feeling miserable and rejected. He was never a good public speaker, being too nervous and excitable, speaking too quickly and wildly, going off at tangents, becoming incoherent. After that first débâcle, however, things got much better and he enjoyed reading various essays and informal discussions round the fire, or at the Pump, as their favourite drinking premises – Rutherford's public house in Drummond Street – was called. In conversation he was always amusing and entertaining – some even considered him dazzling – and very soon he was one of the leading lights of the club, elected as one of the five rotating presidents. 'I do think that the Spec is about the only good thing in Edinburgh,' he wrote.

Sir Walter Scott had been a member of the Spec, as were Lord Jeffries and other notables, many of them lawyers. Charles Guthrie, a fellow member, later a Scottish law lord (and the author of the memoir of Cummy), remembered Louis being one of those who left at nine, after the evening debate was over, and went off to 'buy pencils'. This was a euphemism for visiting the Pump. Guthrie, being a teetotaller, managed to persuade the Spec's servant, known as 'Clues, our worthy old soldier servitor', to stop making 'his vile stuff, a weak concoction made of cheap coffee, dashed with cold milk' and instead produce decent French coffee, with hot milk: 'an elixir which brought down the Pencil trade to zero! Thereafter, Stevenson never left us.' So Guthrie improbably remembered, many years later.

It was at the Spec that Louis got to know Walter Simpson, son of Sir James Simpson; James Walter Ferrier, son of a St Andrews professor and grandson of the writer Christopher North; and Charles Baxter, son of an eminent lawyer, all of them the sort one would expect to find in this society. They were lively young bloods, fond of their drink, often too fond, as was the case with Ferrier. Baxter had a taste for slumming, as well as drink, and remained one of Louis's life-long intimate friends and the most regular and racy of his correspondents. Simpson was a bit older, had been to Cambridge and had returned to Edinburgh on the death of his father to read for the Bar. He had an eye for the women, was fond of practical jokes and ready for most adventures. One of his attractions was that he and his brothers and sisters were technically orphans, though old enough to live on their own, in a New Town house with their own servants. Louis deemed their house 'The Republic', a friendly haven when funds were low, and an ostensibly respectable one, as Louis's parents were never suspicious of anything that went on there. Eve Blantyre Simpson, Walter's younger sister, later wrote a lively if not exactly flattering book about Louis's Edinburgh days, recounting the more harmless of their exploits:

> Louis was an emotional youth, a bundle of nerves, whims and fancies. He never was glum. He might be in the depth of dejection, but it was such a magnified drooping of body and soul as to be farcical. His outlandishness of dress, his mannerisms, his frenchified flourishing of his hands and his transparent modes of attracting attention, used to come in for derisive condemnation. He had to endure a deal of taunting, but he never took offence.

There are many references to Louis's foreign, or Mediterranean, appearance, which pleased him, as he had no wish to look like an Edinburgh New Towner; and also to his feminine mannerisms. As we all know, real Scots do not go around flapping their hands or jumping about. The outlandish clothes were his trademark, making him recognisable all over Edinburgh, an unusual affectation for the time, judging by the many accounts of his appearance; though there was a Greek professor, Blackie, famous in his day, who also wore strange garments and talked to himself, but he sounds like a genuine eccentric. Louis was a poseur, no doubt about it, deliberately drawing attention to himself. At school, where the sporting hearties were the heroes, this had been hard to achieve, but with undergraduates values change: people said to be clever or arty, different or just weird, can be themselves, or anything they want to be, just as long as they can put up with cackles in the street from uncouth locals or jibes from fellow students.

Louis's velvet jacket was his best-known feature, but he also wore a cloak, grew his rather lank brown hair long and straggly and wore flannel shirts. Eve, a sensible-sounding girl, thought the cloak was silly:

> An overcoat, such as his friends sheltered beneath in winter,
> was what he ought to wear. The cloak was not suited for him
> of all people, delicate chested as he was. Such a cloak on a
> wind-swept city like Auld Reekie was dangerously draughty.

She didn't care for his soft flannel shirts, either, preferring the starched white cotton which most young gentlemen wore – she said Louis's never looked clean. In fact she considered that his outfit made him look more like a vagabond than a romantic poet, which was how he saw himself.

It is not quite clear exactly when Louis first put on his romantic vagabond clothes, but I suspect it is somehow connected with the return from Cambridge to Edinburgh in 1871 of his cousin Bob Stevenson. (Bob's father Alan, Thomas's partner, was a brilliant engineer in his youth, designer of the Skerryvore lighthouse, but suffered some sort of mental breakdown and died in 1865.) Bob was three years older than Louis, a man of the world, so he thought, who had inherited some family money and was now set on spending it all and becoming a painter, preferably in France, which was his passion in life. He was sparkling in conversation and ideas, even more so than Louis, and considered by one mutual friend as the Stevenson who might go furthest. Louis had loved him in their childhood and was now as a student clearly in awe of his cleverness and artistic inclinations. 'The mere return of Bob changed at once and for ever the course of my life . . . I was at last able to breathe.' With his brilliant cousin, or the amiable Baxter, as his boon companion, there were no mad notions Louis was not prepared to consider, no pranks he would refuse, and few experiences he did not want to have, if only for the experience.

Most of Louis's stunts and notions were harmless student wheezes, and amused even the reproachful Eve. She describes him experimenting on their family dog, who had a sweet tooth, filling him up with sugar cubes to find out if dogs could be satiated. She remembers him trying gambling, based on a biblical notion from his childhood at Cummy's knee that the Devil always favoured the first ventures of a gambler and let him win, thus trapping him. Louis put five pounds on a gaming table, and lost. 'He was utterly flabbergasted. Satan had made a mistake, if he thought he would ever get him to try his luck again.' Which seems to be true. Gambling was one vice Louis never managed, even for the experience.

One of their longest-running stunts was the creation of a character called John Libbel. This began when Bob, coming home from London, pawned his trousers at Crewe to pay his rail fare, giving the name John Libbel, for no apparent reason. He and Louis then tried to get all the Simpsons to go around Edinburgh with them, pawning objects, using the name of John Libbel. 'We said we did not want to pawn anything,' writes Eve, very serious. Louis and Bob were not deterred. They printed John Libbel calling cards, and flooded Edinburgh with them, leaving them at boarding houses, then calling back to ask for him. They sent messages to him, parcels for his collection, or parcels from him, with Mr Libbel's compliments. They wrote letters from him to leading citizens, harassed hotel staff for messages which were expected from him, tried but failed to put adverts in the *Scotsman* in his name, and walked the streets with clipboards, pretending they were agents searching for the heirs to the great Libbel family fortune. They planned a biography of John Libbel, now that his name was so well known throughout Edinburgh. They would come home, after a hard night drinking and fantasising, singing and shouting, clutching each other, convulsed by their own inventions. In one jeweller's shop, after fifteen minutes making the shopkeeper investigate some order for Mr Libbel, the jeweller looked up and recognised them. 'I know who you are – you're the two Stevensons!' And so they fled, guffawing.

It helped that they had money and family behind them, enabling them to print things like cards and stay out of any real trouble. Louis was on a small allowance, only half a crown a week when he became a student, but he lived at home and was allowed to run up bills at the shops his parents used. He was a spendthrift, when in funds, on himself or on his friends, but he was also fond of giving money to beggars. He once hired a beggar's rags for an hour, so that he could give himself the experience, however brief, of being a down-and-out. Not exactly necessary, as many people missed the point of the arty clothes he normally wore and assumed he was indeed impoverished. The Simpsons took him to visit an uncle of theirs in the country who was convinced that the emaciated Louis – five feet ten inches high but only eight stone six pounds in his early twenties – was an impecunious student of foreign extraction who had to be filled up at every meal.

Louis and Bob considered themselves serious intellectuals, despite the sixth-form antics, true Bohemians in their beliefs as well as in their dress and behaviour. Edinburgh to them was boring, dreary and grey. They were against the New Town's bourgeois values, hated people like merchants and bankers, and despised the hypocrisy of so-called solid citizens. They wanted to live life to the full, experience the underworld, mix with all classes. 'Louis did not hesitate to go into all sorts and conditions of mischief,' writes Eve, ' "to see what it was like".'

When did Louis lose his virginity? Quite quickly, according to his own hints, and eventually outright boasts. With Bob he made a point of frequenting the most disreputable Old Town and Lothian Road drinking dens, the howfs and shebeens, and consorting with prostitutes. Where else could he go for sexual experience? Nice girls, of his own class and kind, did not give way to their own desires or allow such favours before marriage. Most nice boys, brought up in the fear of God and guilt and respectability, managed to subjugate their physical longings until marriage, but a great many of the more daring or randy chaps gave in, looking upon the occasional harlot as part of growing up, a known and acceptable stage in their journey towards manhood. These things were, of course, rarely written about, not even in letters of the period, and in Calvinistic Scotland people tried hard to pretend that such places and such women did not exist. You have to know the codes, the allusions, the whistles in the dark, the smile from a window, working out the slang, the sexual references, and spotting a touch of the clap even before the participator has realised. Louis was unusual in that he made open references in his letters to his sexual activities. 'I have been all my days a dead hand at a harridan, I never saw one yet that could resist me.'

A peculiar boast. Surely it was the feel of his money she could not resist, not his puny body. This was another unusual thing about young Louis. He did not feel guilt, despite all those years with Cummy. He liked to think he befriended the women of the street whom he had used, not ill-treating or dismissing them as others might do. He considered they were more honest than the New Town bankers in that they did not hide their immoral habits behind false façades. Writing about one whom he called Mary H., he described her as a 'robust great haunched blue eyed young woman of admirable temper, and, if you will let me say so of a common prostitute, extraordinary modesty'. Meeting her in the street he was a bit disappointed that she did not acknowledge him, thinking 'of me otherwise than in the way of business'. He met her again, some years later, when she was emigrating to the USA, and this time she did speak to him. Louis shook 'her good honest loving hand as we said goodbye'.

There are tales, still current in Edinburgh, that he had a proper love affair with one woman of the street called Kate Drummond, and had a child by a servant woman. No convincing evidence for either tale has ever been offered, though in the 1920s someone did come forward and maintain he was Stevenson's illegitimate son.

There was a more serious suggestion a few years later that one of the women from his past was about to blackmail him, which obviously worried him, so we have to believe some of the stories about his early sexual adventures. But how much of a rake was he? How far did he sink? He clearly enjoyed being

with the prostitutes and semi-criminal class, for the atmosphere
and excitement, boasting about having to 'keep moving for fear
of the police and magistrates'. Was he perhaps exaggerating his
closeness to them, the frequency with which he consorted and
cavorted with them? Did he do more than any of the other young
bucks from the Spec?

His suggestion of criminal activity is a bit laughable, as his
only known illegal act was to take part in a snowball fight in
1870, town against gown, a traditional sport, not exactly heinous,
though he was arrested and marched by the police over the bridge
from the Old Town, acclaimed a hero by his watching friends. He
was then bound over to keep the peace.

His more straitlaced contemporaries did think he was mixing
with the wrong sort and doing himself harm. Looking back at their
student days, Guthrie describes Louis's 'exaggerated contempt for
many of the restraints of polite society, his indiscriminating thirst
for novelty, his fondness for the bizarre and the gruesome, the
grotesque and the uncanny, his relish of rough jests, his tolerance
of Rabelaisian and strong language, his curious liking for queer
company. . . .' Guthrie, of course, believed that he was really a
Puritan in fancy dress.

Eve Simpson describes an interesting scene when some of Louis's
friends were teasing him about the 'falseness' of the poems and articles he was producing. 'Some of his boon companions lamented that
he was somewhat of a cowardly humbug, for he judiciously kept his
Jekyll reputation so much before the innocent public that the Hyde
in him, which they knew, was never suspected.' They challenged
him to write a 'doubtful' plot, saying they could do better. 'Louis
avoided their company for weeks and laboured sedulously at a
novel which would out-Herod Herod. He laid it before them and
they were startled with its strength, its terribleness, its outrageous
blackness of human depravity. The efforts of Louis's companions
were schoolgirl reading by comparison.'

What happened to this book? Eve says that the manuscript was
kept by one of his life-long friends who 'had it bound as the History
of Peru'. Perhaps all his explorations into Edinburgh's seamy side
were really a search not just for excitement but for copy.

In some of his private letters, especially to his friend Baxter, his language is decidedly racy and rude, and these were naturally not published in the official collection of his correspondence after his death. He mentions some enemy whose testicles he would like to grab, a friend who had given up drink, which made him think he would take up buggery, and, in cursing someone, he wishes that he would 'wallow in the underclothes of shopgirls'.

In his 'public' writings, such as they were at this time, in four editions of a student magazine he helped to edit, and his addresses to the Spec, his language is serious and grave, on such subjects as capital punishment, or light-hearted, as on the philosophy of umbrellas. He was writing from the moment he started at Edinburgh, poems, short travel articles and essays, mostly for himself, not published at the time and many now lost.

Despite the image he liked to encourage that he was an out-and-out Bohemian, living a dissolute life, spending long evenings with loose women, drunks and beggars, he always managed to get home to Heriot Row. Usually for dinner. Then into his own little bed. There are also no known rows with his parents about his personal behaviour – which one would have expected, if he had gone off the rails. He was an only child, so it was hard for him to hide, and there were enough relations and family friends who would quickly have reported him, if he had finally overstepped the bounds of accepted behaviour.

One of the restraining elements in Louis's life was a friendship with an older couple, Anne and Fleeming Jenkin. Mrs Jenkin was having tea with Louis's mother one day at Heriot Row and by chance she heard Louis talking. She decided his conversation was brilliant and went home and told her husband that Louis was like 'the young Heinrich Heine with a Scottish accent'. In his velvet jacket he was supposed to look like a Parisian artist, not a German Jewish poet who had died twelve years earlier, but it was a flattering description all the same. Anne Jenkin was in her mid-thirties, very attractive and cultured. She gave little theatrical parties at her home, part of which had been transformed into a theatre, mainly classical plays, for which her husband stage-managed and did the costumes. He happened to be Professor of Engineering at the university at the time of the Heriot Row meeting, some time in 1868. Louis joined his classes in 1869. Fleeming (pronounced Fleming)

Jenkin was an interesting study, a pioneer of electrification, a scientist who had argued against Charles Darwin, a first-class ice skater, dancer and actor.

Young Louis was invited to join the Jenkins's salon and was given a part in one of their Shakespearian productions. He proved to be a terrible actor, but a positive adornment when it came to champagne and bright, cultured conversation afterwards. He seems to have hero-worshipped Fleeming Jenkin, and probably fancied Anne, but they both kept him in his place, nicely, treating him like a son to whom they could speak honestly and wisely, and he remained firm friends with them for the rest of their lives.

Thomas Stevenson was pleased with this relationship, with people he knew and respected, one of whom was an engineer like himself and made a pleasant change from some of Louis's younger and less desirable friends.

What a surprise, therefore, and what a shock, when in the winter of 1870, after over three years' studying to be an engineer, Louis announced he was giving it all up. Two weeks earlier he had won a prize for a paper on 'A New Form of Intermittent Light for Lighthouses', which thrilled and reassured his parents, even though the title would suggest his papa had helped him somewhat with his homework. Louis recalled a 'dreadful evening walk' to Cramond with his father, during which he told him his decision. There was a heated discussion – his father was very upset – but no open bitter row. Perhaps, deep down, his father had seen the decision coming and had already resigned himself. Louis had shown little talent for engineering, no interest, no will to make a go of it.

Then came the next problem. What are you going to do now? What else can you do? You need to have a qualification, some sort of career path to follow. It's all very well saying you want to be a writer, it's the only thing you like doing, we all know that, but it's not a proper job, you won't earn a living that way, my lad. Best to get something behind you. When you're established, then you can amuse yourself in your free time at your so-called writings. In the meantime, you must learn something. Age-old arguments. Age-old solution.

It was agreed that Louis would change to another course, train for another profession. He would read law and become a solicitor, thus at least he would end up with letters after his name. Not CE, alas, but perhaps WS, meaning Writer to the Signet, a very superior form of Scottish lawyer.

Louis agreed. After all, his allowance would continue, his student days would be prolonged, he could still indulge himself in his various Bohemian pursuits and continue his attempts at writing, without having to work too arduously. Law might turn out to be more interesting or amusing for him than Engineering, so his parents imagined. And so he hoped. 'At college we did not look for Louis at law lectures,' wrote Guthrie, whom he now joined in the law faculty, 'except when the weather was bad.'

One of the most attractive things about Louis, which endeared him to his friends and was admitted even by those who thought him spoiled and a poseur, was that he was young in his youth. His own expression. But would he ever grow up?

4

Heriot Row

Dear Louis,

I did it. I got into Heriot Row. After twice having to cancel me, because of the illness of her husband, Lady Dunpark gave me a definite date. At last, I would get to see your family home.

On the way there, I realised I was walking down Queen Street, where your friend Walter Simpson once lived, on the other side of Queen Street Gardens to Heriot Row. I was early, so I thought I'd have a quick look at number 72. A plaque outside said, 'The home of Sir James Young Simpson from 1845–1870, the Discoverer of the Anaesthetic Power of Chloroform'.

It is now called Simpson House and belongs to the Church of Scotland, not apparently open to the public, but I pressed a bell all the same. A receptionist said they were a counselling centre, helping people with drug, alcohol, marital or sexual problems. A woman counsellor came down the stairs as I was explaining my search and invited me to look at the Discovery Room, a large room on the first floor, totally Victorian, with a huge mahogany dining table and dusty prints on the wall.

It was in this room, on 4 November 1847, that James Simpson gave a supper party for several of his friends and relations. At the end of the meal, he passed round a brandy decanter and each guest was given a glass and asked to sniff it. A few moments later, they passed out and slid under the table. They had all inhaled chloroform in the first 'public' trial of its powers.

Simpson's use of chloroform in childbirth was fiercely attacked by male doctors, who said it flew in the face of nature, until Queen Victoria gave it the seal of approval by using it during the birth of one of her children. Simpson was made a baronet in 1866. On his death, his widow refused the offer of burial in Westminster Abbey, preferring Warriston Cemetery, and his oldest son became Sir Walter. As you know.

Walter used to say he could see your room diagonally across Queen Street Gardens, but this must have been in winter. It was now summer, the trees all out, and Heriot Row was obscured as I walked towards it, round the Gardens.

Lady Dunpark was not at home when I arrived at number 17, and I was shown in by a friend. But she appeared a few moments later, rolling up in a battered Audi, parking it awkwardly outside. She dashed into the house, wearing a khaki-coloured army-style battle jacket as if she'd been on combat exercises. Aged about sixty, bouncy, ebullient, with a lilting Irish accent.

'You could not have chosen a worse day,' she beamed as she led me into the drawing-room, taking me by the hand and clutching it tightly, which I always find alarming. One never quite knows how to adjust one's expressions.

I could see that she too was having problems, such as who was I, what was my name? I suspected she had completely forgotten about my arrival. Why I had come was probably clear enough, as she has a continual stream of visitors on the RLS trail. The house is not open to the public, but she welcomes any RLS enthusiasts, as long as they make an appointment. She sees herself as a custodian of the Stevenson legend, with the self-imposed duty to keep the house as a family home, in the spirit in which the Stevensons kept it, not allowing it to become either a dusty museum or a flashy set of executive offices.

'Now, Trevor,' she said, still holding me tight, 'I have just so much to do this morning, two places I've got to go to, then I've a dear friend coming to lunch, how long have you got exactly, I'll tell you what, Marie will give you some coffee, and you could stay here, look round the house? Hmm? I won't be long,' she said, smiling. 'I don't think. . . .'

I wanted to be taken round by her, the person who knew

the house. I feared she might waltz off, trying to fit in too
many things, and not return for ages. So I offered to come with
her. Perhaps I could carry her things, park the car, as she didn't
seem all that gifted at car-parking.

'Aren't you lovely,' she said. She took me by the arm this
time, out of the door, and whisked me into her car. 'Nothing has
changed in Edinburgh since Stevenson's time,' she said, waving
airily out of the car window. 'A hundred years is but a twinkling
of an eye.'

As we went down Hanover Street, crossing George Street,
she suddenly started peeping the horn and blowing kisses out of
the window. A rather deprived-looking old man on the pavement
corner turned to stare angrily at the car making all the noise, then
he smiled, waved and blew kisses back. Who's that? I asked. 'My
kissing pal,' she said.

I turned back and could see that the old man was a newspaper-
seller, with a bundle of papers under his arm.

'I don't know his name, but we've known him twenty-five
years. He used to sell papers outside the law courts, and when
my husband Alistair was going in to judge some big trial he would
stop him and say, "Now, Alistair, you're not going to hang anyone
today, are you?" '

We went up into the Old Town, heading for the law courts, to the
Signet Library, where she was to meet officials to discuss a National
Trust for Scotland dinner for sixty people. While I waited for her,
she suggested I should walk round Parliament Square and look in
some of the legal buildings. Not very exciting, I thought, till I
remembered that you, Louis, did your legal training here. I had
never realised how magnificent these buildings were, architecturally
richer than the Inns of Courts in London, with ornate ceilings,
elegant staircases, fine paintings.

I wandered into the seventeenth-century Parliament Hall, about
the size of a football pitch, with a huge stained-glass window at
one end, a carved wooden ceiling and walls hung with paintings of
legal worthies, many of them by Raeburn. The floor was wooden
and totally bare, without furniture or seats, which seemed strange
at first, an empty space, surrounded on all sides by such riches.
What could it be used for? From one end I saw two lawyers in

wigs and gowns emerge from a hidden door, walking slowly, side by side, deep in legal talk. Without breaking stride or pausing in their conversation, they got to the far end, did a semi-military turn, marking time with their feet, then progressed back across the enormous wooden floor, still talking. Then other legal men and women came out of side doors, all in their finery, and from a hundred feet away I could feel the floor vibrating, as if I was on the deck of a sailing ship, being rocked by their movement. At appointed moments, they disappeared, off to some unseen court to offer evidence or argue legal niceties, to be replaced by others, entering in full flow, sent on their way by some hidden stage manager, to play their part, walk their appointed route, deliver their lines, then exit.

Did you do all this, when learning about the law, Louis? The weediest young man looked so splendid in his gown, so impressive in this setting, so right and proper, while I, in my street clothes and trainers, seemed a mere interloper. Even their accents, though they could never quite compete with Etonian tones for making outsiders feel inferior, were plummily Edinburgh, the best part, in other words Heriot Row.

'Fellow,' shouted a female voice, with an Irish accent. It was Lady Dunpark, come to collect me. At least I was no longer being called Trevor.

Kathleen Macfie was a widow when she married Lord Dunpark in 1984. She had previously been married to John Macfie, also an Edinburgh lawyer, and lived for many years in Great King Street, round the corner from Heriot Row. Number 17 came up for sale in 1971 and they bought it, though she can't remember how much they paid for it. 'Is it really necessary to know the price of things?' she said when we were back at Heriot Row. I said I just wanted to know any details of the house, what were the problems, if any, of living there.

'There are no major problems. The house is well built and has always been in careful hands. Lord Balfour had it for a while. The house is arranged roughly as it always has been, although I now have two students in what we call the garden flat, but I've made no physical changes, except to replace the astragals [wooden bars in the window panes] to the style they used to be.'

She took me on a tour, starting in the front hall. It was nicely and artistically cluttered with walking sticks, hats, ornaments, a grandfather clock, a bicycle, binoculars and a two-foot-high statue of you, Louis, wearing your leather thigh boots, which she had garlanded with dried flowers. 'I like a little "populous disorder". Now where did Stevenson write that? One of his letters. You must know.'

I didn't actually, but we moved on, through glass doors into the body of the house and I could see that most walls were colour-washed in a dull honey yellow, to give an Italianate effect. 'I haven't painted inside the house for twenty years, except the windows. I am trying for a faded effect, to lend a patina of age, to make things look as good as old. These sort of houses do not respond to over-elaboration.'

Looking up, I could see three flights of stone stairs, with the cupola at the top. Wasn't it a bit cold, having so much bare stone?

'The house is surprisingly easy to heat. The front gets all the sun, as we face south. The north is the cold side. But, in a curious way, the stone seems to retain its warmth, once you have the heating on. Stevenson was grateful to the stone stairs. It meant, when he came back late at night from some student jaunt, he could creep past his parents' bedroom without anything creaking.'

We started in the library, as Thomas Stevenson called it, a smallish room at the back, with a classical frieze around the walls, now used by Lord Dunpark as his study. 'It was in this room that Stevenson had his famous row with his father. Can you imagine the atmosphere . . . ?'

We'll come to that later. Next we went into the dining-room, overlooking the front, with the large mahogany table set for lunch for Lady Dunpark and her friend. 'Nothing has altered here, except Lady Kinross, when she lived here, took the mantelpiece with her. Replaced by another one, in a similar style.' She picked up two silver forks from the mantelpiece and pointed out the initials RS. They were given to her by an American friend. 'The dumb waiter is still here,' she said, opening a cupboard door. 'It still works and goes down to the old kitchen. The Stevenson butler's pantry is now my kitchen.'

Up one flight and we came to the elegant L-shaped drawing-room, with three long windows overlooking the front. In a glass case Lady Dunpark has a collection of RLS mementoes, such as photographs, postcards and an original copy of *The Charity Bazaar*. Remember that? You wrote it when you were in your early twenties, a jokey piece, only four pages long, done in dialogue, very much influenced by *Punch*, which you were very fond of at the time, especially Thackeray's series on Snobs. Your mother sold copies of it at a real charity bazaar in 1875, which she held in this very house. It was your second published work. It's still funny, by the way – much more readable than the dreary *Pentland Rising*. Lady Dunpark also has a printed invitation to your father's funeral, signed RLS, which asks for the 'favor' of your company.

In a corner of the drawing-room I noticed a large model of a lighthouse. I asked whether it was the Bell Rock or Skerryvore. 'I don't think it's supposed to be either. Some schoolchildren made it and gave it to me. I get regular parties of them coming round. They put breath and life into RLS. I had twenty-one of them yesterday from a primary school in Linlithgow. I had forgotten they were coming, so I was rather caught on the hop, but they knew so much about him and the house. They've written a play about him which they are going to perform. Now isn't that marvellous?'

Next door is where your parents slept. It is now the spare bedroom, with Thomas's dressing-room turned into a bathroom. 'It probably was a bathroom in their day, using pitchers of water to wash. There's a letter somewhere describing the water being frozen in the pitcher.'

I looked out of the window at the back garden, a secret garden, so Lady Dunpark says, which people never expect. It gets hardly any sun, but she has created little winding paths and planted a mountain ash. 'That's supposed to keep away the witches.' Most houses in the row had a coach-house at the bottom of their back gardens – later turned into garages or mews houses – but not number 17. 'I can find no record of Thomas Stevenson having his own coach, but I suppose he must have had one.'

Cummy's bedroom is on the top floor, a little room at the back, formerly used by Lady Dunpark's son and still known as his bedroom, though he is now married and lives elsewhere in Edinburgh. Next to it is another small bedroom, known as the cousins' room, where Bob or any of the Stevenson relations slept when they came to stay.

At the front is RLS's room, your so-called study when you became a law student, now Lord and Lady Dunpark's bedroom. I whipped out from my jacket a photostat of a letter written by you, complete with drawing, where you describe some new bookshelves which you'd had installed. I checked the position of the door and the fireplace, both still in the correct place, and tried to work out where the bookcases must have been. 'It is so nice to sit on top,' you wrote, 'especially in the corner, for I have a thorough child's delight in perches of all sorts.' But I couldn't get the position right. Lady Dunpark assured me it was your room. No other could possibly fit in with the basic features, or the countless other references. In the end, we decided that, at some time after the Stevensons left, the top-floor ceilings must have been raised, making them proper rooms, not attics.

By sleeping in Louis's room, did she feel close to him? 'Oh, I love him dearly, as everyone always does, but I don't go along with all that twaddle that was written after his death, making him out to be almost a saint. He wasn't.'

We were chatting so much that we had not heard her luncheon guest arrive. I was introduced to her, once again as Trevor. This time I said, 'Actually, it's Hunter' – and the woman exclaimed. Our paths had crossed thirty years earlier, when we had been exact contemporaries at Durham University. Naturally, I was invited for lunch, then Lady Dunpark said, why not come back and stay the night, to get the real atmosphere?

To fill in the afternoon I went to Lady Stair's House, a museum on the Royal Mile. This is where all the RLS mementoes were moved after Howard Place was sold and became a private home, and today it's the only place in Edinburgh where RLS fans can gaze at your relics. That's the good news. The not so good news is that you are sharing the house with two other great Scottish writers, Walter Scott and Robert Burns.

You are in the basement, which I took as something of a slight,

as one could easily miss you, while Scott is on the ground floor
and Burns upstairs. Your bit begins with an illustrated biography
of your life and from it I learned you wrote 'forty novels', which is
stretching it a bit. It probably seemed like forty to you, but by my
count you wrote only ten novels, including some in collaboration
and some unfinished, plus five collections of short stories.

There are then two rooms devoted to RLS objects and memorabilia, all of them fascinating – and all supposedly used by you.
There's a golf ball you used to hit at Swanston, with your initials scratched on; a copy of *The Pentland Rising*; a *Christmas
Bazaar*; two pairs of your cufflinks; your pipe; cigarette papers
of the style you might have used; your umbrella with '17 Heriot
Row, Edinburgh' inscribed on the handle; your fishing rod and
basket; a large mahogany bed-head, taken from the bed on which
you were born.

The museum attendant, sitting upstairs at his desk, did not
know how many people visited the house – entry is free – but
he reckoned Burns got most visitors, followed by Stevenson. 'The
Japs love Burns while Stevenson is most popular with Americans.
They are very knowledgeable. They know a lot about him and
have been to see his two museums in the States. We get calls all
the time from Americans wanting to know what we've got here.
Yesterday someone rang from Honolulu to get our opening times.
Some Americans actually think he was American.'

There's no statue of you, as yet, in Edinburgh, but there's that
wall plaque, done by St Gaudens. It's in St Giles Cathedral, which
I'm sure will please you, but I'm afraid it has been tampered with.
You know the one, where you're lying down, rug over your legs,
book on your lap, cigarette in your right hand. Well, as it is a kirk,
they decided to change something, purely on grounds of taste. You
now have a pen in your hand, not a cigarette. . . .

That evening I returned to Heriot Row, letting myself in with the
key which Lady Dunpark had kindly given me. You used to moan
that for a long time your own father wouldn't let you have a key (an
incident you used in *The Misadventures of John Nicholson*). I made
sure I got in reasonably early, just after ten o'clock. Lady Dunpark
was still up and escorted me to the guest bedroom. She had laid

out for me a copy of *Catriona*, for the description of Edinburgh in the first chapter, a copy of the Vailima prayers, a decanter of whisky and a cut glass goblet which had engraved on the side the heads of RLS and of John Knox. I don't think the latter would have approved of drinking in bed.

Then she took me upstairs, to Cummy's bedroom at the back, to admire the setting sun over Edinburgh and beyond to the Forth. It was spectacular, an urban foreground, then a broad sea view and above, as if in the sky, the hills of Fife.

My room was on the first floor, where your parents used to sleep, with its own spacious bathroom. It was filled with books, fine paintings, old prints, choice pieces of china, mirrors, scarves, silver ornaments, boxes, caskets. I spent about an hour just looking at all the objects.

I could hear Lord and Lady Dunpark above, going to bed. The stone stairs might have hidden your nocturnal arrival but, once you were in your bedroom, they would have detected you by the creaking floor boards. I could also hear an ancient water pipe gurgling somewhere in the distance and the faint hum of traffic from the front of the house, but this soon ceased. When I thought my hosts were both asleep, I tiptoed to the front drawing-room, and looked out on Heriot Row. Below me, the front lamp was lit, automatically, thanks to the wonders of electricity.

I meant to lie awake as long as possible, imagining conversations in this very bedroom, Maggie and Thomas discussing their beloved only son, why is he so late home, where is he, do you think he'll ever qualify as a lawyer, have we done the right thing, should we have been tougher on him, it's all your side of the family of course, that's where it comes from, but what with the glass of whisky and very comfortable bed, I'd fallen asleep before I'd finished the first page of *Catriona*.

5

Law and Love
1873–6

On 31 January 1873, just over a year after Louis had started reading for the Bar, he had a terrible quarrel with his father. The occasion was not wine, women or song. Getting drunk, chasing whores, singing in the street or even being arrested in charge of a snowball had not led to any parental disagreements.

They had not worried either about his appearance, even though his unkempt Bohemian clothes drew derision from people in the street. 'Hauf a laddie, hauf a lassie, hauf a yellow yite' – so uncouth boys yelled at him. They kept his allowance modest, but continued to pay any reasonable bills. They even financed a trip to Germany and Belgium which Louis took with Walter Simpson in 1872.

Nor was it anything to do with neglecting his legal studies. They seemed quite happy with his progress, despite the fact that they must have known he was spending a great deal of his time writing non-legal notes, walking round Edinburgh with a little book at the ready. It appeared on the outside to be an academic exercise book, but inside were his thoughts and observations about people, incidents, books read, authors hated, Edinburgh life, human attitudes. In one of his more frantic creative moods, he would stay in his room all day, writing up his jottings into essays and articles, leaving meals sent up to him uneaten outside his bedroom door. His parents accepted all that. Idle jottings of a fairly idle fellow.

But there was one thing Thomas could not possibly accept.

As soon as he found out, he called Louis into his study. He had chanced upon a copy of the constitution of a new club Louis and his friends Baxter, Ferrier, Simpson and Bob Stevenson had formed, the LJR. The initials stood for Liberty, Justice and Reverence. Thomas was deeply perturbed because it appeared to question the existence of God. 'In the course of the conversation,' wrote Louis to Baxter, 'my father put me one or two questions as to belief, which I candidly answered.' And the answers revealed that Louis was an atheist.

Thomas had always encouraged intellectual discussion. He himself had unusual views on many topics, and liked to hear Louis take an unorthodox stand and argue his case. At the dinner parties he and his wife gave in Heriot Row for Louis and his student friends – a sure sign that Louis had never strayed very far from his family – visitors commented on the conversation. 'Louis was at his recklessly brilliant,' recalled one young woman guest, the daughter of a professor. 'His talk was almost incessant. I remember feeling quite dazed at the amount of intellection [*sic*] he expanded on each subject, however trivial in itself. The father's face at certain moments was a study – an indescribable mixture of vexation, fatherly pride and admiration and sheer bewilderment at the boy's brilliant flippancies, wit and criticism.'

There were no mixed emotions this time. Thomas could stand almost anything, except a rejection of God. 'You have rendered my whole life a failure,' he told Louis. Thomas wished he had never married, never had a son, and would have preferred his son dead rather than an atheist. When his mother was told, her reaction was almost as intense: 'This is the heaviest affliction that has ever befallen me.'

It is hard for most Westerners today to understand Thomas's anger, when Christianity arouses so few emotions. A hundred years ago, however, good, sincere Calvinists like Thomas Stevenson were beginning to feel their whole belief coming under threat – from Darwin, socialism and atheism. Louis probably made things worse by appearing flippant and off-hand. His mouth and lips did have a habit of mocking, even when he was not.

Afterwards, Louis thought it might have been better to have lied, as he had done in the past, but he had been sincere in what he had told his father and did not wish to go on living a falsehood: 'And now they are both ill, both silent, both as down in the mouth. O Lord, what a pleasant thing it is to have just damned the happiness of (probably) the two only people who care a damn about you in the world . . .'

A chill descended on Heriot Row for many weeks, the Devil had arrived and taken Louis's soul, there seemed no help for him. Thomas flayed himself, for his own mistakes, for having bred and raised a 'horrible atheist'. And yet, good man that he was, he meted out no punishment to Louis, except the mental and emotional ones of living with someone whose views were abhorred. Louis contemplated escape, naturally enough, suggesting he should transfer his studies to Cambridge, that he should go to London and read for the English Bar, but his father refused. In the end, Louis gained. He was given his own study, next to his bedroom, and those handsome shelves put up for his convenience.

Come the summer, he was given another holiday, not this time swanning off round Europe with his friends, but a more sedate jaunt to Suffolk, to stay with one of his Balfour cousins, Maud, of whom he had always been fond. She had married the Reverend Churchill Babington, a cleric who was also Professor of Archaeology at Cambridge. Summer in a remote country rectory would be just the thing to calm down a horrible atheist and perhaps bring him to his senses, so his parents hoped.

While Louis was away, one of his young cousins, on his deathbed, asked to see his uncle Tom. He said that he could not die without passing on an awful warning about 'a moral blight and mildew' which he had observed at first hand, namely that the mortal soul of young Louis was being corrupted by . . . Bob Stevenson. Yes, his very own cousin was the one who had been filling Louis's head with wicked thoughts.

Not long afterwards, Thomas met Bob in the street, and confronted him with his evil. 'Bob answered that he did not know where I had found out that the Christian religion was not true, but that he hadn't told me,' wrote Louis in a letter. 'I think from that point the conversation went off into emotion and never touched shore again . . .' Thomas parted from Bob by shaking his hand, wishing him happiness in life, but adding that he never wanted to see him again.

In a way, Thomas now felt a certain relief. He could believe that his son was simply betraying a 'childish imitation of Bob' – and thus was a victim, not evil in himself.

Meanwhile, at Cockfield Rectory, near Bury St Edmunds, Louis had met an interesting house guest who was already in residence. This was Fanny Sitwell, a dear friend of his cousin Maud. She was thirty-four, very attractive, even voluptuous, cultured, lively and exceedingly well travelled. She had been born in Ireland, née Fetherstonehaugh, but had lived in Europe, Australia and India. Louis had always got on well with older women, judging by his friendship with Mrs Jenkin, and was fascinated by people who were well travelled. Fanny turned out to be married, to the Reverend Albert Sitwell, and to have an eleven-year-old son, Bertie, but there was some cloud over her marriage. She was soon to be separated, for reasons never quite stated, except that she was in 'refuge from her uncongenial husband'. The rumour mentioned drink, plus possibly wife-beating.

Fanny Sitwell was captivated by the first sight of Louis. 'I was lying on a sofa near an open window when I saw a slim youth in a black velvet jacket and straw hat, with knapsack on his back, walking up the avenue.' He talked shyly about his walk from Bury St Edmunds in the heat, then her son Bertie, who also had been staring at Louis's large limpid eyes, took his hand and led him off to go fishing. Any friend of Bertie's must be all right in Fanny's estimation and so they spent the evening talking together. 'Then the hours began to fly by as they had never flown before in that dear, quiet old Rectory,' Mrs Sitwell recorded. 'Laughter and tears too followed hard upon each other till late into the night and his talk was nothing I had ever heard before, though I knew some of our best talkers. . . .'

Louis was thrilled to find a woman who was willing to listen avidly to his troubles back home, about how he had so upset his parents. Fanny was comforting and sympathetic to all the anguish in his life, but was also positive and encouraging when it came to the other topic that burned away in his soul – his desire to be a writer. Why, he had a few scraps on him, which he could show her, should she be interested, and of course she was. She pronounced them absolutely wonderful.

After three days, Fanny wrote to a dear friend of hers at Cambridge, twenty-eight-year-old Sidney Colvin, a brilliant young man who was Slade Professor of Art and very well connected in the literary world, begging him not to delay his promised visit. He would be sure to love Louis's work as she did, but, even better, would help with critical comments and give advice on how to get published. And it all came true. Professor Colvin duly turned up, was equally impressed by young Louis and gave him invaluable guidance on his literary endeavours. There was a minor problem, which took some time to sink into Louis's infatuated but very sensitive mind – Colvin was Fanny's Intended. There appeared to be some unspoken bond between them. Not in the physically intimate sense, but they had an understanding that, if Fanny ever became free, Sidney would be the one. Or was he just one among many? Louis soon discovered that, in her wake, Fanny had left a trail of adoring swains, mostly young like Louis, many of them well-established and successful in their chosen careers, such as Colvin. Louis was clearly not in this league, but with his velvet jacket, his lovely brown eyes, his youthful enthusiasm, his sparkling conversation and his obvious if embryonic literary skills – here was a young man she could easily grow to like a great deal. And love? Of course she did. No question about this, in the nicest, purest sense of the word. As for Louis, only one word will do: besotted.

Over the next two years, whether he was back in Edinburgh supposedly studying, on holiday in Scotland or abroad, Mrs Sitwell was never out of Louis's thoughts. He wrote almost every day when they were apart, sometimes several times a day. They met in London the following year when Louis was receiving medical advice, apparently to see if he was fit enough to study for the English Bar, which he was not. This whole London stay might well have been a device to enable him to see Fanny. Then he did fall ill, and was ordered south, to the Mediterranean again. The letters continued, passionate and intimate.

Did anything untoward occur between them? The consensus amongst biographers and literary experts is that nothing carnal happened. Louis was a young, impressionable fellow, getting his mixed-up emotions off his chest, and she was a loving, caring, older friend who helped and guided and listened to him when he was at his lowest.

Colvin came out to see Louis in France, which would indicate that he did not see him as any sort of deadly rival for Fanny's favours, and he proved to be an invaluable friend and adviser. Thanks to Colvin, Louis found a market for his first properly, professionally published piece of work – an essay on 'Roads', inspired by his visit to Suffolk, which was rejected by the *Saturday Review* but then accepted and published by the *Portfolio* magazine in December 1873. The fee was three pounds eight shillings. Not a huge amount – his allowance from his father was ten pounds a month at the time – but an enormous boost to the morale. Under Colvin's guidance, he then started on a longer essay, 'Ordered South', written from France, which appeared in *Macmillan's* magazine and was very well received.

It was Colvin who got him elected in 1874 as a member of the Savile Club, a new London club, which he had helped to found. It was meant to be more relaxed and less formal than the traditional stuffy London clubs, with gentlemen eating together without having been introduced. Louis enjoyed going there, meeting the young stars of literary and artistic London, and tried to visit it whenever he was in London. Through Colvin he was introduced to Andrew Lang and made contact with Leslie Stephen, editor of the *Cornhill* (and father of Virginia Woolf), who commissioned an article from him on Victor Hugo.

Stephen in turn introduced him to another young literary type, the same age as Louis, who happened to be in Edinburgh. This was William Ernest Henley. He suffered from tuberculosis, had had one leg amputated and was now being treated in an Edinburgh hospital by Joseph Lister. Stephen took Louis along to the hospital to meet Henley, large, bearded, jovial and learned – he had taught himself two languages while lying in hospital – and they immediately became close friends, planning to write poetry and plays together and generally change the world.

The arrival of Colvin therefore had a huge effect on Louis's life, introducing him to the literary and magazine world, encouraging him in his ambitions and helping him achieve his first minor successes. But during these two years most of his letters are not to

Colvin but to Mrs Sitwell. A lot of them are sentimental, dwelling on his love for her, or very pretentious, breaking into French and German, or pathetic, begging for sympathy. 'I do not know, but I hope, if I can only get better I shall be a help to you soon in every way and no more a trouble and burthen.'

They started when he got back to Edinburgh, after their first summer meeting, telling her that hostilities had broken out again with his father. 'I say, my dear friend, I am killing my father – he told me tonight that I am utterly alienated from my mother – and this is the result of my attempt to start fair and fresh and to do my best for all of them.' He says he does love his father, no matter what has happened, and hopes very soon to hear the noise he knows will show things are better – his father whistling.

In France, he reveals that he is taking opium, not unusual in those days, and describes two Russian women in the hotel who have befriended him. One of them has clearly taken a fancy to him, yet another older woman attracted by his youthful energy, but Louis affects not to have realised at first. Mrs Sitwell doubtless did.

He keeps her informed about all the articles and essays he is trying to write, a series on eminent Scotsmen, on French writers, on Walt Whitman, claiming one moment that he deserves to get on, as he is working so hard, then another time saying that he has 'given up all hope of literature – I have not the capacity for it'. If Colvin believes he cannot support himself by writing, he will take a job in an office, so he says. He bewails the fact that he has 'the poetic character and no poetic talent'. Then on another occasion he boasts that he owes it to civilisation to keep going, after all the help and money he has had. 'Modesty is my most remarkable quality.' He sends most of his work to Colvin first, for his approval and advice. On one occasion Colvin loses one of his essays, when moving rooms. 'One masterpiece fewer in the world,' writes Louis.

In light-hearted moods, he writes funny descriptions about the people he meets, witty observations, bits of dialogue. Several times he tells Mrs Sitwell about children he has met or overheard playing. He sees two little American girls and plans to abduct them. He admits he has 'such a longing for children'. He does not say with whom, but presumably Mrs Sitwell can think of the person he has in mind.

All the while, he is supposedly preparing himself for his final Bar examinations, though most people think he has little chance of qualifying. So much of his time has been spent writing, being ill, travelling or thinking about Mrs Sitwell that it is a surprise, reading the letters, to find that he is still technically a law student.

Even Guthrie, who is never knowingly unkind, fears that his fellow student will not succeed. He admits Louis is a clever and brilliant fellow, but cannot see where his cleverness and brilliance are going to take him – an observation often made about creative people in their youth, when nobody at the time knows where they are going. Certainly Guthrie cannot see him succeeding at the Bar, and cites four main reasons: Louis is poor at public speaking and debate; he has no interest in the law; he has 'not the iron physique necessary for distinction at the Bar': and he 'is the child of well off parents and far too well provided for'.

This last observation was made by many of his contemporaries, seeing him still in his twenties as a wealthy spoiled child, who has been indulged too much, who has not acquired the good Scottish Presbyterian work habits which they all have. Louis himself acknowledged it: 'I fall always on my feet, but I am constrained to add that the best part of my legs seem to be father's.' The popular view was that he would remain a waster.

'The mass of students knew very well that we should have to earn our own living by the sweat of our brows,' wrote another contemporary. 'Our course at the University was the highest privilege we were ever likely to enjoy. We could not afford to mix ourselves up with apparent idlers.'

Louis should have ended up a waster. The elements were all there, with his over-excitable, often unstable temperament, his interest in low life, his sudden and whimsical passions, his wanderlust, his generous parents always willing to indulge. Why did he not? Simply because he had found something he did want to do, which was not seen or understood by most of his contemporaries, nor by his parents. They thought he was messing around at writing. They could not see it as a proper occupation for a gentleman, only an activity for the margins of one's life.

To everyone's surprise and delight, Louis passed his Bar examinations on 14 July 1875, after some strenuous last-minute efforts. Guthrie, who also passed that year, says that the final hurdle included payment of a fee of £350 (for the Advocates' Library, a pension for widows, stamp duty, etc.), which makes it clear why the law tended to attract the well-off middle classes. Louis's four years as a law student, plus the four years before studying Engineering, his travels abroad, his medical bills, his monthly allowance to cover his books, beer and tobacco, not to mention velvet jackets, must easily have cost his father between £2,000 and £3,000. In today's terms, that is about £100,000. But his father was so delighted that he gave him the £1,000 which he had promised as an extra inducement for passing, an advance on his patrimony, to help Louis set himself up as a lawyer.

Louis dressed in a tailcoat for the ceremony, as required, looking like a drunken Irishman, according to one of his friends, and then his parents drove him to Edinburgh from their country cottage at Swanston in an open carriage, with Louis on the top, whooping and yelling, telling passers-by his great news. He sent an ecstatic note to Mrs Sitwell, scrawling his initials like a serpent's tail, announcing that he had *passed*. A brass plaque was put up outside 17 Heriot Row: 'R L Stevenson, Advocate'.

Louis's mother had a set of photographs taken of him in his wig and gown. Since his childhood, she had collected photographs of him at significant stages, keeping them in a special folding case which she carried with her all her life. They range through infant-in-arms, toddler in a frock, young boy with hair fiercely middle-parted, serious schoolboy with book on lap, student in his velvet jacket, well-travelled young gent in amusing hat and then the advocate, my own dear Louis, looking suitably solemn, in wig, gown, white bow-tie and stiff shirt. In this photograph, he is also wearing what looks suspiciously like a moustache, not quite a grown-up variety, but a defiantly wispy attempt. When she proudly showed Louis the completed album, which she always told friends and visitors represented 'her large family', she said to him: 'There you are, Louis, from Baby to Bar. My next collection is going to be from Bar to Baronet.' 'No, mother,' replied Louis. 'From Bar to Burial.'

That should have been a clue to Louis's real emotions and ambitions. Nonetheless, he did turn up at the law courts, promenading the famous boards of the Parliament House, warmed his legal bottom on the open fire, invested in a fifth share in a clerk – whom he never knew by sight – and waited for briefs. Family friends did put one his way, which he accepted on 25 July, but it did not require his presence in court. Just as well, for the next day, he was on his way to London, en route to France to join his cousin Bob.

He never did practise at the Bar, despite a few outward signs to please his family. He considered he had done more than enough to keep them happy by the act of qualifying and getting into his mother's album, allowing them to think that, if all else fails, at least he will have something to fall back on, the salve of every parent, fretting in the night about their children.

He now had one thousand pounds to live on, which he had no intention of using to subsidise his legal work. It would not go very far, as he intended to treat some of his friends, help a few of the needy, pay off some debts, keep himself alive while he got down properly to his real job in life.

Those who presumed he was a waster, going nowhere, were unaware that he had already shown a remarkable amount of self-motivation and application to the art of writing, considering his low capacity for hard work in any other sphere. Where had it come from? His father was a reader, with a large library, and had published books himself on technical matters. His mother, in her letters, shows a fluency and wit, at least for letter-writing, which people often assume, wrongly, means they have a book in them. The capacity for hard work was in the family, on both sides. That was fortunate, as all talents, artistic or otherwise, require hard work to make them flourish. Once Louis found he enjoyed writing, could get his thoughts down in a fluent, readable, entertaining way, he deliberately set out to improve himself, reading authors like Scott and Balzac, memorising whole passages, trying on their style to see if it fitted him, hoping all the time to find his own voice, his own means of expression. From the age of about sixteen, he was never not writing. And he never stopped.

Writers write. They do not wait to be published, or wait

for approbation. Thoughts, experiences, have to be committed to paper before they make sense, almost as if they do not exist until they are turned into a literary form. Louis was doing this before he knew what he was doing. Once he realised, once he saw this was the one activity which could give him total pleasure and fulfilment, as well as disappointment and depression, there was never any doubt in his mind what he wanted to do with his life.

6

Love Letters

Dear Louis,

I hate to jump ahead with your story, and I did make a vow not to refer to people or places in the future, but I might as well mention here what eventually happened to Fanny Sitwell.

Your passionate friendship with her lasted at its height for around two years. After that, you were good friends. Her other friendship, with Sidney Colvin, went on, and on. By the time they married, in 1903, their courtship had continued for three decades. I knew that would amaze you. She was by then sixty-two and Sidney was fifty-six. All this time, she had acted as his hostess at dinners he held in Cambridge or in London, when he took up a job at the British Museum, but they always returned to their respective quarters and innocent beds. No scandal was ever associated with them. One problem, all these decades, was the existence of her unfortunate husband. Being a cleric, the Reverend Sitwell could not consider divorce, so they had to wait till after he died. They then had twenty years of happy married life, so all was well in the end.

The real point of jumping ahead is to record that Colvin went on to be the official editor of your collected letters. But he carefully edited or omitted some of the franker letters which you wrote to the woman who became his wife. At his death, he left instructions that these letters should not be made public until 1949 (presumably because that would be fifty years after the first selections were published). Furnas had a look at them, for his biography of you which appeared in 1952, but he quotes from only a few of *your* letters. The letters which Mrs Sitwell wrote to you do not exist, anywhere, as far as is known. The evidence is that she insisted you should burn them. Out of guilt? Fear of discovery? Certainly. She was a married woman and your correspondence was rather steamy. That's why she sent them to you at the Spec, not to Heriot Row, just in case any prying eyes should see them.

The bulk of your letters, and the best collection of RLS manuscripts and papers, are today in the USA, safe at Yale University, but the unpublished letters to Fanny Sitwell are in Edinburgh, in the National Library of Scotland. This is on George IV Bridge, a rather dour but fairly informal building. Unlike the British Museum, you don't need endless permissions or to wait weeks for the right tickets to let you in. You can get a day ticket, at the door, with proof of identity, and see their treasures straightaway.

I headed for the South Reading Room, where the manuscripts and rare books are kept. Umbrellas, wet coats and briefcases are not allowed. Any note-taking must be done in pencil.

I asked for their RLS catalogue and was directed to several boxes, full of filing cards. Behind me an Australian was asking for material on medieval farming in Scotland while a Japanese gentleman was enquiring about William Blake.

A bearded man, who had been sitting waiting, came forward and complained that something he had asked for had not arrived. The assistant explained that he had not filled in a form correctly. 'It must be my accent,' the bearded man said sarcastically, in clear and educated Edinburgh tones. 'That's why you can't understand me. So sorry about that . . .' Then he sat down and waited, very huffily. Looking around, and listening to the voices, it did seem to me that most people were foreign, or at least non-Scottish.

I got distracted at first by some of your university lecture notes, written in pencil, appalling handwriting, very scruffy, done when you were supposedly paying attention to a law lecture. Now and again you did manage to jot down a few words of Latin, a bit of Roman law, the price of slaves, slivers of jurisprudence, but mainly the sheets are filled with funny faces, doodles, sketches and samples of your own adolescent poetry.

Amongst them was a new purchase, which I did not know existed, three pages, apparently unpublished, written by you in 1871, describing a drunken outing you and some fellow-students made to the Glasgow area. It's in brown ink on legal-looking lined notepaper. The library bought it from the Heritage Book Shop, Los Angeles, California, in June 1988, at a cost of $8,500.

The RLS–Mrs Sitwell correspondence is contained in two massive boxes and consists of 104 letters, all written by you. They vary in length, from one to twenty pages. In all, they cover 902 pages. Colvin, when he made his selection, even for the four-volume collected letters of 1911, used only half of them, and the ones he did use were not always in their entirety. I was looking for letters I had not seen so far.

The letters in the boxes start on 6 September 1873, just after you have returned to Heriot Row, after your summer idyll. Mrs Sitwell is not addressed in the letters by name, or even pet name, and there is no clue to the recipient's identity. Was this to keep it all secret, or were you in a panic to get the first letter in the post and were not sure how to address her? Obviously Mrs Sitwell knew, and Colvin would have realised, when he was working on the letters. (It is interesting that she kept your letters, yet told you to burn hers.)

The first words, on the first page of the first letter I picked up, said:

> I went away so happy on Saturday night, my dear friend, I could not contain my happiness and all the people that passed looked at me with a point of interrogation for a long way. . . . You need not be afraid of my writing so, it is all right and I cannot tell you how good a thing. . . . I am content [underlined] . . . I hate the place.
> Ever your faithful friend, Robert Louis Stevenson.

Not many secrets there, or much to examine, but there is a strong hint of love in the air, or at least in young Louis's mind. (I'll refer to you in the third person here, as you probably would hardly recognise him yourself.)

The letters pour out at regular intervals, almost daily, still without addressing her by any name, going straight into the first sentence; though, as time goes by, he alters his signing-off words.

Nothing dramatic or significant. Usually 'Your faithfullest friend, RLS'. He moans when her letters are late, or she hasn't written. He includes some of his own poetry and philosophical thoughts, and has even more French and German quotations than in the published versions, so Colvin did well there, editing them down. He moans about Edinburgh, and moans about being without her. After a month, he does properly begin a letter, but only with the words 'My Dearest Friend'. There is still no hint of the recipient's name.

The letters are mainly on short pieces of headed notepaper, all from 17 Heriot Row. The lettering of the address is rather modern, more like 1930s typography, almost art deco, than 1870s. The H in Heriot is particularly fancy, with the cross bar going up in the air, while the R in Row has a tail which goes down to the line below. Presumably, this headed notepaper belonged to your parents. If so, someone had good taste in typography.

Over the winter, he continues to write, from Heriot Row or the cottage at Swanston, and then in the summer, while travelling, from Dover to Menton. He is now beginning to sign off rather lavishly: 'God Bless you, my dear.'

It is clear that one of the objects of his travels south is so that they can meet in London. Their arrangements beforehand go on for pages, and get very complicated, trying to keep any meetings as secret as possible. His handwriting at times is a bit hard to read, made worse by lack of proper punctuation, words missed out or shortened.

'PS. I am due in London, Euston at 2.30,' he writes from Wales. 'Shall I go to the Savile Club for orders. Do have orders there for me and let them be to come early. I shall eat my hand [or perhaps it's "heart"] off after I am once there. Adieu, no fear [or "my dear"]. I shall be good, and you shall get well.'

He then starts to use certain abbreviations for his beloved, calling her LS, which from internal evidence stands for Lady Superintendent, referring to a job she has taken up.

In December 1874, writing from Edinburgh, presumably after he has seen her, he signs off 'Ever your faithful friend, and son and priest – Robert Louis Stevenson'.

From this stage, and their London meetings, the letters become increasingly weird. Not only does he address her as his mother, but as the Madonna. 'So Madonna, I give you a son's kiss this Christmas morning and my heart is in my mouth, dear, as I write these words. . . .'

'Dearest Mother . . . je vous embrasse de mon coeur . . . goodbye darling mother . . . ever your son, dear mother of my soul. . . .'

In another letter, he does mention a real name for once, though not Fanny's. 'I want to know where Bert is, and also how. He has dropped out of our correspondence.'

Bertie was her son, who had taken Louis's hand to go fishing, a fairly sickly son, whom she must have mentioned in one of her letters.

'Sorry to hear about Bert,' writes Louis in the spring of 1875. 'I hope I'll be at the next concert with you. I shall pay a visit at Brunswick Row sometime in the course of Sunday. . . .'

This meeting does take place. After it, there is a scribbled note from Louis in which he is clearly ecstatic about something: 'Oh God, I am Glad! How, When, where would you like me. Yours from top to toe. You will get well yourself because. . .'

In 1875, he is abroad, writing from France, and the letters become for a while less passionate. He addresses her simply as 'My Dear', without the Madonna bit. 'Think of me a little if you can, I think of you 3 hours out of 24 – ever your faithful friend, RLS. Love to all.'

The following year, back in Edinburgh, he returns once more to the Madonna image. In the main he is fairly restrained in his letters from now on. 'Look here, you and Colvin are God's holy angels.'

This is the first mention of Colvin in the correspondence. In this letter, Fanny is named, for the first time, as if any secrecy were now over. But, in the next letter in the box (and it could be wrongly dated), he returns to the old sentiments. 'Thanks Madonna. I kiss your hands for that with all my heart. I'll come . . . yes, I do want to put my head in your hands and tell you lots of things. And besides, I must tell you about my work. . . .'

This, however, marks the end of the 'intimate' letters. By now he has someone else in his life. The letters to Mrs Sitwell have already become rarer, and shorter, but he keeps them going over the years, usually to keep her up to date with his health.

The last letter is written from Samoa and dated April 1894. In it he calls her 'My dear friend' and says he is sending some photographs. 'Do not altogether forget me. Keep a corner of your memory for the exile. . . .' The rest of the words are not clear, but he does sign the letter Louis, which is unusual.

So what brought the relationship to an end? It could just have petered out – or for some reason, she said enough is enough. Before or after you had gone too far? There does appear to have been some crisis in 1874. You were both sexually experienced, after all. You had had your obliging harlots. She had had some contact with her loathsome husband, enough to have provided her with two children – one of whom died young. There was definite physical contact between you, a lot of heads being held, hands touching, heads on breasts, possibly even more, judging by some of the suggestive codes and cryptic clues, enough to make her feel guilty enough to want it all kept secret. But was it more than that? The moment it became really serious, was that when she asked you to desist? She might have been taken by surprise, thinking you were safe or far too moralistic to venture over the unspoken boundary.

The sexual element was there, but whether you always withdrew at the last technical moment, we shall never know. I suspect you did, once, go too far, and that was it.

7

France and Fanny
1876–8

It is surprising how active Robert Louis Stevenson managed to be, considering his delicate nature and poor health. By the age of twenty-five he had walked round large parts of Scotland, the Lake District, the West Country. By canoe he had paddled round the Firth of Forth, usually with his friend Walter Simpson. 'Will it paddle?' became a joke phrase, meaning 'Will it work?'

It was this activity which led to his first book. He had managed to place a few essays and articles in various magazines, but only a hard binding would prove he was a proper writer. He fancied doing a travel book, but realised the subject had to be a bit out of the ordinary if it was to be accepted: 'A book about a journey from York to London must be clever; a book about the Caucasus may be what you will.' His means of conveyance were unusual for a travel book, and the route was foreign enough, if not exactly exotic.

He and Simpson set off on another canoeing trip in the summer of 1876, this time starting on the canals south of Antwerp, on the Belgian border, then paddling by river into northern France. Simpson and his canoe are referred to as Cigarette while Louis is Arethusa. No dramatic events happened on the journey, which lasted only eleven days, and there are no great encounters with particularly fascinating people. It is all fairly leisurely and whimsical, two young chaps wandering abroad, amusing themselves.

The writing is gentle and relaxed, with no attempt to be informative, drag in local history or explain the geography, but Louis does manage to throw off a few neat remarks along the way. Such as on health: 'only necessary for unhealthy people.' On eating: 'to detect the flavour in an olive is as perfect as detecting the beauty in scenery.' On idleness: 'there should be nothing so much a man's business than his amusement.' When paddling through some woods, he muses about trees, describing a forest as 'nature's city'. An old man tells them to go home and he comments, 'A tree would never have spoken to me like that.' They see some local girls, who cheer them on from a bridge, then some glamorous Parisian types, which makes him think about 'fallible males'. Later he writes, 'I like to be a bit of a rogue with women,' but does not elaborate. There are a great many thoughts about death, for a fellow so young, but his main philosophy is that you should enjoy everything while you can. Not an original thought, but he puts it nicely: 'If a man knows sooner or later he will be robbed, he will have the best bottle in every inn and gain much on the thieves.' Very true of Louis, all his life.

There is one accident when he crashes into a low branch and is knocked into the water. 'On my tomb, if I have one, I would like "He clung to his paddle." ' They pick up some letters, but he decides he does not want to be reminded of home. He wants to remain on holiday from himself. 'Out of my country and myself I go.' He does feel he is going out of his mind at one point, when paddling mechanically along, reaching a state of Nirvana, which he observes is better than taking drugs.

They are taken for pedlars in their scruffy clothes, which amuses Louis, as of course his companion is a fully fledged baronet. The only real drama is when Louis is arrested, deemed to be a suspicious foreigner. Louis retails his cross-examination by the police, which is very funny, though probably exaggerated. (This incident happened earlier, but he worked it in as an 'epilogue'.)

He worked harder on the preface than on the book, which was basically his diary copied, and it is very witty, but he was not very proud of the book itself. 'I want coin so badly and besides it would be something done. I should not feel such a muff as I do, if once I saw the thing in boards with a ticket on the back.' He was fortunate to have Walter Crane do the illustration for the frontispiece. Writing to Colvin about it, he said it should show a river, not a canal. The book was eventually published as *An Inland Voyage* in May 1878 by Kegan Paul.

The reaction of the public was lukewarm, sales were slow and it was five years before the book went into a second edition, but he did get some good reviews. 'It contains passages of feeling, humour, insight, description, expressed with fluency and finish in the best manner of English prose,' pronounced the anonymous critic in the *Athenaeum* of 1 June 1878. In fact it was Sidney Colvin. 'Charming in itself, and charming in an even greater degree by reason of the glimpses it affords of the author's personality,' said the magazine *London* on 27 May 1878. The author of those unsigned words was almost certainly W.E. Henley. But there were other equally admiring reviews by strangers, and George Meredith, one of Louis's literary heroes, did write to say he loved it, though he was not keen on the preface.

By the time *An Inland Voyage* was published, resplendent between hard covers, Louis had been working away solidly in the magazines, with over a dozen pieces published, mainly in the *Cornhill* and *London*. Henley himself took over as editor of *London* in 1877.

Louis's magazine articles fell into two distinct types during his first few years as a writer. There were his travel pieces, starting with 'Roads', and his essays on literary, historical or philosophical matters, which were more intellectual, or trying to be, as if he imagined he might be the new Francis Bacon. They later came out in book form – under the titles *Virginibus Puerisque* (1881) and *Familiar Studies of Men and Books* (1882). They are hardly read today, being rather pretentious and dated, but it is interesting from a biographical point to see him, as a young, unmarried man, laying down the law on things like marriage. 'Man becomes slack, selfish, fatty, and it causes degeneration of his moral being.' Women are told not to marry a man who is teetotal or vegetarian, while men are told not to marry a woman writer. 'Marriage,' he states, not very originally, 'is like life itself, a field of battle not a bed of roses.'

He has some interesting comments on parents, which makes one wonder if he was thinking of his own. 'Parents form an imperfect notion of the child's character, formed in gales of youth and they adhere to it, so youth gives up the effort to speak the truth.' On death he writes, 'Old or young, we are all on our last cruise.' He also repeats a favourite theme, as if convinced he will die young: 'Better to lose health like a spendthrift than waste it like a miser.'

In one of these essays, entitled 'Apology for Idlers', he remarks aptly, 'There is no duty we so underrate as the duty to be happy.' But he also says, not so happily for his fellow writing hacks, 'Books are good enough in their own way, but a bloodless substitute for life.' He argues that apparently busy-looking people are not really busy, in that when stuck somewhere, or waiting for something, they are at a loss what to do. 'Extreme business is a symptom of deficient vitality.' In an essay called 'El Dorado' he has a go at an aphorism to which he returns in another form later on: 'To travel hopefully is a better thing than to arrive.'

In December 1877, before his first book had appeared, he received his very first fan letter – all the way from Melbourne in Australia, from a gentleman called A. Patchett Martin who had read some of his essays in the *Cornhill*. Louis was naturally well pleased. 'Are you not my first, my only admirer? People who write for the magazines are apt to suppose their works practically unpublished.'

Mr Martin enclosed a copy of his own poems, presumably hoping for a favourable reaction, even a mention in some magazine. Louis accepted the present, telling the man not to worry about appearing egotistical by sending his poems: 'I am a rogue at egotism myself, and to be plain, I have rarely liked any man who was not. When I see a man who does not think pretty well of himself, I always suspect him of being right.'

In June 1878 he received an important letter from Leslie Stephen of the *Cornhill*, important in that it encouraged Louis to expand his two specialities – travel and essays – and in that it showed the feeling of London's literary world at the time, explaining why Louis was taken up so easily by it: 'It has occurred to me lately that you might help me in an ever-recurring difficulty. I am constantly looking out rather vaguely for a new novelist. I should like to find a Walter Scott or Dickens or even a Miss Brontë or G

Eliot. Somehow the coming man or woman has not been revealed. Meanwhile, I cannot help thinking that, if you would seriously put your hand to such a piece of work, you would be able – I will not say to rival the success of *Waverley* or *Pickwick* – to write something really good. You might start a few chapters and then let me see whether I thought them available for the *Cornhill* purposes. But of course I do not want to push you, only throw out a hint which you can deal with as you please. I have a strong persuasion that if a good subject struck your fancy, you could make a good piece of work.'

It is the cry of any editor throughout the ages, looking for the next bright young thing or, failing that, a new version of the bright old things. There did appear to be a dearth of new novelists. Scott was long gone, dead in 1832. Dickens had died relatively recently, in 1870, Thackeray in 1863, the Brontës by 1855. Where was the next wave coming from? Stephen's remark about 'even a Miss Brontë or G Eliot' was rather disagreeable, or a sign of simple male chauvinism. An older, more experienced hack than RLS might have thought the underlining tone of his suggestion somewhat patronising. It is not a commission, despite the flattery, but an attempt to get a young writer to do something on spec, which he might or might not use. Nonetheless, Louis was delighted by the suggestion.

He was already trying to write fiction. Only a few months earlier he had written to Mrs Sitwell saying that he was changing his writing. 'Vividness and not style is now my line; style is all very well, but vividness is the real line of country. If anything is meant to be read, it seems just as well to make it readable.' He was also motivated by the need to make more money. 'I want money and money soon,' he wrote to Colvin, 'and not glory and the illustration of the English language.'

His first published and signed attempt at fiction, *Will o' the Mill*, appeared in the *Cornhill* in 1878, a rather sentimental story, like a children's fable, about a country boy on a mill who wants to visit cities, but never does. After that came a string of much stronger, more satirical stuff which appeared mostly in *London* magazine. Perhaps Stephen did not like these pieces; perhaps Henley would print anything Louis gave him. *London* collapsed after two years, and it was said that Louis's 'crawlers', as he sometimes called them, had helped to finish it off. (They appeared later, in 1882, in book form as *New Arabian Nights*.)

The most interesting and unusual of these early stories is *The Suicide Club*. The original idea was Bob's, thrown off in one of his stream-of-consciousness semi-drunken narrations. He span a story about people wanting to commit suicide who cannot quite face it, so they join a club where lots are drawn for one member to be killed and another member to do the killing. He then threw out a second variation of this theme in which the choice of a random executioner is replaced by a train on which all members of the Suicide Club travel, a luxury train with a dining-car furnished with the best dishes and finest wines, and a dancing-car for dancing in; then the track is cleared, the train crew leave and the train goes over the cliff at Dover.

Louis used the first idea, writing it almost like a serial, in little episodes, with teasing beginnings, so you cannot quite see the connections at first. It is nicely bitter and satirical on the meaning of life, with some good contemporary jokes at the expense of the young gentlemen aesthetes of the time (in other words, of himself and his friends). One club member's desire to die is the fault of Darwin: 'I can't bear to be descended from an ape. . . .'

The stories were written quickly, always starting off at a great pace and very often running out of steam when he could not think of an ending, but they are still enjoyable to read today and are often reprinted. They carry their messages lightly and are far more fun than his more intellectual or literary essays.

Louis's first book is remembered today, and highly valued by collectors, simply because it *was* his first book. But there is another, biographical, reason for its importance. After he and Simpson had finished paddling, they did not return to Edinburgh. Instead, they carried on to Paris and headed south to Fontainebleau, for an artists' colony at Grez, on the river Loing. It was there in September 1876 that Louis encountered another Fanny, also a married woman, also ten years older than he, also a mother who had lost a child.

According to later accounts, Louis vaulted through a hotel window and into the dining-room. 'The whole company rose in an uproar of delight, mobbing the newcomer with outstretched hands and cries of greeting,' wrote Lloyd Osbourne, son of this new Fanny, who at the time was around eight, a few years later. Louis had not taken a random jump through a random window, but had staged an entrance to amuse his cousin Bob, who he knew would be there, along with a group of other arty young Bohemian men from France, Germany, Scandinavia, the USA, Ireland, Scotland and England who congregated at Grez every summer. Walter Simpson's brother Willie was also a regular, spending what was left of his family money on drink and other amusements. Louis had been for a short stay before, so he knew what to expect. This time, sitting amongst the group of some sixteen men, there were two women and a child. Fanny Osbourne was thirty-six and with her were her daughter Belle, aged eighteen, and little Lloyd. When the screams and shouts subsided, and Louis had been introduced all round by Bob, he sat down – next to Fanny.

Had he met her earlier? It is not clear. If so, it was only in passing, and no relationship had been established. This time it was love at first sight, according to later legends. This is hard to believe, as Fanny was not immediately swept away by Louis. He seemed a bit strange, and not very attractive. She much preferred Bob, his cousin, but then most people did, considering him the handsomer, cleverer and more entertaining of the two Mad Stevensons. Fanny had several other suitors in tow, floating around her, young gentlemen ever willing to carry her paints and her easel, but most hearts were throbbing for the delectable young Belle, so sweet, so simple. Bob fancied her more than he fancied Fanny, but Belle was in love with an Irish painter. It was all very complicated.

Grez had been a noted artists' colony for some years, frequented by Corot and Millet, but both of them had died the previous year and its most eminent painters had gone. Now it attracted an international community of younger painters and would-be painters, idlers using art as an excuse to loll around, drink and talk, enjoy the summer, and now and again take a boat out and do a bit of painting, especially if any female models were on offer. Fanny was not a model, or anyone's mistress. She appeared to be a fellow-painter, which made her unusual in this all-male company. She was also something of a mystery. What had happened to her husband? Where did she get her money from?

Despite what both Louis and Fanny later said, the romance took some weeks to blossom. They went about in a gang for a while, painting in little groups during the day, eating and drinking in bigger groups in the evening. Fanny also had Belle's virtue to keep an eye on and young Lloyd to amuse, though Louis came in handy there. He had always loved young children and, being a child himself, could think of endless ways to entertain them, just as he had done with Fanny Sitwell's young son.

The attractions for Louis are easier to understand and were probably more immediate. We know he liked older women. This Fanny was not as elegant, as pretty or as voluptuous as Mrs Sitwell, being smaller, squatter and rather swarthy in complexion, but she too had seen life, travelled in far-away places and had her share of troubles. Her baby son Hervey had died just a few months previously and she was still in mourning for him. She was, however, a great deal more fun than the other Fanny, drinking and smoking, even rolling her cigarettes, very open, very honest and forthright, with strong opinions which she was never afraid to offer.

Louis followed her back to Paris where she was then living and where Bob had a studio. Louis later used her address as his address, when letters were sent to him, which shows a degree of intimacy.

Next year, they met again at Grez, and again in Paris. This time Louis fell ill, with an eye infection, and thought he was going blind; then Fanny developed some trouble with her foot. They came to London together for medical help, and Fanny was put up by Mrs Sitwell – who was, after all, Louis's friend, and the friend of his friend and mentor Colvin, so naturally she helped. Fanny Osbourne met most of Louis's London friends, such as Henley, and appeared on the surface to be getting on well with them. She discussed with Louis the articles and essays he was doing and gave constructive opinions.

Intimacy took place some time in 1877. There is no doubt it happened. All modern biographers of RLS agree on this. (The early ones had the salient letters hidden from them, or declined to use them.) 'I'm a miserable widower, but as long as I work

I keep cheerful,' wrote Louis to Henley from Edinburgh. 'And do I not love? Am I not loved? And have I not friends who are the pride of my heart? O no, I'll have none of your blues. I'll be lonely, dead lonely, for I can't help it; and I'll hate to go to bed where there is no dear head on the pillow.'

While still in Paris, Louis had told his parents about Fanny, if only about her existence as one of his new friends. It is hard to imagine he told them the truth – that he was sleeping with a married foreign woman, ten years his senior, with children and no obvious means of support. Louis was not so stupid, or obsessed by having to tell the truth.

He was by now running short of money, and needed to maintain good relations with his father. The £1,000 had gone and his earnings from the magazines averaged no more than fifty pounds a year up to 1878. He tried to raise money through Henley and from Baxter, with no luck. His father came to Paris and visited him, which seems strange. The details of their discussions are not known. Was there some other family drama we do not know about? Or was it just to discuss Fanny? Thomas apparently did not see her, but was presumably told a few more details about her. He returned to Edinburgh and remained calm: there were no rows or strong words on the subject of Fanny as far as is known, but nor was there any more money. Thomas and Maggie's strategy was to keep out of it, neither to hinder nor to help, and hope it would blow over. Louis was now twenty-seven, and growing up fast, if belatedly.

He was trying hard to improve his relationship with his father. In February 1878 he wrote him a rather confused letter saying he felt 'lonely, sick and out of heart'. The letter is mainly about Christianity, in which he appears to say he now believes, though in exactly what is not clear. 'Christianity is amongst other things a very wise, noble and strange doctrine of life.' He adds a postscript which appears to refer to his above thoughts on Christianity, but it might also cover other matters: 'I have taken a step towards intimate relations with you. But don't expect too much of me. Try to take me as I am. Usually I hate to speak of what I really feel, to that extent that when I find myself cornered, I have a tendency to say the reverse.'

Whatever the reasons for his confused state, it looked as if his parents' strategy had worked. Fanny decided to go home to her husband. In August 1878, Louis took her, and Belle and Lloyd, to the boat train in London, bound for the USA. He saw them on to the train, then walked away, miserable, without looking back.

Was that it? Was another two-year affair with a married older woman over? Had they had rows, which was why he felt so depressed? No doubt Thomas and Maggie Stevenson were very relieved.

The following month Louis left Paris, heading south for the heart of France. He was off on another travel book, this time without Walter Simpson, who would not accompany him. The kind reviews which *An Inland Voyage* had received six months earlier weighed on his mind. 'The effect it has produced on me is one of shame,' he wrote to his mother, who was now keeping a cuttings books of his articles and reviews. 'If they liked it so much, I ought to have given them something better, that's all. And I shall try to do so.'

He was not paddling but walking and riding this time, with the help of a donkey he hoped to hire. There was one other companion, but only in his head. Fanny Osbourne. The first Fanny had been bombarded with letters from the moment he met her, receiving an avalanche of purple prose and tortured passion. This time he was not going to write to her, so he said. 'All that people want by letters has been done between us. We are acquainted; why go on with more introductions? I cannot change so much, but she would still have the clue and recognise every thought.'

So, this new book would serve as a message to Fanny, for she would understand what he was trying to say, even when he did not say it. But would the message be a farewell, or something else?

8

The Cévennes Today

Dear Louis,

I thought I'd choose a female, just as you did. There were about half a dozen of them lined up for my inspection in André du Lac's barn. Mirabelle looked nice and friendly, her hair a suitably donkey-brown colour, except for her soft grey-white nose and chin. Enormous ears, of course, flopping like deflated leather footballs. I walked round her, inspecting her fetlocks as if I knew what fetlocks were, or how to inspect them. A few bare patches at the back there, André, looks a bit nasty. André explained that she had developed a habit of rubbing herself at night in the barn. His voice tailed off. I decided not to pry further into Mirabelle's personal life. I'll take her. Saddle her up ready for me, I'll be back tomorrow morning.

I was just outside the village of Monastier, deep in the Massif Central, which is miles from the Cévennes but, despite the title of your book, the place where you started your *Travels with a Donkey*. Monastier is quite a large village, a small town really of some 1,800 souls, a grey, dour stone village, no signs of tourism, no signs of much life, in fact a decidedly dreary village. Why on earth did you start here? Someone must have recommended it to you, I suppose, or you picked it at random from a guidebook. Presumably it was slightly livelier in your day, before most peasants left the land, but even so you rather damned it by saying it was only interesting for three things – lace-making, drunkenness and bad language.

I'm surprised they acknowledge you here after that, but they do. There's a plaque on a stone slab outside the post office, put there by an American, stating that this is where you started your journey, and the local museum has a 'Salle Robert Louis Stevenson', which sounds impressive but is very disappointing. It does consist of a whole room, but most of it is bare wall and some dried flowers. The RLS memorabilia amount to a few faded cuttings and photographs, badly framed. The exhibition of old ploughshares in the next room is much more exciting.

In the library I met an Englishman called Peter, the town's only resident Brit, who works there part-time. He came to this area eleven years ago with his wife and children. 'It reminded me of Yorkshire.' They sold their house and arrived with no jobs, thinking that would be the easy part. Nor did he speak any French. For a while, he bred rabbits, till he found that the price of feeding the rabbits was more than he was getting by selling them. After that, he did a sequence of jobs. He got to know the Monastier people through taking his daughter to majorette classes. I thought I had misheard. The idea of young girls doing American-style marching and baton-twirling in this remote peasant village seemed bizarre, but Peter said no, there really was a majorette band in Monastier.

Every month in the spring and summer a few dozen British people arrive in Monastier to do the Stevenson walk. A company called Sherpa in Isleworth (where you went to school, Louis) was doing the organising, booking hotels on the route and arranging for baggage to be carried from hotel to hotel. In 1978, on the centenary of *Travels with a Donkey*, an attempt was made to waymark the route, but this was half-heartedly done. Peter had recently been painting out marks on trees because they were the wrong colour. Personally, I never noticed one of them. There are also plans to improve the hotels in the area, all of which are very modest, verging on the primitive. Monastier is certainly not a tourist centre, and probably never will be. The French have not heard of it and the British on the RLS trail are never liable to be more than a trickle.

During 1978 a competition called La Coupe Stevenson was inaugurated for local village football teams, and has proved very popular. You don't appear to have played football, being a seven-stone weakling, or even attended a football match, judging by your letters and memoirs, not even in your Edinburgh days, though you had no lack of opportunity. (After all, Hearts was founded in 1874, Hibs in 1875.) But I notice that you used a footballing metaphor on the first page of *Catriona*: 'having the ball at the feet'.

According to local rumour in Monastier, you left a child behind. Yes, I know, those rumours are silly, you expect them in Edinburgh but not here, where you only spent a month, finishing off some writing, planning your journey, hiring a donkey. Quite a long time, a month, now I think about it, so I went to look at the pension where you lived, Chez Morel, in the main street – 14 Rue Saint-Pierre. It is now a private house, but I was told that a descendant of Madame Morel was still alive, living locally in an old folks' home.

The gate was open, so I walked through into a courtyard, which had splendid views over the valley. There seemed to be no one around but I could hear sounds of eating from an upstairs window. A young man came out of a side door. Aged about thirty, wearing a black leather jacket. I thought at first he might be a security guard. I asked if he knew a Madame Morel. He shook his head, but said he would help me to find her. He turned out to be a village priest, Father Jean Jacquet. I asked him why he didn't wear a dog-collar. 'Everybody knows me,' he said.

I told him about my journey and he said he knew about Stevenson and the local connections, but had not read many of his books. He led me into a sitting-room where various old men and women were sitting silently alone with their thoughts. I recognised the sights and the smells. Several nodded and waved at him and he went over and clasped their hands and exchanged a few words. None of them knew a Madame Morel. He then went to a board and found a Madame Morel, in room 51, second floor, so off we went up the stairs.

Going down a long corridor, looking at the door numbers, I began to be worried. I was presumably trespassing on state property, about to burst in, without her permission, upon some poor old woman, who might turn out to be the wrong woman, but Father Jacquet seemed to be enjoying our quest. He knocked at the door, waited and went in. An old lady was in bed, half-watching football on TV.

I let Father Jacquet do the talking. It took him some time to explain who I was and why I was bursting into her life, unannounced, but then she held out her hand. She said she was Madame André Morel, born 1903, the daughter of Rose Morel. I asked who her grandmother was. Irma Morel, she said.

That's it, I exclaimed to Father Jacquet. She was RLS's land-lady. Yes, she knew about RLS staying with her grandmother, the family had often talked about it. I tried to ask her if she'd ever heard any family legends or folk tales, handed down, about him having a girlfriend while he was staying with her grandmother. She looked confused. I asked Father Jacquet if he could explain it better, but he looked a bit confused as well. I decided not to push it further. I explained that her grandmother became quite famous in Scotland, thanks to RLS, though not quite as famous as Cummy, and that, when she died, the *Scotsman* did an obituary of her. Madame Morel didn't know about that and, anyway, who was Cummy? I apologised for disturbing her, and left saying I'd try to get her a copy of her grandmother's obituary.

Next morning, I went to pick up Mirabelle. A young French couple were just leaving with their donkey, all saddled up. I made some jokes about hoping their donkey would not be as awkward as Modestine. They looked at me as if I was a lunatic. I presumed my schoolboy French had confused them, so I told them I was following the trail of RLS. Still they looked confused. They had never heard of you. In fact, according to Monsieur du Lac, very few of his customers have heard of RLS. And he would like to keep it that way. Oh, come on, I said. You have eight donkeys which you hire out, with special cane luggage panniers, and you send people off with maps, names of hotels or camping sites, an unusual rural holiday, with literary connections – surely you must be cashing in on RLS's fame?

'Pouf,' he said, or sounds to that effect. 'Steff Enson, 'ee was very bad publicity for donkeys.'

He has read the book, in French, and quite enjoyed it, but was most upset by your treatment of Modestine. In his opinion, you were horrible to her, beating her till she bled, trying to make her do things she couldn't do, treating her all the wrong way.

'Steff Enson was not a rural person and he wasn't practical, so he didn't know how to control a donkey. He should have used a rope about ten metres long, not a short one. He did not know how to make the right panniers. That was a big mistake. He had bought a donkey which was used to pulling a cart, not carrying things, so no wonder she objected.'

You should have realised that, Louis. When you did your haggling for Modestine, and handed over sixty-five francs, plus a glass of brandy to that nice old man, you should have been suspicious. When he demonstrated how equable she was, he put two children on her back – and they immediately fell off. But of course, as ever, you were in love with the romance of it all, the madness of the idea, the daftness of the mode of transport.

I loaded up my things. Just a few simple objects, straw hat, pullover, bottle of wine, notebook, camera. You were on the road for twelve days, so your needs were a bit more elaborate – cooking utensils, candles, a lantern, jackknife, clothes, chocolate, a bottle of Beaujolais, several tins of Bologna sausages, mutton, white and black bread, notebook, a pistol in case of wolves and a special blanket of your own devising for sleeping in the open air. That was probably the world's first recorded use of a sleeping bag, by the way.

Mirabelle and I set off down a hill. The sun was shining, the fields awash with colour, and not a car did we see in the first hour. We made steady progress, but no one could call it fast. Her normal walking pace was slower than mine. Nothing I could do would make her increase it, but it was very soporific, listening to her clop, clop, clop, clop, the beat coming in fours, gently rhythmic, like water lapping on the side of a boat.

We came to a small village, Saint-Martin-de-Fugères, and I worried that Mirabelle might embarrass me, but she was still swinging along, slow but steady. The sun was really hot and I wished I'd worn shorts. We arrived at the village *boulangerie*, terribly French, and I decided to have a refreshment stop. I bought a long French loaf from the shop and sat outside with Mirabelle, tearing off bits to feed her. An elderly peasant in a bright blue boiler-suit and tatty tartan slippers came out of what appeared to be a barn door and stepped over me, tutting and clucking. I gave him my best smile and most fluent *bonjour*, but he just glowered.

Did he hate all foreigners? Did he blame me for the EEC food mountains?

As I was trying to charm him, Mirabelle grabbed the whole of my baguette. I heard laughing behind me and a little boy and girl, about three and five, were watching me from the shop doorway. I said hello, what are your names? as one does, as you always did, come and say hello to Mirabelle. They disappeared, then came out again with fresh croissants and sticky cakes. Not for me, or even themselves, but for Mirabelle. Then their mother came out, the shopkeeper, in her pinafore, to watch Mirabelle eating. When she'd had enough, I tied her to a rusty bar in an old window, then opened my wine. I drank a few glasses, sitting in the sun, thinking this is the life, this is the way to do research.

I could hear loud angry shouting, so I stood up, a bit woozy, but couldn't locate the voice. I noticed that Mirabelle had deposited a monster pile of manure, still warm and steaming. The shouting was coming from inside the old window, which I had presumed was part of a derelict barn. Inside was the peasant, standing on his tartan-slippered toes, waving and shouting at me. I had tied Mirabelle to his front window.

My travels with a donkey lasted only one day. The rest of the route I did with a Ford Escort, not quite as romantic, but a great deal quicker. I stayed at Goudet that night, just twelve kilometres from Monastier, the first place you stayed at. Compared with Monastier, it was quite pretty, an affluent little place, with well-kept stone houses, very popular with fishermen who come to fish in the Loire. As I was parking my hired car, a man came across to exclaim at its registration number. '*Soixante-quinze*.' Seventy-five. I looked at it, bemused. 'Paris!' he said. Well, I suppose they don't have a lot of excitement in Goudet.

Your route does have its own map today, produced by the French ramblers' association, 'Sur les pas de Stevenson'. A lot of the tracks you took are now road, so it's easy to follow. In a bookshop in Volagne I bought a new edition, in French, of your *Journal de Route en Cévennes*, a very scholarly work, published by the Club Cévénol (1991), which has copious and erudite footnotes, plus all the bits that were cut out of the final, printed edition. (The original manuscript is in the USA, complete with your drawings.)

I sat reading it in a café on the main street, sharing a table with a young woman with short peroxide-blonde hair, aged about twenty-one, who was writing postcards. We got talking and she said she was about to go to Scotland, taking up a job as a French assistant at a school in Kelvinside, Glasgow. She was worried it would be full of football hooligans. I assured her Kelvinside was a very nice area.

I explained my journey and she said the only book by RLS she had read was *Robinson Crusoe*. I said English people make that mistake. She was on holiday, staying with her cousin, who spoke brilliant English, so I must come and see him. She got up and led me round the corner, opened a door beside a health food shop and led me up some stairs. I stepped into a warm, colourful, artily chaotic living-room cum kitchen where a meal was being prepared by a woman at a stove, a couple of children were rushing around and a man with long hair who looked like a hippy was sitting reading a book. It felt like going back to the Sixties.

I was immediately greeted like a long-lost friend, as if they had all been expecting me, made to sit down and given a glass of Beaujolais. I introduced myself and the man said he was Michel Eudes, a part-time farmer and teacher, his wife was called Fifi and one of the children running around was their son Kevin. He said yes, he knew Kevin was a joke in England, but he had named him after a New Zealander he had once known, in the days when he lived in a hippy commune.

Today, he is still part of a commune, in that he is in partnership with five other couples, producing raspberries, honey, Beaujolais. Together, they run the health food shop below, Le Loup Vert. The Green Wolf. Interesting name, I said. Stevenson was frightened of wolves. Michel said wolves were a local legend, even then, but haven't existed for centuries. This area of France, he said, has quite a few ex-hippies, attracted by the cheap land, the cheap living. The rest of France, if they know about it, assume all the people round here are poor, rude and archaic. 'And they are,' he said, laughing.

My next stop was at Luc, a village off the main road, which looked very backward and unfriendly. 'Why anyone should desire to go to Cheylard or Luc,' you wrote, 'is more than my much inventing spirit can embrace.' This is the sentence immediately before the best-known lines in the whole book. 'For my part, I travel not to go anywhere, but to go. I travel for travel's sake. The great affair is to move, to get down off this feather bed of civilisation and to find the globe granite underneath strewn with cutting flints.' Poor Luc. Probably just as well no one remembers how this famous paragraph began.

You stayed the night in the village inn, where the dinner was good – 'a capital trout, stewed hare and a famous cheese' – but the bed was straw and you were so cold you put two table napkins over yourself and did 'penance all night long in gooseflesh and chittering teeth'.

When you were here, the big excitement was the erection of a huge statue of the Madonna on top of the ruined thirteenth-century château which looms above the village. Fifty donkey-loads were needed just to get the statue up the hill, which you clearly thought was a pointless exercise. I walked up to look at it and read a noticeboard which lists all the famous events in the ruined castle's history. It begins in 1380 with 'combat victorieux des trois co-seigneurs contre 2,000 Anglais'. It finishes in 1878, the year you passed through, with the 'érection d'une statue de la Vierge sur le donjon'. How lucky to have been in Luc, during its last big event.

In the village, I studied a poster announcing that Jacky Bruel was coming soon to play his accordion. I went into the post office, thinking they might have a nice card of the Madonna on the castle, but they had none. The postman behind the counter was young, eager-looking and wearing a sparkling clean shirt. I'd expected a crabby peasant, with or without slippers. I told him what I was doing and he put his fingers to his lips and said come with me.

Another ancient retainer who once knew someone who once knew RLS? More tales of left-behind offspring? I followed him out of the post office, which he left open and unattended, down the street and up some stairs on which were neat piles of little shoes and boots. He leaned against a closed door and listened. Nothing at first, then I heard the following, all in English.

'How is the sky today?'

'The sky is grey.'

He opened the door to reveal a little schoolroom, with thirteen children, aged between three and six, well dressed, bright, colourful, fresh and keen, listening attentively to their teacher, who was asking them questions – in English. I was astounded.

'How are you?' the teacher asked one little girl.

'I am a girl,' replied the girl.

Hmm. Not so good. Marie-France Coupard, the teacher, was a bit embarrassed. She repeated the question till the correct answer was given. 'I am fine.'

She used to teach in Avignon, but gave up the big city when she got divorced and came to live here three years ago. She takes the children for English twenty minutes every morning – her own idea, being an ardent Anglophile. She had been to London at Easter, visiting once again her favourite part. 'Do you know the Ealing Broadway district? I always stay at the same Bee and Bee.'

I left them working on a Ladybird book of animals. 'What is it?' she said pointing to a dog. 'It is sheep,' replied a boy. I could still hear their eager replies as I walked back down the street to my car. How dangerous it always is to sum up a place, or a person, as backward and unfriendly, dour or dull, when one is only passing through.

The highlight of your tour, judging by the space devoted to it, was your stay at a Trappist monastery, L'Abbaye de Notre Dame des Neiges. It is still there, situated near a village called La Bastide, about twelve kilometres south of Luc. It took me some time to get its phone number, then to get anyone to answer, but I had got through in the end and booked a room in their Maison de Retraite.

The monastery was most impressive, surrounded by woods and hills, like a stately home or a grand country hotel. The original buildings were destroyed in a fire in 1912, but the new ones, on the same site, have been done with taste and style. There seemed to be a great deal of them, with signs pointing in various directions.

I found the Retreat House where a notice warned: 'Hôtellerie du Monasterie réservée aux retraites spirituelles.' It is not meant for passing travellers, or travelling writers, so on the phone I had not revealed I was writing a book. Assuming my most solemn expression, I rang the bell. Eventually the Père Hôtellerie, Father Raphael, appeared, wearing a worn apron over his white habit. He stared at me rather accusingly. I was too early. My room was not ready. I had to come back at six o'clock.

'I have rarely approached anything with more terror than the convent of our Lady of the Snows,' you wrote. 'This is what it is to have had a Protestant education.' In the event, you were welcomed and the monk in charge of the guest house, Father Michel, gave you a glass of liqueur, till it was time for dinner.

I wandered round the estate and followed a sign saying Audio Visual. This turned out to be a slide show in a little theatre, all about life in the monastery, complete with moody music and an excruciatingly slow commentary. Next door was a souvenir shop, full of women buying religious statues and booklets, assorted trinkets, soft toys, soap, slippers. One very popular line is a snow scene inside a glass bowl, a moving memento of one's visit to the Lady of the Snows.

Another sign directed me to Les Caves. The door was open so I walked in. It was like a cave, dark and moist, with what looked like thick red blood trickling along the floor from under a far doorway. I opened that, blinking in the light, and realised I was in a wine vault. Two monks were cursing and arguing as they tried to fasten a connection on a huge pipe, leading from what looked like an oil tanker to one of the vats. In another large building, I could see wine being bottled.

But the biggest surprise was when I walked into a huge cash and carry warehouse. I had noticed quite a few cars outside, but had presumed they belonged to pilgrims, come to commune spiritually, *comme moi*. They were queuing up, silently waiting their turn for one of the monks to serve them at a long counter. They were buying wine by the case, as well as cheeses, hams, sausages, chocolates and other foodstuffs. At one end, a group of six very worn, scruffy old peasants were sipping thin glasses of liqueur, trying out the various tastes, smirking at each other, pleased at their cunning at getting a free drink.

Has your monastery, my dear friend, now sold out to the

great god Mammon? Catering for the consumers rather than the worshippers? What fun you could have had, describing the scene in that supermarket, a monk in his full habit, ringing up prices on his till. Monasteries have traditionally had some sort of business, to bring in money, usually selling nice things like incense and candles. La Trappe happens to be in the wine and food business, yet the overall atmosphere is still one of peace and reverence. The church itself is totally church-like, with no modern gimmicks, and the monks in their own quarters live a life of prayer, when they are not working in the kitchen, the Retreat House, the shop, the winery, the farm or the sawmill. I tried to get into their quarters, but a locked door barred my way.

At six o'clock, I went back to the Retreat House. Father Raphael was at the back of the building, in his apron and dirty wellington boots, feeding some rather smelly geese and some huge rabbits. I waited on his pleasure, as he seemed no keener to welcome me than he had been earlier in the day. Eventually he gave me a key to my room, number 16, on the second floor. The corridor was dark, with no windows, and an institutional smell. My room was small and bare but adequate, with a bed, a sink, a table. A leaflet prohibited the use of the radio in my room or having any visitors, and asked one to respect the atmosphere. In bold letters, I was warned that 'l'hôtellerie n'est pas une maison de vacances'.

There was also a list of all the offices, starting at 4.30 in the morning with Vigiles, then Messe at 7.00, Tierce at 7.50 and 10.30, Sexte at 12.15. None at 13.00, 14.15 and 17.00, Vêpres at 18.30 and finally Complies at 20.30. Quite a full day for any monk, and any visitor of a genuinely spiritual disposition. I looked at my watch, saw it was a few minutes before 6.30, so I rushed and was just in time to get into the upstairs public gallery for Vespers.

I watched the monks file in, all in creamy white, with their hoods up. During the day, while working, they wear a black armless tunic over their white, with perhaps an old apron for dirty work. Now they looked mysterious and magisterial, part of a secret society lesser mortals were excluded from, on a direct line to God. They came in one by one, crossed themselves, then knelt down, in their own space and own time. I wondered if each day their routine changed, if they had different thoughts, different

1a: Thomas Stevenson (1818–87), father of RLS: one of thirteen children, from a distinguished family of lighthouse builders, became a civil engineer and hoped his only son would follow in his footsteps

1b: Margaret Isabella Balfour (1829–97), mother of RLS; also one of thirteen children, and from a distinguished family, daughter of the manse, married in 1848 aged nineteen

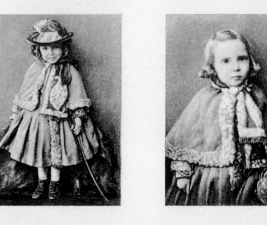

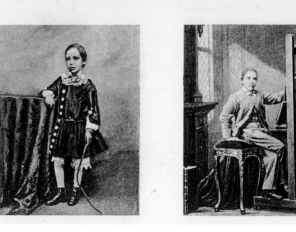

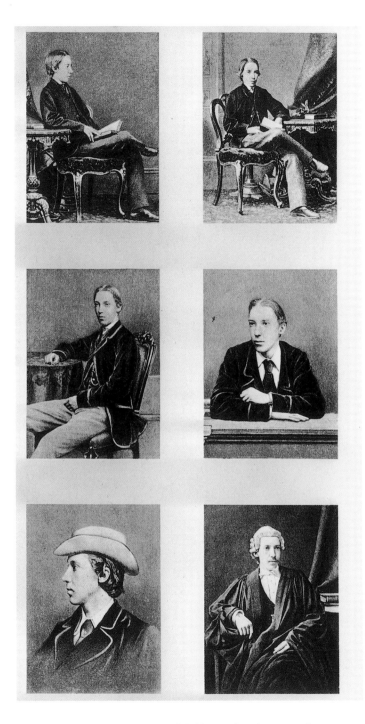

2–3: From Baby to Bar: RLS's mother kept an album
of Louis's progress, through his childhood,
student days to qualification as a barrister
in 1875, aged twenty-five

4a: Alison Cunningham, known as Cummy, RLS's God-fearing nanny

4b: 8 Howard Place, Edinburgh, birthplace of RLS on Nov 13, 1850

4c: 17 Heriot Row, Edinburgh, family home from 1857 onwards

5a: William Ernest Henley: friend of RLS as a young man, later the model for Long John Silver

5b: Sidney Colvin: Cambridge scholar, literary mentor to RLS

5c: Mrs Fanny Sitwell: RLS's first passion, despite the fact that she was married to a cleric. She later married Colvin

6: Robert Louis Stevenson in 1876,
aged twenty-five, around the time he fell in love
with Fanny Osbourne

7: Fanny Osbourne: aged thirty-six when she first
met RLS, already married, mother of three.
Married RLS in California, 1880

8a: Monterey, California, where RLS stayed while waiting to marry

8b: La Villa Solitude, Hyères, South of France:
home of RLS and Fanny, 1883–4 and where he said he was happiest

expressions, different ways of bowing, crossing, kneeling. If you attend ten services a day, every day, perhaps it is like clocking in and clocking out. It is their job. I counted twenty-seven monks, so eight were missing, either ill or otherwise occupied. As I looked down, I could see a lot of bald pates. Average age about sixty, with one bent old monk who looked ninety. Then I noticed three youngish ones, in their thirties. They were sitting together.

The singing was soft and gentle, rather than deep and sonorous. Some cleverly positioned microphones ensured that the twenty or so of us in the congregation, almost all women, could catch every note. I noticed that Father Raphael, last seen in his dirty boots, was the main singer.

Most of the congregation turned out to be day visitors. In the *hôtellerie* that night, as we gathered for supper, there were only four other residents, all women, all French. Three appeared to have taken a vow of silence, or been warned not to speak to strange men. Only one was friendly. She was on Retreat for a week, which she had done every year for fifteen years. Her husband had been against it at first, but now encouraged her. She always returned home in a better mood: 'Staying here washes out the mind.'

On the table laid out for us was a litre bottle of wine. I stared at it thoughtfully, wondering how far it would go between five. But I was in luck. The non-speakers were also non-drinkers, so I got through most of it. It was the house wine, or rather the monastery wine, so I was helping consumption.

The first course was soup, brought in a large metal tureen, followed by rissoles whose contents I could not even guess at. It reminded me of school dinners during the days of rationing, or hotel meals in Russia. Afterwards, I had a walk round the woods, then came back in time for Compline at 8.30, the last service of the day. They turned out the electric lights, and we all sang the last psalm of the day in candlelight, which was very atmospheric. Then I went straight to my bedroom. There didn't seem much else to do. My lady friend had confided that she was setting her alarm for the 4.30 service.

I was awakened at 6.30 next morning by someone getting up and washing in the next room. I could hear every splash through the hardboard walls. I had presumed my whole corridor was empty, as the women were along the other corridor. I never found out who it was. At breakfast, we were the same five people. My talking friend had made the 4.30 Vigiles, but then she had gone back to bed and slept in, arriving for Mass half an hour late.

It was coffee and bread for breakfast, rather good, real coffee with hot milk, served in soup bowls. All four Frenchwomen drank their coffee in the same way – dropping large pieces of bread into it, stirring it all up, then supping it with a spoon, as if it was porridge. I drank mine, *sans* bread, holding it up to my mouth, pretending it was just a large cup. There are not many differences between us these days, now we are all good Europeans, but I think that over breakfast I could always spot a genuine Frog from a Rosbif.

All Trappists are supposedly under a vow of silence. I had asked a monk serving in the shop if it was true. 'We are silent,' he said, 'but not mute.' It means that for important things they are able to speak, such as working or praying. Otherwise, they do not converse idly amongst themselves. But they do have fifteen minutes set aside each day for 'Chapitres', when they can gossip away.

I asked Father Raphael if he could spare a few minutes for a chat. He agreed, reluctantly, taking me into his office, and stood there, arms together, waiting for me to ask him questions. I revealed I was writing a book. My French is perfectly adequate, and had been with everyone so far, but it needs the other person to be willing to meet me halfway. Father Raphael was either not willing, or under instructions not to talk. I asked some harmless questions about the people who stay on Retreat. Some 3,000 a year, he said, which includes school parties. He was sorry. There was little else he could tell me. Why didn't I speak to the abbot? I said fine. Alas, he said, the abbot was away. I felt I had been caught up in some Aristotelian dialogue.

You were lucky on your stay, Louis. One of the monks was Irish and was thrilled to meet an English-speaker. All the monks seemed to go out of their way to talk to you – mainly trying to convert you to Catholicism. I bet your father didn't like that bit.

It was when I got to Florac, in the Cévennes proper, and the first really pretty tourist town on the trail, that I was given an explanation. I was telling someone about La Trappe, and the poor welcome I'd got, and he said they might have been worried I was a foreign spy, come to investigate their wine dealings. The other year, apparently, they had been taken to court for using cheap Moroccan wine as a basis for their own wine. They are not allowed to do this, under the terms of their government-controlled wine authorisation.

One of the undercurrents in your book, Louis, is sex. Right at the beginning in Monastier there is the 'stripling girl with a bashful but an encouraging play of eyes'. Then remember when you were captivated by a young serving girl called Clarisse. 'Her huge grey eyes were steeped in a sort of amorous languor. Her features though fleshy were carefully designed. It was a face capable of strong emotions and, with training, it offered a promise of delicate sentiments. It seemed to me pitiful that so good a model should be left to country admirers and a country way of thought.' A bit condescending, and also rather rude when you described how she waited at table: 'With a heavy placable nonchalance, like an educated cow.'

Two of the bits missed out, in the final version, are about girls. In one of them 'a stout, homely wench brought a basin of new milk to my bedside'. Did you worry you might be teased about that? The other scene could easily be misconstrued. This concerns some banter between you and a farmer about his daughter, pretending you had bought her for ten pence. The daughter takes it as real, and runs out of the kitchen in tears.

Did anything sexual happen along the way? I sense the trip was an attempt to get away from all that, retreating from the temptations of the flesh, following a hair shirt of a journey, away from towns and tourist facilities, making yourself suffer, travelling simply but symbolically with a donkey, sleeping under the stars, on straw beds, in a monastic cell. A punishment for having slept with a married woman?

You do say of course that the book was a letter to Fanny, which I find strange. There is no reference to her, though you do refer to some woman, unnamed, when you are describing your struggles with your brown-faced stubborn female companion, Modestine. 'Once when I looked at her, she had a faint resemblance to a lady of my acquaintance who formerly loaded me with kindness.' Was this a dig at Fanny?

Fanny would, of course, recognise many of your observations, thoughts and longings, particularly one on your last day, during a moment of sudden elation. 'I moved in an atmosphere of pleasure, and felt light and quiet and content. But perhaps it was not the place alone that so disposed my spirit. Perhaps someone was thinking of me in another country. . . .'

9
Fanny and California
1879

Frances Matilda Vandegrift, always known as Fanny, was born in Indianapolis on 10 March 1840, the oldest of six sisters and one brother. She had lovely feet, everyone said so, small and dainty, and even as a grown-up she never had to wear more than a size four. Her feet were a quiet joy to Fanny when often her other attributes did not fit in quite so well with the required notion of feminine beauty. Her complexion, for example, was olive, her eyes dark, her hair black, whereas in the circles in which she grew up girls had to be blonde and fair-skinned to be considered pretty. She should have been blonde. Her parents were of Dutch-Swedish Presbyterian stock, but for some reason she had arrived looking Latin.

As a little girl, she did not like her name, and asked to be called Lily. 'You are a tiger lily,' said her mother, a reference to her temperament, but Fanny took it as a gardening hint and ever afterwards tried to grow tiger lilies wherever she lived. Her grandmother was so worried about Fanny's skin that she tried to wash it whiter with soap, before deciding it was hopeless. 'She is that colour by nature – God made her ugly.'

These alarming titbits were later recounted in a family history by one of her sisters, Nellie, who no doubt thought them touching, but she did have the grace to add that, despite her dark looks, Fanny was the prettiest in the whole family. She was small, but far from fragile, joining in the boys' games, roaming the woods, fording streams. At school, she was not much interested in lessons, except for art and composition.

She was playing on stilts, aged sixteen, when she was first spied by the dashing Sam Osbourne, tall and blond and handsome, good family, good job, fine prospects – he was private secretary to the Governor of Indiana. They were married on 4 December 1857 when Fanny was seventeen and Sam was twenty.

In 1861, when the Civil War broke out, Sam joined the army of the North and became a captain, but left after six months. Not enough fighting, not enough adventure, so he headed for California and then to Nevada to make his fortune, so he hoped, mining for silver. Fanny joined him there with their daughter Isobel, known as Belle, who had been born in 1858, the year after the wedding. It was a tough, male environment, living in the outback in wooden shacks with the other prospectors, but Fanny adapted well, cooking over an open fire, using a shiny tin pan as a mirror when brushing her hair, learning to roll her own cigarettes, handle a gun and, after a fashion, handle Sam. Part of the adventure in life he was looking for was other women, and he would often disappear for several days, prospecting for other females. There was little choice in the mining camps. At one dance, so Nellie describes, there were fifty men and only seven women. Among the men who danced with Fanny was a clergyman. When asked for his name, he told Fanny to call him what everyone else did, 'Squinting Jesus'.

Sam went off into Indian country, looking this time for gold, and was away for so long he was reported dead. Fanny considered herself a widow and went to San Francisco with Belle and got a job as a French dressmaker. This time her complexion came in handy, as she could pass herself off as French. She became very friendly with a young Englishman staying in the same boarding house; his name was John Lloyd and he worked as a bank clerk. He played with Belle, took her on outings and read her fairy tales. One day, who should turn up at the lodging house but a tall man in a wide hat who picked up young Belle in his arms and asked, 'Is this my little girl?' The bold Sam had returned. He whisked his family off into what Belle remembered as being a very fine house and she was given a wax doll for Christmas.

Not long afterwards, once the Osbourne family had settled down again, Fanny had a son, born in 1868, whom they named Samuel Lloyd, after her bank clerk friend. Could Mr Lloyd have been the father? That has never been suggested. Fanny had several male friends around, especially when Sam started to go absent again, and she wrote them rather intimate letters, particularly to a lawyer friend, Timothy Rearden, with whom she had held hands. It is not clear where Sam was getting his money from, but perhaps the mining had eventually paid off for, in 1869, he moved his family across the Bay to Oakland to a pretty cottage with a garden where, in 1871, another son, Hervey, was born.

By then, the marriage had collapsed. Belle remembered an evening when Sam was reading *Vanity Fair* and had just reached the bit where Captain George Osborne has been unfaithful to his wife Amelia. 'I wonder, Captain Osbourne,' burst out Fanny, 'that you can read your own story.' Belle was sent from the room before any quarrel developed.

According to the Vandegrift side of the family, it was all Sam's fault. 'Her husband's infidelities had now become so open and fla-grant that the situation was no longer bearable,' writes Nellie. We do not, alas, have the Osbourne point of view, and there are always two sides to every split marriage. There are hints that he found Fanny's temper hard to live with. 'Fanny was deeply wounded and humiliated,' says Nellie, but, instead of thinking about divorce, she threw herself into the San Francisco art and cultural world, meeting Virgil Williams, director of the local School of Design, through her well-connected lawyer friend, Mr Rearden. She went to art classes, along with Belle, built herself a little studio at home and also took up the new art of photography, developing the wet plates on her own. Fanny was obviously a highly adaptable, resolute young woman, whether mucking in with the rough miners, or mixing with San Francisco's artistic set.

In 1875, aged thirty-five, she decided to go to Europe, alone with her three young children. A strange decision. If all she wanted was to get away from her unhappy marriage, she could have moved houses, or moved towns. The lure of Europe was its art, says Nellie, to give Fanny and her daughter 'the advantage of instruction in foreign schools of art'. Another attraction was that

Sam agreed to pay, which shows he was not quite as bad as the Vandegrifts often suggested. It probably suited him well. Another young woman moved into the Oakland cottage with him not long after Fanny departed.

So Fanny and her brood hit the high seas, along with a woman helper called Kate who apparently did not receive a wage but came along for expenses, to help with the two younger children. Belle, aged sixteen, did not need much help. On board ship, a thirty-year-old Kentucky businessman proposed to her. His offer was gently declined. Belle in theory had a boyfriend back home, a handsome young artist called Joe Strong who had painted her portrait.

They arrived in Antwerp, where the indefatigable Fanny found lodgings, settled in her family and began calling herself Van de Grift, which sounded much smarter than Osbourne. She then discovered that the Antwerp Academy did not take women pupils. Instead she and Belle went to local art classes, doing life drawings of nudes, but after three months she decided there was more chance for women artists to study in Paris, and lodgings there would be cheaper.

In Paris, Fanny existed frugally on black bread and smoked herring but lived well artistically, enrolling with Belle at the Julien School of Art and befriending many young foreign art students, cooking them meals, joining in their Bohemian life. Alas, little Hervey, aged only four, fell ill. Scrofulous tuberculosis was diagnosed and he slowly began to wither away. Fanny wrote to Sam, telling him the awful news, and Sam arrived in time to sit at the death-bed of his little son. He then returned to the USA – on his own. For whatever reasons, they had decided to live separate lives, but stay legally married. Sam's arrival shows again that, despite everything, he was not a totally uncaring father and husband. He continued to support Fanny and the two remaining children, accepted the life she was leading, mixing with all these young male art students, and left her to recover from Hervey's death at Grez with her young friends. And that was where young Louis jumped through the window and into her life.

'There is a young Scotsman here,' wrote Belle in a letter home, 'who looks at me as though I were a natural curiosity. He never saw a real American girl before and he says I act and talk as if I came out of a book. He is such a nice-looking ugly man, and I would rather listen to him talk than read the most interesting book. We sit in the little green arbor after dinner drinking coffee and talking till late at night. Mama is ever so much better and is getting prettier every day.'

Why did not Louis go for Belle, which was what Bob did, as Belle was so young and pretty and much nearer his age? (In the summer of 1876, when the romance started, Louis was twenty-five, Belle eighteen and Fanny thirty-six.) Perhaps his preference for older women was because of their sexual, not just their worldly, experience. Fanny was attractive-looking, if not in a conventional sense. She is wearing a neck-tie and a jacket in the photograph taken around the time she met Louis, which gives her a studious, boyish appearance, but her hair is up, her eyes bright, as if to say, I am a modern woman, I am ready for anything.

It was Bob who suggested to Fanny that she should continue writing to Louis, perhaps to take her mind off him, Bob, so that *he* could get on with trying to court Belle, which in the end came to nothing. Meanwhile, the Fanny–Louis relationship flourished. In one sense it was love at first sight, in that, once it had started, it was passionate and intense and excluded all others. But were Fanny's original motives anything less than pure? Was she, perhaps, after his money? Several biographers, including a recent one, Frank McLynn in 1993, have suggested that Fanny was on the make. It is true that in her first letters home after they met she mentioned that Louis was said to be wealthy, but she also lists other assorted 'facts' she had picked up about him – that his family was unstable, there was mental illness around (Bob's father), that the Stevensons were all a bit mad, in ill-health or dissolute, and likely to die young.

She was alarmed by Louis's sudden fits of rage and passion, by his habit of bursting into tears of laughter or anger. In a Paris restaurant, he sent back a bottle of wine that he said was off. A new one was brought, which was also faulty. Louis felt they were trying to cheat him, as an 'ignorant Englishman', sending back the same bottle, so he marched across the restaurant, whirled the bottle round his head and smashed it against the wall. Another time, while driving in a cab, Louis had a fit of hysterics so violent that

Fanny bit his hand till blood was drawn. Only then did he stop. After that, her usual method of calming him down was to bend back his fingers till he screamed in agony.

There has to be love somewhere, to put up with all that, not just an interest in money. Anyway, she soon learned from Louis that, though he was an only child, from a well-off family, his relationship with his father was far from perfect. Who could tell if he would ever be left any money, or receive any more? He was certainly not flush, earning only fifty pounds a year from his magazine work.

During the first two years of their affair, Fanny threw herself into his life, as well as allowing him into her bed. She clearly enjoyed the literary world, a new area for her, but one she was determined to understand, just as she had survived in various other spheres. She did have cultural aspirations, fancying herself as a critic and as a creative person, and had a story published in Paris.

On the surface, Louis's London literary friends had been friendly enough at first, but people like Henley had private doubts, thinking Fanny was a bit too uppity and bossy, and she was not even very pretty, nor had she any money. Fanny, of course, had never been easily intimidated, getting herself accepted into much stranger circles than this one, but she was not totally insensitive to the impression she was creating in this sophisticated, awfully English world:

> It seemed most incongruous to have the solemn Mr Colvin, a professor at Cambridge, and the stately beautiful Mrs Sitwell sit by me and talk in the most correct English about the progress of literature and the arts. I was rather afraid of them but they didn't seem to mind but occasionally came down to my level and petted me as one would stroke a kitten.

She kept up with her American friends, writing regular letters, still as teasing and intimate to Rearden and Lloyd, both of whom had clearly been possible suitors. Each also did well in his career – Rearden becoming a judge and Lloyd a bank president. If her motives had been mercenary, she would have been more sensible to have hitched herself to one of them rather than to a struggling, impecunious, rather hysterical, often unbalanced and sickly writer.

Was that why she returned to the States? The given reason, in the family memoirs, was that Sam stopped supporting her, she had no more money, so had to go home. If this was the only reason, and they both were truly in love, she could have survived somehow in Paris or London, as she had done in San Francisco on her own. It seems more likely that Fanny was still unsure of herself and Louis. She could not marry him, without a divorce, and that would be very difficult. She wanted to go back to her homeland, sort herself out, think of the options, consider what she really thought about Louis.

Louis was very busy after he returned from the Cévennes. He had the book to write, articles and essays for the magazines, and also another book to see through the printer, *Edinburgh: Picturesque Notes*, which appeared first in episodes in the magazine *Portfolio*, then came out as a book in December 1878, making it his second published work. This was not a travel book, in the travelling sense, nor a nice topographical study, as the twee title might suggest – more a piece of invective aimed at his own native city. No wonder the good citizens were incensed. Even today, Edinburgh folk become rather sensitive about its contents, especially those who like to believe that, deep down, RLS always loved his birthplace. They can, of course, dig out many affectionate memories from his later life, and prefer to dismiss this book as juvenilia, but his main complaints against Edinburgh were meant seriously and remained with him.

First the awful weather, which of course no one can do anything about, but Louis did punch a bit unfairly by saying, 'The delicate die early, and I envy them their fate.' Then he had it in for the double standards of the bourgeoisie, their ostentation, their indifference to social inequalities. He lashed out at the Old Town, likening parts of it to the black hole of Calcutta. He had a go at advocates, the craven young lawyers putting in the years till they can be made Sheriff of Lerwick – 'an arduous form of idleness'. He hated the new villas in Morningside and Newington, and suggested that the locals rise up and burn them. Strong stuff, easy to read, sometimes bitter, sometimes witty, especially if you happen to come from Glasgow. In the introduction to the book, he mentions that local people have already been upset by his opinions (when they appeared in magazine form) but adds a warning: 'I have not yet written a book about Glasgow.'

Picturesque Notes got only one review, a rather sad one in the *Scotsman* on 21 January 1879, regretting Louis's cynical humour, his over-lofty belief in himself, saying that his 'tone was of a well bred lounger, a flâneur, not deeply interested in anything'. This must have made him smile. 'It is not good form nowadays for youths to be earnest or enthusiastic about anything under the sun.' Such a shame, continues the reviewer, that Mr Ruskin or Mr Carlyle had not written the book – 'by either of whom it would be rather better done'. That must have made him furious – there is nothing authors hate more than critics dragging in other authors. The anonymous reviewer does finish with some hope for the future: 'Happily Mr Stevenson is a young writer and if he eschews such errors of youth he may make his mark in letters; and we trust to see him soon more worthily occupied than he is here laboriously spinning pretty sentences on his own romantic home town.'

In June 1879, *Travels with a Donkey* was published, with a frontispiece again done by Walter Crane. In a letter to Bob, Stevenson repeats that it is for Fanny, and wonders about its reception. 'It has good passages, some stuff in it in the way of writing, but lots of it is mere protestations to F, most of which I think you will understand. That is to me the main thread of interest. Whether the damned public – but that's all one. I've got thirty quid for it, and should have had fifty.'

His father wrote to him from Edinburgh saying the book was 'a very bright one'; he was sure it would be successful, but he found the same fault as in *Inland Voyage*: 'There are three or four irreverent uses of the name of God which offended me and must offend others. They might have been omitted without the slightest damage to the book. So much for your absurdity in not letting me see your proof sheets.'

Interesting, that Thomas should have expected to see proofs, but then he had been supporting his son in his writing career and expected to be involved.

The first reviews of *Travels with a Donkey* were excellent. The *Fortnightly Review* in July used the words brilliant, delightful, comparing him with Sterne and Addison, though it was a shame he had to beat the donkey so hard. *Fraser's Magazine*, while mocking those who have a soft life but invent artificial hardships in order to get a book out of them, welcomed 'a new name which in all likelihood will make itself very well known ere long'. It also picked up and used the quote about 'I travel not to go anywhere, but to go'.

But then in late September came a really damning review in the *Spectator*. 'Why did you not send me the *Spectator* which slanged me?' Louis wrote to Henley. Then later to Colvin he tried to be amused by the nasty review: 'The delicious article in which the *Spectator* represented me as going about the Cévennes roaring for women and only disquieted at the monastery because it was not a bawdy house for which more congenial scene I accordingly aspired.'

The *Spectator* did not quite allege this, but their unsigned review did list all the sexual references, to pretty engaging young hostesses, his longings for the softer sex. Worse, it mocked his style and his superficial views on religion. From then on, Louis always referred to the *Spectator* in his letters as 'Grandmamma'.

Fortunately, he was abroad when the *Spectator* review came out, thus softening the blow. Not back in France on another jaunt, but in the United States. Had he planned it all along?

The call came some time around early August 1879. A cable arrived from Fanny, and almost immediately Louis made plans to leave for America. The cable has not survived, so no one knows exactly what the message contained to make him pack his bags. A few of his friends thought darkly that it was all part of Fanny's scheming, and that silly old Louis fell for it. Having slept with the damned woman, he apparently now felt he should do the decent thing and marry her.

Some have suggested he had a row with his father. He wanted more money, to go to the States to see Fanny, and his father refused. There is no evidence of this – but it seems clear he went off to America secretly, leaving behind a letter to his father. That could indicate some sign of worry or guilt, knowing how upset his parents would be by this foolhardy move.

His dramatic action, leaving his London life just when his

books were beginning to come out, does presume some sort of dramatic telegram, but Louis never needed definite commands, requests or suggestions to get up and go anywhere. He acted so often on whims and fancies, especially if he could see copy in it. It seems more likely that Fanny's message simply said that she missed him and mentioned in passing that she was not well. He indicates as much in a letter to Bob on the day of his departure: 'F. seems to be very ill. I hope to be back in a month or two; but . . . it is a wild world.' He fancied a trip to the New World, as prophesied all those years ago; he wanted to see Fanny again; and, whatever happened, he would probably get a book out of it.

While he appeared to think he would return fairly soon, his friends, having failed to persuade him not to go, were convinced they would never see him again. Edmund Gosse, bidding farewell to him in Berkeley Square, bet sixpence with himself that he would never see Louis's face again. Louis made a will before he left, but this does not imply he did not expect to return – it was a normal and understandable thing to do when about to cross the Atlantic in 1879.

He departed from Greenock on the Clyde on 7 August on the *Devonia*, under the name Robert Stephenson, not much of a disguise, though it might prevent his father finding him, should he make a last-minute search of the passenger list and try to dissuade him from leaving. It was a secret departure in the sense that he wanted his whereabouts kept quiet, giving Baxter his address as 'c/o Joe Strong, Monterey, California', and adding that no one must be given it, 'no one, not even the Queen'. Joe Strong was Belle's boyfriend. Presumably any correspondence with Fanny had to go to this address, so that her husband would not find out.

The *Devonia* was not technically an emigrant ship, as is often imagined – because Louis produced a book based on his voyage called *The Amateur Emigrant* – but a normal liner with different classes, some of whose passengers were emigrating. Louis opted for the second class, price eight guineas, as opposed to steerage, six guineas, which gave him a small table on which he could write. Ever the professional, he had work to finish, and this new experience to record. Even at highly emotional, unsettled periods of his life, he always managed to fit pen to paper. Where else was he going to get an income? He was running away from his family and its purse strings, and had with him little more than his thirty-pound *Travels with a Donkey* payment from Kegan Paul ('The vile Paul', as he usually called him in his letters. Sad how some authors refer to their publishers behind their backs.).

Most of the voyage was spent with the steerage passengers, which was where Louis usually drifted in life, given a choice, and almost all were emigrants. His descriptions of them and their problems mark a big advance in his writing – full of social observation, far more realistic and with much stronger opinions and more direct language than either *Inland Voyage* or *Travels with a Donkey*. By comparison, those were extended literary essays, with most things happening in his head. *Amateur Emigrant* was a social documentary, which is why it is still fascinating to read today (and why certain people hated it when they read it).

He found the emigrants older than he expected, mostly over thirty, and much milder and sadder, realising that in a sense they are a 'shipfull of failures', containing the idle, the incompetent, the drunk who couldn't make it at home, but who hoped that, by some magic, the fact of emigrating would change their luck. 'Emigration has to be done before we climb the vessel. An aim in life is the only fortune worth finding.' He describes the stench in steerage, people being sick, being terrified, screaming that the ship is going down. He interviews stowaways and confidence tricksters, charmers and amateur philosophers, and one young sex-mad Devonian who fancies every woman on ship and manages to have his way with an Irishwoman with accommodating eyes, apparently inside a stoke-hole.

In the book, Louis is sometimes on the side of the proletariat, advocating that Britain needs a revolution like the USA, to give the working man a chance; then at other times he writes about their fiddles and skives, how roofers employ someone called a tapper whose job it is to pretend that work is going on, while the roofers are in the pub. He remarks that it is 'a relief to find the poor so little oppressed by work' and observes how they consider there is 'no dishonesty in half an hour's work for one hour's pay'. By comparison, he knows men who do 'hard literary work all morning', then physical work in the afternoon. He may have been thinking about himself.

It could be argued that Louis was up to his old tricks, a gent slumming for the sake of the experience, and the copy, knowing he did not have to live their life for ever, but so what? Most travel writers do that. If what is exposed and revealed is true and important, then that is what matters. The result was perhaps the best of his travel books, and one which is regularly reprinted.

On arrival in New York, he found cheap lodgings and encountered his first Americans on their home soil. The city virtually felt like Liverpool, except for the people. He liked their open-air life, not constrained in parlours, which kept them from being dreary or self-denying. Americans, he observed, were either rude or kind; often the same people, who started off rude, turned out to be very kind. Despite travelling quasi-steerage and using cheap lodgings, one of the first things he did in New York was look for a good meal, money no object, with real French coffee. When his clothes got soaked in a downpour, he left them behind. Underneath the scruffy exterior, there still lurked the wealthy, middle-class boy.

He then travelled by train right across America to California, again capturing the experience on paper: it came out later in book form as *Across the Plains*. He fell in love with the name Susquehanna, met his first negroes and pitied the way they were treated, even by kind whites – 'like a young master treats a good looking chambermaid'. He met some Chinese whom he liked and found very clean, but said that everyone else hated them. He was against the eviction of Indians and was generally liberal in all his views and observations, but the book is thin and unsatisfactory. It does not have the characters and incidents of the boat voyage, nor does he make it clear why he is on the train, what his object is – which of course he cannot do, if he is to protect Fanny's reputation as a respectable married woman. He also fell very ill, which sapped his energy for vivid writing or documentary interviewing. The two-week train ride left him far more exhausted than the boat trip.

His welcome in Monterey, where Fanny was with her sister Nellie, was not exactly ecstatic. They must have known he was on his way, at some time, somehow, as there had been a letter waiting for him in New York, saying that Fanny was still ill, but by the time of his arrival the case had altered somewhat. Various dramas had taken place. Different arrangements had to be made. Belle, still only twenty, had just eloped with Joe Strong. Tongues were wagging locally, about the young couple, and about Fanny's own personal life. She appeared to be living apart from her husband, though he did make occasional visits from San Francisco. Most worrying of all from Louis's point of view, arriving weak and ill after over a month of tough travelling, full of romantic expectations, was that Fanny's relationship with Sam Osbourne might not be as clear-cut as he had led himself to believe.

Young Lloyd, aged ten, heard heated conversations between his parents, intense discussions and whispers, including an exclamation from Fanny which concluded with the phrase, 'Oh Sam, forgive me!' What could that mean? That she was confessing some misdemeanour and was now wanting to patch up their marriage? Sam was still in funds, and still dutiful enough to visit his wife and remaining child. Compared with the weakling at the front door, who was now saying he had cut himself off from his father, and therefore his only real chance of money, Sam might still turn out to be the better bet.

Fanny had not seen Louis for over a year. In London he had been fit and well, bustling about his literary business, quite a fellow in his way, someone going places, with smart friends and good contacts. Even young Lloyd had noticed how much more dapper and successful, more grown-up and mature, Louis had appeared in London, compared with his memories of him hanging around his mother's apartment in Paris.

Louis was turned away. It was not quite as brutal as that, but the effect was much the same. He was urged to go away for a while, make himself scarce. The given reason was that things were too delicate for him to be seen with Fanny. If a divorce were ever to happen, and who knows if it would, then it was vital he was not seen to be in contact with her.

So off he went into the wilds, where he immediately fell so ill he was convinced he was going to die. 'My news is nil,' he wrote to Baxter. 'I know nothing. I go out camping . . . and now say goodbye to you, having had the itch and a broken heart.'

IO

Monterey Today

Dear Louis,

You appear to have enjoyed your three months stuck in Monterey. In your day, it was a small frontier town, very Mexican, sand on the streets, adobe houses, wooden sidewalks, horses tied to street posts, but as you walked the coast around Monterey Bay you could see signs of change. The final paragraph of your essay 'The Old Pacific Capital', written in 1880, rather put me off:

> The Monterey of last year exists no longer. A huge hotel has sprung up in the desert by the railway. Three sets of diners sit down successively to dinner. Invaluable toilettes figure along the beach and Monterey is advertised in newspapers as a resort for wealth and fashion. Alas for the little town! It is not strong enough to resist the influence of the flaunting caravanserai and the poor quaint, penniless native gentlemen of Monterey must perish like a lower race before the millionaire vulgarians of the Big Bonanza.

I like 'Big Bonanza', another of the words and phrases you used a hundred years ago which still seem to us so modern. I've got a list of slangy, colloquial expressions I compiled while reading your letters, the sort which if you used them in a made-up mid-Victorian letter today people might think were anachronisms. Naturally, in your lovely, well-polished essays, you normally stuck to proper prose. Some of them I've already quoted, such as 'blues' meaning sad, 'dead' used as an adjective, 'quid' for pound. I also noted 'o golly', 'blooming bad', 'gushy', 'other fish to fry', 'feeling chipper', 'beastly', 'slated' in a review, 'blow the gaff', 'feeling tip top', 'bloody' (as a swear word), 'flash house', 'huge lark', 'measly', 'collywobbles', 'no great shakes'. In America, you also picked up American English such as 'quit writing'.

I took soundings before arriving in Monterey and booked into an inn called Merritt House in the heart of the old town. Jeff the Innkeeper, so his card said, welcomed me to historic Monterey. 'People come here for the history, and because it's so damn pretty.' I said it was RLS I was after, and he said sure, they still remember him. 'There's a Robert Louis Stevenson High School in Pebble Beach and a golf course called Spy Glass, after *Treasure Island*, which of course he based on the Monterey Peninsula.' I was not convinced by the claim.

One of the inn's brochures directed me to Dennis the Menace Park. It was designed by the cartoonist Hank Ketchum, who lives in Pebble Beach. Or I could visit Monterey Bay's world-famous aquarium and see the Planet of the Jellies.

Next morning I walked through Old Monterey to the offices of the Monterey State Historic Park. I was pleasantly surprised to find that Big Bonanza has not done its worst. Apart from one large hotel, the old town has been well-preserved, with neat and tidy two-storey adobe buildings, most of them with plaques outside, telling you just how historic they are.

Jonathan Williams, Superintendent Ranger of the State Historic Park, was on the phone. He looked like a colonial district commissioner in his immaculate khaki uniform. On the wall behind was a notice which read: 'THIS LIFE IS A TEST. It is only a test. If this were an actual life you would have been given further instructions on where to go and what to do.' I was still puzzling this out when he stood up, smoothed down his already immaculate shirt and checked his mobile phone hanging in a hip holster like a gun.

He is in charge of the fourteen historic properties which make up the Old Monterey Historic Town Trail, most of them named after local nineteenth-century worthies who once lived there, such as judges and merchants. Stevenson House is the only one named after an outsider, yourself, Louis, despite your very short stay. Strange, isn't it, you were only passing briefly through Monterey, hanging about, waiting to see how life and love would work out, yet they have a whole house in your honour. Better than Edinburgh, your picturesque home town, where there is no single building devoted to your memory. I asked how many people go to Stevenson House.

'You mean annual visitations?' He guessed around 15,000 a year. Stevenson House is second in popularity to Larkin House, which gets around 25,000 a year. (No, Philip Larkin never made a quick trip to Monterey. This is Thomas O. Larkin, a local merchant who served as the first and only American Consul to California from 1843 to 1846.)

I said I only wanted to visit the Stevenson House, not all fourteen, thank you very much, so he summoned up the appropriate guide on his walkie-talkie, checking when her next tour would be. 'I want you to have the opportunity to converse with her.'

Stevenson House is at 530 Houston Street, a rather dignified two-storey building, flat-fronted, with neat shutters set in pretty gardens. It reminded me of Keats's house in Hampstead. On the front wall, at the top, I could just make out the faded lettering from the days when it was a hotel. It was owned by a Frenchman, when you stayed there, Juan Girardin, and known locally as the French Hotel. However, after you'd left, and news came through about the success of *Treasure Island*, Monsieur Girardin smartly changed its name to Stevenson Hotel. I'm sure you would not have minded.

Rosemary Smith, the guide, was waiting outside the front door. On the stroke of ten, a couple arrived, middle-aged Americans, and Rosemary opened up the house and let the three of us in. She explained that only some of the upstairs bedrooms were rented out in Louis's day – you'll be pleased to hear she pronounced your name with an s on the end – while downstairs there were workshops. The house was cool and spacious and graceful, with stone floors and grey shutters and a remarkable amount of original Stevenson material – furniture, photographs, paintings, memorabilia. Some had been bought at auction in New York, but mostly it had come from Belle, Fanny's daughter, who had ended her years in California. I was thrilled to see your little flageolet. I noted your binoculars, your wine glasses, decanter, inkwell, two statues of Buddha you used to own (with photographs to prove it) and a large Dutch cabinet which appears in the famous portrait of you by Sargent. The portraits and paintings were particularly good, by Joe Strong, Fanny and others, some of which I had not seen before in any books. They have the wall sculpture of you by St Gaudens, the original version, with a cigarette in your hand. Rosemary explained how you had written a sweet little letter to St Gaudens's son, Homer, after the sitting. It sounded just the sort of nice thing you would have done. She said she got that titbit from St Gaudens's biography, something else I didn't know existed. It always amazes me how many people remembered you passing through their life.

Their biggest item is the massive mahogany dining-table which came from Heriot Row, round which your young friends were entertained by your dear parents, a Stevenson family heirloom which you later dragged round the world. Rosemary pointed to a scratch in one corner. 'That was made when they rested Louis's coffin on the table.'

Rosemary, formerly a teacher, didn't know much about you till she got the job in 1979. Now she has even called her dog Bogue, after one of yours. Only ten per cent of visitors know anything about RLS when they step through the door, so she says, most of them are simply doing a trail of Monterey's historic houses. But, when she mentions *Dr Jekyll* or *Treasure Island*, almost everyone has heard of you.

Upstairs, she led the way to your bedroom, at least the room it's thought you occupied. It does tally with a description in one of your letters. The large cracks are more recent, the result of the 1906 earthquake. On the bed was one of your velvet jackets. I could hardly believe it. While Rosemary was talking to the couple, I stepped over a little rope, put up to keep people like me away from the bed, and picked up the jacket. I felt it might fit me, as I'm roughly your size and frame, similar moustache, though no longer quite as thin. I opened the jacket and found a label inside: 'J M Sandford, 2 Aston Place, New York'. Surely you couldn't have bought one as smart as this when you were penniless in Monterey. It must have been a later purchase, perhaps donated by Belle. You did have a large collection of them, though, run up by tailors round the world.

We came out into the sun through an upstairs door. The other visitors were from Clovis, California, and had been as delighted as I with the tour. They had heard of RLS before, but knew nothing of his life. 'I never realised he'd been so sick,' said the woman.

Every year on your birthday, they have a special party in Stevenson House with readings and performances and the guides all dress up in tartan shawls and ribbons. Rosemary said that even bigger and more splendid festivities would take place in 1994.

Before I left Monterey, I had a look at its real claim to fame, as far as the average American is concerned. This concerns another author, long after your time, who put Monterey on the national map. He was a local chap, born in 1902 in Salinas, who grew up on Monterey Bay and went on to win the Nobel Prize for Literature in 1962 – John Steinbeck, author of *The Grapes of Wrath*, *Of Mice and Men* and *Cannery Row*. When the last was published in 1945, there were nineteen local canneries processing 235,000 tons of fish a year. By 1948, this had dropped to 14,000 tons. By 1951, it had all vanished. No one quite knows why the fish fled – overfishing, contamination or changes in ocean currents. The result was that the Sardine Capital of the World disappeared – to be replaced in the Sixties by a Tourist Trap version of Cannery Row, the old warehouses being restored or added to and turned into hotels, restaurants, shops, walkways and other excitements.

I walked to the end of the row and had lunch overlooking the bay in a fish restaurant where I watched seals basking on the rocks below. On the way back, on a newly made, environmentally friendly bike lane, I came across some words on the path, stencilled in green paint: 'Steinbeck fucked sheep.' You'll be pleased to hear that no one in Monterey has a bad word to say about you.

11

Marriage

1880

There were no literary agents in the 1870s. No middlemen taking ten or fifteen per cent for doing deals. No professional buffer state, working on your behalf, who would read your humble efforts, suggest changes, then decide which publisher to approach. Such an animal had not yet been invented. A writer submitted his or her stuff direct, then took whatever a publisher or magazine editor offered, or refused it and tried elsewhere. He or she had to organise the legal and financial arrangements without professional assistance. Royalties – whereby the author received a certain sum per book, usually on a sliding scale, depending on the number of books sold – existed, but you had to fight for them. Publishers preferred to pay a set price, outright, for a book, regardless of how well it might sell.

So what did a British author do, who ended up abroad, say out in the wilds, or even the Wild West, well away from the London literary world, without fax or telephone? The post was reasonably fast, around three weeks from California to London, and there was the new-fangled telegraph, by which urgent messages could be sent across huge distances. (The first permanently successful telegraph cable system across the Atlantic was laid in 1866.)

The vital thing for an exile was to have friends at home, acting on his behalf, friends who knew his aims and ambitions, who would keep him in touch, receive manuscripts, give immediate comments, then try to sell them and finally chase up the payments, if any, and get them to him. That was often the hardest thing of all, transferring money between continents.

Louis was fortunate throughout his whole writing career that he had such good friends working on his behalf – mostly unpaid, as far as can be seen – who took tremendous trouble in organising his writing and business life. Colvin was his chief literary adviser, with Henley in a secondary capacity. Both were based in London, but he also had Baxter in Edinburgh. Baxter was the friend from the Speculative days, a bit of a rake in his younger years, now becoming a distinguished lawyer, Writer to the Signet, whom Louis trusted with his money matters, when he had any. (Baxter eventually took a percentage in the 1890s, when he formally acted as Louis's agent.)

When he returned to Monterey, after nearly dying out in the wilds, Louis soon settled down to work. He booked into the French Hotel, made friends at a local restaurant and began writing. His relationship with Fanny was kept as discreet as possible. He made occasional visits to see her, but left her to sort out her affairs and decide what she and Sam were going to do, if anything.

In October 1879, he wrote to Colvin, telling him he was hard at work on *The Amateur Emigrant*, which he thought would be a good seller. 'Can you find a better name? I believe it will be more popular than any of my others; the canvas is so much more popular and larger too. Fancy, it is my fourth.' He was also working on a story called *Pavilion on the Links*, but he was not as hopeful of that, so he told Henley. 'Carpentry, of course, but not bad as that, and who else can carpenter in England, now that Wilkie Collins is played out? It might be broken for magazine purposes. It is the dibbs that are wanted. Dibbs and speed are my mottoes.'

By December, he had finished the first half of *Amateur Emigrant* and sent seventy-one pages to Colvin, telling him that he must press for royalties, and that in the finished book he wanted an advertisement on the page opposite the title page, in the French manner, he said, which 'must have all my books advertised'.

Good friends, of course, are bound to tell you the truth, as they see it, and when you are stuck on your own 6,000 miles away the truth, as they see it, can be pretty hurtful. They still thought he had been stupid, running off after the awful Fanny, putting his life and career in jeopardy. Even worse, Colvin did not like *The Amateur Emigrant*. He thought it too brutal, too realistic, and not what RLS should be about. Henley didn't like it either. Some time later, Thomas Stevenson also caught sight of it – and he absolutely hated it. So much so, that he bought up the rights, to stop it being published. (Which it wasn't, not in Louis's lifetime.)

Louis was in sporadic contact with how his parents were in Edinburgh, but the tensions were obvious. They felt hurt and let down by his actions, believing that he had brought shame on them by what he had done, and were in no mood to advance him any more money. In one letter, Louis is told that Thomas is ill, which he half-suspects is a ruse to bring him home, but he refuses to go. Fanny is ill. He needs to stay in Monterey.

There is some good news in December about *Travels with a Donkey* going into its second edition, but then Henley happens to mention in a letter that he didn't actually like it much. 'If you despise the Donkey, dear boy,' replied Louis, 'you should have told me so at the time, not reserved it for a sudden revelation just now when I am down in health, wealth and fortune. But I am glad you have said so. Never please delay such confidence any more. If they come quickly, they are a help. If they come after a long silence, they feel almost like a taunt.'

Perhaps to get a little of his own back he tells Henley that their plan to collaborate on plays is hopeless. 'Plays are madness for me now.' He also feels he cannot do any journalism, which is not his forte. He did manage to get a commission from a local newspaper in Monterey, but only one article ever appeared. In fact, why is he bothering to write anyway, when things are going so badly? 'I am going for thirty now,' he wrote to Edmund Gosse, a few weeks after his twenty-ninth birthday. 'And unless I can snatch a little rest before long, I have, I may tell you in confidence, no hope of seeing thirty-one.' However, he intended to keep plodding on, and perhaps write something good before he died.

By mid-December, it was decided at last. Fanny was getting a divorce from Sam, despite the wishes of her brothers and sisters, who considered divorce a disgrace on the whole family. She had moved to San Francisco, back to the cottage across the bay in Oakland, and at the end of the month Louis, too, left Monterey.

The cold and fog were getting him down, as was the gossip. 'To live in such a hole, the one object of scandal, gossip, imaginative history, well, it was no good.'

He took lodgings in Bush Street, San Francisco, far enough away from Fanny to preclude any gossip, but near enough to meet her from time to time. He had already been considering her as his wife-to-be for some months. 'In coming here I did the right thing,' he wrote to Baxter. 'I have not only got Fanny patched up and in good health, but the effect of my arrival has straightened up everything. As now arranged, there is to be a private divorce in January . . . and yours truly will be a married man as soon thereafter as the law and decency permits. The only question is whether I shall be alive for the ceremony. . . .'

It would be hard to accuse Fanny of marrying Louis for his money. He was at this stage a penniless, shattered wreck, estranged from his parents. His letters to Colvin and Henley were all about money, saying it was coin he wanted, not sermons. Sam had apparently lost his job as a court stenographer, so Fanny had no means of support either. As his money ran out, Louis restricted himself to twenty-five-cent lunches and tried to live as frugally as possible. His Irish landlady, Mrs Carson, who was at first suspicious of this scruffy stranger with the rotten teeth, allowed him scraps left over from her table while he helped to nurse her sick four-year-old son.

'For four days I have spoken to no one but my landlady or restaurant waiters,' he wrote to Colvin on Boxing Day, 1879. 'This is not a gay way to pass Christmas, is it?' Fanny was presumably spending Christmas with her family, possibly even with Sam, so Louis was unable to be with her. But, by 10 January, he was feeling a bit more chipper, giving Colvin a sprightly account of his typical day in San Francisco: 'Any time between 8 and 8.30 a slender gentleman may be observed leaving 608 Bush and descending Powell with an active step . . . to a branch of the original Pine Street Coffee House, no less. He seats himself at a table covered with waxcloth and a pampered menial, of High Dutch extraction, and indeed as yet only partially extracted, lays before him a cup of coffee, a roll and a pat of butter. A while ago RLS used to find the supply of butter insufficient; but he has now learned the art to exactitude and butter and roll expire at the same moment. For this refection, he pays ten cents, or five pence sterling.

'Thenceforth, from three to four hours, he is engaged darkly with an ink bottle. Yet he is not blacking his boots, for the only pair that he possesses are innocent of lustre. The youngest child of his landlady remarks several times a day, as this strange occupant enters or quits the house, "Dere's de author." Can it be that this bright-haired innocent has found the clue to the mystery? The being in question is at least poor enough to belong to the honourable craft.'

Note how he refers to himself as RLS, as if he were his own creation. A couple of months later, the boy fell seriously ill: 'My landlady's little child is dying. And O, what he has suffered. It really has affected my health. O never never any family for me! I am cured of that.'

Was this a genuine vow, or said in the despair of the moment? Perhaps he was thinking of his relationship with his father, and the heartbreak he had caused him. Perhaps his bride-to-be had already said she did not want any more children. Most biographers think Louis meant what he said, but I find it hard to believe. He had been entranced by children all his life, making passes for their affection, going out of his way to amuse and entertain them.

The little boy recovered, but then Louis fell ill, seriously ill, and for the first time in his letters 'Bluidy Jack' makes his appearance. Louis began to haemorrhage from the lungs and stomach, his mouth filling with blood. Fanny took him to her cottage at Oakland and nursed him, believing he had what she had first diagnosed in Paris – tuberculosis.

For the last six years, his health had been good. He appeared to have outgrown his sickly childhood and enfeebled schooldays, following the pattern of the Balfour genes in growing increasingly stronger with age. Paddling in Belgium and France, donkey-pulling and walking in the Cévennes, camping under the stars, had shown he could lead a fairly normal life. California was proving to be the wrong place for him, or he was at the wrong stage in his life for California. True, he had arrived in a weakened state after his long and arduous journey, but it was made worse by roughing it in the wilds of Monterey. The fogs and cold and winter winds of

San Francisco, combined with not eating properly, plus all the emotional worries of his impending marriage and his distraught parents at home, exacerbated his condition. There was no known cure for TB, only rest and perhaps a change of climate.

From then on, thoughts of imminent mortality became more frequent in his letters; sometimes he was amused, mocking himself, but at other times they are only too serious. In February 1880, writing from Bush Street, he sent Colvin the first version of his requiem – 'when I die of consumption, put it on my tomb. . . .

> Robert Louis Stevenson
> Born 1850, of a family of engineers, died . . .
> Home is the sailor, home from sea
> And the hunter home from the hill.'

Then he relapsed into the old Louis, saying that this verse, which he might write better one day, was taken from 'a beatyootiful poem by me'.

He was clearly shocked and alarmed at being so ill, when in the last few years he had tried to act like a fit and well human being, even if he was not, but there was also part of him which appeared to be enjoying contemplating death, being cynical and satirical about it, to amuse or perhaps shock his friends back home. It became a topic to play with in words, like so many other events in his life, big and small, on which he could try out a few philosophical thoughts, or the odd joke, capturing the subject on paper and, in doing so, feeling for a moment that he was in control.

'I have truly been very sick. I fear I am a vain man, for I thought it is a pity I should die. I feel as far from having paid humanity my board and lodgings six years ago when I was sick at Mentone.' This was in a letter to Walter Ferrier in Edinburgh in early April 1880, a theme he repeated a week later to Edmund Gosse: 'For about six weeks I have been in utter doubt; it was a toss up for life or death all that time, but I won the toss, sir, and Hades went off once more discomfited. This is not the first time, nor will it be the last, that I have a friendly game with that gentleman. I know he will end by cleaning me out; but the rogue is insidious, and the habit of that sort of gambling seems to be part of my nature; it was, I suspect, too much indulged in youth; break your children of this tendency, my dear Gosse, from the first.'

At the end of April, he received some wonderful news from home. 'My dear people telegraphed me in these words "Count on 250 pounds annually",' he wrote to Colvin. 'You can imagine what blessed business this was. And so now recover the sheets of the Emigrant and post them registered to me. . . .'

Only a couple of months previously he had been writing to Henley that he was now reconciled to the fact that he would never get any money. 'I am glad they mean to disinherit me . . . I always had moral doubts about inherited money, and this clears me of that forever.'

News of his TB had reached Edinburgh, and Louis's determination to go ahead with the marriage, whatever happened, had softened his father's heart, which in any case had never set against his son. There appeared to be no strings attached to the money, except that it was hoped Louis would leave a decent interval between Fanny's divorce and the marriage. Judging by the letter to Colvin, it would seem that Louis was going to withdraw the *Emigrant* from publication, to please his father.

The money from home was better than any medical treatment. Louis had his teeth done on the proceeds, and then married Fanny. The ceremony took place on 19 May 1880 in San Francisco. The Reverend W.A. Scott, a Scottish Presbyterian minister, president of the local St Andrew's Society, married them, but the simple service took place at his house, not his church. Louis gave the minister a copy of his father's book on Christianity, which he had carried with him all the way from Edinburgh. Dora Williams, husband of Fanny's art school friend Virgil, was the witness. Louis was twenty-nine and a half. Fanny was forty.

A few days later they began their honeymoon. Louis had been desperately ill, but now at last they had money on the way. So did they go off and enjoy some luxury in a nice resort? No – they went camping, roughing it once again. They took the train to Calistoga, then proceeded by stagecoach up the Napa Valley to a disused silver mine where they found a derelict wooden hut, with no glass in the windows, no amenities, and there they proceeded to squat for the next couple of months.

We know Fanny had already proved herself a dab hand at roughing it, and that Louis fancied himself as the outdoor type,

though so far his limit had been a couple of weeks, usually with a
hot bath and French coffee at the end. The romance of it all was
a big attraction. There was also the health element. By travelling
only seventy miles or so inland from San Francisco, they were up
in the mountains, well away from the coastal mists and fogs. Then
there was that element which occurred in almost all of Louis's
decisions – copy. Out of their honeymoon came *The Silverado
Squatters*, his first 'American' book – American in content and in
the sense that it was published first in an American magazine. It
is sharper, less pretentious than *Travels with a Donkey* or *Inland
Voyage*, strong on characters and setting, without any dragged-in
history and fewer philosophical digressions. It is also more personal than his previous works. Fanny is mentioned; so is Lloyd,
and Joe Strong, Belle's husband. He joined them for a while, made
some good omelettes and drew the frontispiece for the book. The
language shows an American influence – 'bit the dust', 'taking his
whack', 'gotten'. Louis, on the way there, sees his first telephone
and meets people who drink cocktails. The local people are well
described – the Jewish shopkeeper, the indolent hunter and the
con-man Scotsman. Louis muses on Scots abroad, decides that he
has no desire to live in Edinburgh ever again and would prefer to
die elsewhere, but he would like to be buried there. 'There are no
stars as lovely as the Edinburgh street lamps.'

It was Fanny this time who fell ill, with diphtheria, and
they had to go to Calistoga for medical attention, but mostly
they stayed in their hut, on a hillside, not far from a toll house
on a road where there was a shop with basic supplies. The life
seems to have suited Louis, according to Fanny's first letter to
his mother: 'As to my boy's appearance, he improves every way
in the most wonderful way.' She also enclosed a nice photo of her
little boy, just the thing to endear her to her new in-laws.

Louis got up first each day, so he boasted, made the porridge
and coffee, then let Fanny take over the household chores while he
sunbathed naked on the roof of the hut, did his calisthenics, wrote
his notes, looked out for rattlesnakes, listened to the animals. He
fantasised about discovering a new creature, such as a kangaroo rat,
and becoming famous in science, and conjectured whether it was
true that the quietest animals were the longest-lived. He did not,

however, put forward the corollary that the noisy died young. He could have had fun with that – thinking of his own morbid thoughts.

He explored the disused mine and its derelict buildings where once there were 1,500 miners, some of them drinking champagne to celebrate rich finds, now all departed to other El Dorados. Towards the end he said that the whole mine was in fact a sham, that the silver had been smuggled in by stock jobbers on the San Francisco stock exchange in order to swindle investors. That was the story someone had told him, but no facts or names were given. It sounds the sort of explanation Bob Stevenson would have thought of, and that a novelist would have latched on to.

Fanny and Louis, plus Lloyd and their dog, returned from their honeymoon in July 1880. In August, they left America by boat, the beginning of yet more adventures.

San Francisco and Silverado

Dear Louis,

I don't know how you survived San Francisco in winter, in your physical condition, in your poverty, in your state of mind. Yet you had the cheek to criticise Edinburgh weather. At least in a Scottish winter you know what to expect, and prepare accordingly. I got caught, as even other Americans get caught, by imagining that the whole of California is a beach-boy paradise, sun and sand, all year round. It was January, and perishing, in a nasty, insidious way, so that you look out of the window and think, oh good, no frost or snow and only slight drizzle, I'll chance it, and it turns out like Siberia.

Fortunately, I'd booked into San Francisco's newest and smartest hotel experience, an architectural wonder in itself. It was reading your description of Mrs Carson's dingy, depressing boarding-house that made me decide I wasn't going to slum it. The Ritz Carlton Hotel was built in 1909 as the West Coast headquarters of the Metropolitan Life Insurance company, a 'temple of commerce' it was called, the size of a palace, occupying a whole block on Nob Hill, with seventeen neo-Ionic columns at the front. Insurance companies used to take themselves very seriously. Solid, impressive structures meant solid, impressive finances and solid, rock-like souls. Just like your own dear New Town.

Next morning, I walked the few blocks to Bush Street, to number 608, to find your Irish digs. Still cold and windy, beggars not up and around yet. There are a lot of them today in San Francisco, thanks to the recession which has hit California's pride as much as its pocket. For two decades, California seemed recession-proof, the state of opportunity, attracting millions hoping to make their fortune. Gold and silver in your day, silicon chips and military might today. California did not trim itself and keep lean when there were warning signs elsewhere, till in 1993 it woke up to find itself the worst-hit state in the Union with ten per cent unemployment, compared with seven per cent nationally. The ending of the Cold War meant the arms race was over and the American defence budget had to be reduced. Southern California, traditionally the home of the arms industry, lost most, but further north San Francisco also suffered.

The original two-storey wooden building at 608 Bush Street has gone, replaced about ten years after your marriage by a much bigger block called Nob Hill Apartments. Outside is a plaque marking your residence, from December 1879 to March 1880, erected in 1972 by 'admirers of the author in co-operation with the California Historical Society'. Not bad, for a mere three-month stay. Above the plaque, I noticed an old-fashioned lamp, but that could be pure chance, rather than a poetic allusion.

I stepped into the hallway, expecting a security guard to stop me, and there were two men deep in conversation, discussing a crime which had just taken place. Someone had stolen a framed photo of RLS which had hung for years inside the hall, just beside the lifts. It must have been someone carrying a goddamn screwdriver, said one. Yup, it was firmly fixed to the wall, said the other man, who was big and burly. He turned to me, suspiciously, and I said no, this is a pen round my neck, always carry one, handy for notes. I explained my purpose and he said he was the block's manager.

'Stevenson's left, he don't live here any more.'

I said yes, I knew that, thank you very much.

'We get them all the time – English, Germans, Japanese. Someone usually asks if I'm Stevenson, so I say yes, but I ain't done much writing recently.'

He became more serious when I asked about the flats, thinking perhaps I might want to rent one, telling me what a great bargain they were, classy but not expensive, and very secure. 'Despite the theft of the photo?' I asked.

'I'm real fussy about who gets them,' he said, ignoring my remark. 'The cost is 500–700 dollars a month. Lovely studios. A lot of people sleep in the closet, it's so goddamn big. I set the deposit at only 300 dollars a month. It should be double, but I'm only a dumb Irishman.' From Dublin, not straight off the boat, fifth generation, but still Irish.

Outside in the street we could hear two police cars screeching to a halt, so we all trooped out to investigate. Across the road, two middle-aged Chinamen were standing outside the Five Ocean Café, looking very worried, frantically trying to open the café's front door. It didn't look like a working café, more like a warehouse, with the windows boarded. The police jumped out, guns at the ready, and started banging on the door.

'They think there's some guys inside,' explained my Irish friend. 'Robbers, got themselves trapped.'

The pavement was soon filling up, people arriving from nowhere, iron filings attracted magnetically to what had been an empty street, all looking forward to a shoot-out, but keeping a safe distance.

'That's where Dashiel Hammett got killed,' said my Irish friend, pointing across the road to what looked like a plaque on the wall, a few yards from the Chinese shop. I didn't know Dashiel Hammett got killed. 'Oh yes, on that very corner. His office used to be there. They shot him in the head. Right there.'

More Chinamen had arrived, with more keys. More banging and shouting, then the door suddenly opened and the cops burst in. Dead silence for two minutes as we all listened for gunfire. Just as suddenly they dashed out again, glared at the Chinamen, jumped into their cars and drove off. False alarm. There had been nobody inside.

When the disappointed crowd had cleared, I went across to check out the scene of Hammett's murder. On the corner of Bush and a narrow turning called Burrit Street was a plaque which read, 'On approximately this spot, Miles Archer, partner of Sam Spade, was done in by Brigid O'Shaughnessy.'

So much for my Irish friend. No mention of Hammett at all. This was a reference to his novel *The Maltese Falcon*, made into a film starring Humphrey Bogart. They'd put up a plaque to a *fictional* incident. I suppose San Franciscans don't have too many real people to celebrate, which is why you've done so well.

In the heart of Chinatown, in Portsmouth Square, is the main focal point for anyone in San Francisco on the RLS trail, a large memorial, some fifteen feet high, put up in 1897 by the RLS Fellowship. The inscription is long and fulsome, with a quotation from one of your essays, hard to read, because they have squeezed in too many lines. On top, there is not your fine head, which I would like to have seen, but a large Spanish galleon in full sail, as if they were using up a chunk from a Columbus statue, left over from the 1892 celebrations. Nevertheless, a fine monument. Let's hope Edinburgh follows suit one day.

The square was filled with elderly Chinese in baggy jerkins and cheap trainers playing checkers under pagoda awnings. Now and again one of the players gave a deep whooshing sound, a heavy intake of breath, to signify he was winning, or it might have been losing, I couldn't tell. The checkers looked like bottle-tops. The betting money was real.

I walked round the square and discovered a lot more plaques, celebrating famous San Franciscans, so I take back my snide remark. It was in this square that Andrew Smith Hallidie, born in London, set up the world's first street cable car in August 1873. It was also here that 'the dramatic and authoritative announcement of Gold Discovery was made by Sam Brennan on May 11, 1848, who displayed glittery samples to crowds on the plaza'. Now it's Chinese checker players, hoping for gold.

I went in search of St Andrew's Church, which from the telephone directory appeared to be in Post Street, wondering if there was still a Scottish minister in charge. I passed lots of British names on the way, such as Laura Ashley, Jaeger and Burberry, but failed to find St Andrew's. Perhaps I had the wrong church. Your wedding in San Francisco was a very quiet affair. Now it seems to have been forgotten.

There are clear signs leading to the Napa Valley all the way from San Francisco, out over the Golden Gate Bridge and on to Route 101 North, but for a long time the landscape is most uninspiring. Mud flats, dusty roads, exhortations to drive with headlamps on, for no apparent reason, but everyone was doing so.

I was about halfway up the Napa Valley on Highway 29 before it began to turn pretty, the verges landscaped rather than dusty concrete. Hills appeared on either side, then slowly I could see the vineyards, neat rows of them, knitted carefully without knots to fit the hillsides exactly, designer pullovers for green giants, looking as immaculate as they do in France or Tuscany or the Rhine Valley, so that you wonder how human fingers can be so painstaking on such an unhuman scale. It could well be the Mediterranean, till your eyes come down from the hills and take in the châteaux, some in the French style, some Tudor stately homes, German castles, but mostly pure Hollywood, so that the overall impression is of *Dallas*. Many of the châteaux have authentic European names – Beaulieu, Domaine Carneros, Château Chèvre, Robert Mondavi. But the majority sound all-American – Pine Ridge, Johnson Turnbull, Flora Spring – as do the large notices at the front driveways: 'A deliciously crafted wine experience – savor brunch with the finest Napa wines.'

The normal theory about you, my dear Louis, is that you went to the Napa Valley for health reasons. You did make a surprisingly quick recovery, considering you were near death. I think the big attraction was the Napa Valley wine. Even in 1880 it was well established. And very cheap.

The first vine cuttings were planted in the 1820s by Russian émigrés, but these were purely for domestic use, by local farmers. The first winery was opened in 1861 by a Hungarian, the Buena Vista Winery, the oldest in California. By then farmers in the Napa Valley and the adjoining Sonoma Valley were rushing to make money out of the new crop. Disaster came in 1873 with the arrival of phylloxera, a little louse which wiped out the local vine culture. The cure was found locally, by Emil Dresel in Sonoma, who successfully grafted some European vines on to local wild roots which proved to be resistant to the infestation. (Years later, when the French vineyards were struck by the same pestilence, they imported back Californian roots to re-establish their vineyards.)

By the time you hit the Napa Valley in 1880, they were suffering from a different problem – overproduction. Wine was down to ten cents a gallon. Not considered very good, for those tipplers like yourself who preferred the best French Burgundy, but not bad, when you're squatting.

I arrived in St Helena, the largest town in the valley (Napa calls itself a city), named after Mount St Helena, on the slopes of which you had your honeymoon. It looked very gentrified, clean as a Cotswold village. I made for the Harvest Inn where I had booked a room, equally neat and tidy, except it didn't look like an inn, more like a mock Tudor motel. Where's the inn? I asked a girl at a reception area. 'This is it,' she said. Not an inn, as I know it. 'Oh yes, indeedy. We've got seven acres, so we're an inn.' Just because you've seven acres, how does that it make you an inn? 'It's the speciality of North California, these inns. Just like pensions in Paris. Have a nice day.'

She gave me a key for my room, in one of the little brick buildings on the estate, which I was told to drive to and park outside. It was pretty and cottage-like – but absolutely freezing. San Francisco had been wet and miserable but this seemed cold enough for snow, something which is never supposed to happen in the Napa Valley. There was a fireplace, but it was empty. No kettle to make tea and no fridge. All I could find was what appeared to be a large packet of sliced bread in a greaseproof wrapping. I turned on the television to be told that, after six years of drought, North California was having its wettest winter for years, with worse to come. Tomorrow I'd planned to climb the mountain and find your squat. Perhaps I'll go to the Silverado Museum first instead. In the north of the state, continued the TV news, a young couple and their baby had been snow-bound in their car for eight days – on a highway. He had had to walk for five days to get help. Unbelievable. Could this be the USA, 1993? Now he was being besieged with offers for the book and film rights to his saga. Yes, this is America.

I rang reception, asked what time dinner started, to find there was no dinner. What kind of inn is this? We only do breakfast, she said, but there are lots of really neat restaurants in town.

I picked up the sliced loaf, thinking, if all else fails, I'll have a few slices of dry bread. It was solid, as if it had been frozen, and gave off a faintly chemical smell. 'Duraflame,' it said on the wrapper. 'Californian cedar – burns over three hours, in colors.'

I should have read the wrapper earlier. It was a packaged log. I laid it in the hearth, lit where indicated, and it burst into flames.

It was still burning beautifully when I walked back from supper in town at the Spring Street restaurant, which was excellent, ditto a bottle of the local house wine. I wasn't pregnant, nor driving, which was fortunate: 'According to the Surgeon General, women should not drink alcoholic beverage during pregnancy. 2. Consumption of alcoholic beverage impairs the ability to drive a car.' These warnings now appear on American wine bottles. Cummy would have loved it.

The Silverado Museum in St Helena is the brainchild of an ex-advertising man called Norman H. Strouse, one of those American enthusiasts who become so entranced by a subject that they spend all their spare time and cash tracking down memorabilia, then they set up a museum in honour of their collection. Not to make money, but to preserve their collection, together, in one place, for ever, for the rest of the world to enjoy.

Mr Strouse read John Henry Nash's private press edition of *Silverado Squatters* when he was a young man, and at once became an ardent RLS fan and collector. When he retired as chairman of J. Walter Thompson, he moved to St Helena and in December 1969 (the seventy-fifth anniversary of your death) he opened his museum to the public and provided a foundation to run it. At the time it had 800 RLS items. Now it has over 8,000. I'd hoped to meet Mr Strouse while in St Helena, but he was too ill. (He died a week after my visit, on 19 January 1993.

The museum, which is beside the public library, looked modernly grim and forbidding from the outside, but inside it was a delight. I stared in amazement at all the treasures and didn't know where to begin. Unlike at Monterey, there is no guide and you wander round at will. It consists of an enormous room, about the size of a tennis court, plus two smaller rooms. Every surface is covered with RLS objects, thousands of them, far more than you personally ever had in your lifetime. The RLS memorabilia industry started even before you died, and has continued ever since.

I rushed to the books first, to the ones from your own personal collection, which you had till the end. I picked out and held in my hand your own copy of your first book, *An Inland Voyage*, trying to feel your sensations of delight when you first held it. I caressed the copy of *A Child's Garden of Verses* you gave to Fanny. I looked at the non-RLS books, to see what you were reading at the end of your life, or at least what was on your shelves. Several by your friend Henry James; Lockhart's *Life of Scott*, one of your heroes; Marvell's *Poems*; *The Professor* by Charlotte Brontë; *Little Men* by Louisa Alcott; various books by Lord Lytton, Fielding, Smollett, Dickens, Sterne. I flicked through a *History of US Nurses in War* and wondered why on earth you had that. Was it Fanny's? Perhaps one of her relations had been a nurse.

It was touching to see you had kept a couple of your father's works – one of them, *Lighthouse Illuminations*, was signed in a rather shaky hand, Thos Stevenson 1842. The other was *Description of Harbour Screw Clamps*. They were proper hardbacks, but, on examining them, I decided perhaps they were learned papers which had appeared in scientific magazines and then been specially bound.

I dashed about looking at all the portraits, paintings, drawings and photographs, exclaiming every time I found something I had not seen before. I studied three paintings by Fanny, trying to decide if she did have any talent, or had simply used her interest in art as an excuse to get away to Europe. Two were very dull and amateurish landscapes, but one of the village of Grez, dated 1875, was pretty good. In a note beside this painting, it said that her art teacher in San Francisco, Virgil Williams, had later painted in three figures for her – because he thought the street looked a bit deserted. Even more interesting, another note said that this was the painting she gave to Timothy Rearden, the attorney who arranged her divorce. I'd always wondered how she'd paid for it. He, of course, was an old friend and admirer. His fee should have been a hundred dollars, but instead Fanny gave him the painting. (Rearden was the one who later became an eminent judge, and his family left the painting to the museum.)

They also have the actual copy of the divorce, another item I'd not seen reproduced in any book. It was issued on 15 December 1879 – not January, as you mentioned in one of your letters. The wording is annoyingly elliptical. Fanny, as the plaintiff, had lodged complaints about S. Osbourne, the defendant. The

Referee, Edwin I. Wheeler, agreed that the 'allegations of the complaint are sustained . . . and are sufficient in law to entitle the said plaintiff . . . to have the marriage dissolved'. Alas, it does not spell out the complaints against S. Osbourne. The document also gives F. Osbourne 'custody and control of Samuel Osbourne, the minor child of the plaintiff and defendant'.

They have a copy, not the original, of your wedding registration and I noticed that you were born in 'Edinboro', were living in Oakland, Cal, and that you gave your age as thirty. You were not actually thirty till five months later. I suppose you were trying to shorten the age gap. Fannie, spelled thus, gives her true age, which was forty, but she is described as widowed. Was this for the sake of social propriety or to persuade the minister to give you a clerical wedding?

Beth Atherton had recently taken over the job of curator of the Silverado Museum and was still in the middle of her RLS researches. She took me into a private back room to show me a painting they had recently been given. It showed a horse and a foal, exceedingly dreary, in glaring colours, badly done, the sort junk shops sell for a fiver. It turned out to be a painting which Thomas Stevenson had owned, to which you later gave pride of place, according to a note written in 1939 by Austin Strong, Belle's son.

They have a few pieces of your furniture on display – a rocking chair, a walnut cabinet and a little desk said to have a secret drawer at the right-hand side. Naturally, I opened the drawer and found a copy of another letter from Austin Strong. It described how he used to play with this desk as a little boy in your house, turning it into a castle or a fortress, just the sort of game you loved as a boy.

There is a large collection of your own toys from your Heriot Row days – your lead soldiers and childhood tea-set – plus family dishes, plates, a mustard container with the initials RLS, a silver inkwell, cigar-holders, letter-opener, knife, chess set and signed cheques drawn on the Wilts and Dorset Bank, Bournemouth branch. I wish you'd been with me, Louis, to see these treasures, if only to say you didn't recognise half of them. How can we tell, a hundred years later, if that lead soldier was really the one your infant fingers moved into battle?

Many items do have proof of ownership. On the front of an envelope containing Henry James's glove are the following words: 'Henry James's glove left in my house and dishonestly confiscated by me, F V de G S.' I had to puzzle out the initials, then realised it was Fanny Van de Grift Stevenson. Almost as interesting as the glove itself. There's a badge in Fanny's name which she won at the Art School in San Francisco, proof that she did study, and one of her small shoes, incontrovertible evidence of her dainty feet.

I opened a little box you made as a youth and inside were some words from your mother. She explains how you were once sent to carpentry lessons by your father, despite the fact that you had no manual dexterity. All you ever made was this box. It started off quite large, but you could never get all six sides to fit, so you kept on cutting down one side, then another. It got so small your mother feared 'it would disappear all together'. In the end, you had to be helped to finish it.

Equally charming are two carefully preserved locks of your hair. One of them, when you were aged one year and eleven months, is signed by your mother: 'Dear Little Lewis' hair, Nov 8, 1852.' So your name was at one time spelled the correct way. With it is a lock of Cummy's hair, dated the same day. I can imagine that cold November day in Heriot Row, too bitter to venture out, with your second birthday celebrations coming up in five days, so you and Cummy stay cosy in the nursery and cut each other's hair, then dear Cummy takes them down to present to your Mama.

Most embarrassing, if you had to come back today, is one of those childhood portraits that makes you look like a girl in a blue dress. This original and splendid print is of you aged four, done by J. Archer, Edinburgh, on 18 December 1854.

I suppose the most valuable item, as opposed to the most fun, is an original page from the manuscript of *Dr Jekyll*. This is in the back room, not on show. Along with it are some of your original notes for *Treasure Island*, some pages from *St Ives*, quite a few letters and a telegram. You wouldn't believe the price your handwriting fetches today. Most of your letters are in Yale or Edinburgh, so they rarely come on the market. I was recently offered a scrap by a dealer near Oxford, a bread-and-butter letter, one page only, from you to your cousin Henrietta, thanking her for some present. The price was £2,250, about double the going rate for a comparable letter from Dickens, Thackeray or Henry James.

Next day, as the weather looked a bit better, I headed for Calistoga, the nearest settlement to your Silverado honeymoon. It was founded in 1866 by Sam Brennan, the gold-rush man, California's first home-made millionaire. He knew about the presence of hot mineral springs and decided to develop a spa resort. That all sounds true, so far. On the grand opening, after the guests had quite a bit of the local Napa Valley wine, he stood up to make his speech. What he meant to say was that his new development would be California's answer to Saratoga, the health spa in New York state. What he said was, 'We'll make this place the Calistoga of Sarafornia.' And the name stuck.

Calistoga is another eight miles up the valley from St Helena and I thought I might stop there for a coffee and walk around. I expected a pretty spa town, perhaps not quite like Bath or Harrogate, but with some fine buildings. While St Helena has gone up in the world, done well for itself, preserved its looks and hidden its wrinkles, Calistoga has slipped down market and is showing its age. Tatty, gawdy, rather sad. Huge signs everywhere offering cheap accommodation and cheap medical treatments. 'Acupressure Face Lift (½ hour) – 29 dollars,' announced Dr Wilkinson's Hot Springs and Mud Baths. 'Dr Wilkinson's Cerofanga for Hands and Feet (1 hr) – 50 dollars. Grapefruit and Aloe Facelift – 20 dollars.' A leaflet informed me that 'Doc has been in business so long, some people say that the mere mention of his name can relieve stress and relax the soul. Come see for yourself . . .'

The road rises steeply after Calistoga and begins to climb the slopes of Mount St Helena. I couldn't see the top for mist and as I got higher, negotiating hairpin bends, I ran into snow along the roadside. The mountain is 4,343 feet high, almost the same height as Ben Nevis.

At the summit of the road you come to . . . The Robert Louis Stevenson State Park. They've turned the whole of the mountain and surrounds into a national park, named after you, Louis.

I parked the car on the spot where the old toll house used to be, where you came down the mountainside from your log cabin to buy provisions. A signpost informed me that it was a one-mile walk up to the RLS Monument, five miles to the summit. It also warned me against the triple-leaf poison oak and the 'black-legged tick with harpoon-like barbs in its mouth'.

The walk up the mountainside was well laid out along a dark red, zig-zag path with little marking posts every tenth of a mile. I spotted a couple of deer and a squirrel, but no sign of black-legged ticks. Once I was away from any road noises, I walked in total silence, apart from faint misty drips from the bay trees and the murmur of little unseen burns. Your honeymoon was in summer, so you got all the noisy summer insects.

All the log cabins have gone, long since. The mountain has been tamed and landscaped, covered in trees, as wild as a Forestry Commission plantation. If it were not for the monument, marking your honeymoon spot, no one would know anyone had ever lived here. But first you have to find it. It's very small, only three feet high, very discreet, done in the shape of an open book, very arty, standing on a little plinth. The book itself hardly looks like a book any more as it's now overgrown with moss and lichens. It was erected by the Clubwomen of Napa County. I wonder if Fanny would have joined them today. No, she was too independent, too strong-minded, too outspoken.

Before finally leaving the Napa Valley, I bought a bottle of wine to take home, from the St Helena Wine Center, a very smart wine shop on Main Street, St Helena, where a very smart young man called Mark Vaughan told me that the local wine available to you, in 1880, was terrible. 'We'd call it plonk,' he said. So perhaps that wasn't an attraction for you after all. 'They were still recovering from the first wave of phyllox,' he explained.

The first? Yes, the bad news is that Napa has been suffering again. This time the local experts have produced a new rootstock called AXR-1 which resists the phyllox, but it's very expensive to use. Mark shouted over to an old farmer called Bill who was in a corner of the cellar. Bill said it cost $25,000 an acre to replant with the new root, which he couldn't afford. 'That little critter can ride in the back pocket of someone's jeans or on their tyres. So what ah do is not let folks on ma property.'

Modern honeymooners beware. There's little chance of squatting in the Napa Valley today.

13
Europe
1880–84

Louis arrived at Liverpool on 17 August 1880 on board the *City of Chester*, a year and ten days after he had left. He had gone out alone, second class, with very little money, cutting himself off from his parents, not knowing what the future held or what his welcome might be when he reached his destination. He came back first class, thanks to his £250 a year from his father, complete with a wife and a twelve-year-old stepson, material for three books and assorted articles, knowing that his future was as a family man with several mouths to provide for, but not sure of his welcome. Would his parents hate Fanny? Would his old friends still criticise him, now that he had done what they had counselled against?

First on board to greet him, fresh off the night mail from London and hopping straight on a tug-boat, was Sidney Colvin, the advance customs official for the London literati, come to examine the boy wonder. Colvin, the worthy, serious, solid Cambridge academic, five years older, was always willing to dash across the country, or the continent, at his own expense, to minister to Louis's needs, ever loyal, ever caring, convinced that Louis was the bright hope of English letters, entranced by a personality he thought dazzling and unique.

In his report back to base, to Henley in London, Colvin noted that Louis's teeth were in better shape and had filled out his cheeks, but that he still looked so thin 'you could put your thumb and finger round his thigh'. Overall, he thought Louis did not look too bad, certainly not like a dying man, but he was not so complimentary about Fanny. Few of the London friends were. 'Whether you and I will ever get reconciled to the little determined brown face and white teeth and grizzling hair,' continued Colvin, 'which we are to see beside him in the future, that is another matter.'

Poor Fanny. Elsewhere Colvin described her as having 'the build and character that somehow suggested Napoleon', that she could be a 'dragon indeed' when fussing over Louis's health, and that her 'eyes were full of sex and mystery'. One can imagine Louis being sexually captivated by Fanny at this time, in the full flush of their new marriage, but it is hard to believe she was sending any signals for Sidney to pick up.

On the quayside, waiting their turn, were Thomas and Maggie Stevenson, ready to welcome home the prodigal, to take him back to the bosom of the family, and to meet their new daughter-in-law, the only one they were ever likely to have. 'The old folks put a most brave and most kind face on it indeed,' Colvin observed.

They had prepared their brave face on the way down, making good Christian vows to think the best of everyone. Maggie had told a cousin that 'doubtless she is not the daughter-in-law that I have always pictured to myself'. But she, unlike her husband, had the temperament to cope, being naturally optimistic, able to wipe unpleasant things from her mind and from her sight, taking matters as they came, ready to move on blithely. Thomas would be a harder rock to crack, or even to soften round the edges.

After only a few days back in Edinburgh, they no longer needed to pretend or make allowances for this funny little brown foreign body in their midst. Fanny was a success. Maggie took her into her dressing-room, showed off her fine New Town silks and satins, insisting that Fanny tried on and kept anything she liked. She opened up trunks and cupboards, revealing the smart clothes she had bought for Louis, which he had always refused to wear. She got out the albums of photographs and the old scraps of stories and childhood drawings, and they cooed over them together.

Tom had not been too keen on some of Fanny's own clothes, and had made it clear he did not approve of black stockings, even if it was the American fashion, so she straightaway gave them up.

When it came to verbal jousting, she held her own, stuck to her opinions, but did so gracefully and politely, addressing her father-in-law as Mister Tommy, which rather charmed him. Perhaps the most surprising thing of all was not that they took to her as a wife for their son, quickly deciding she was good for Louis, appearing genuinely concerned about his health and well-being, fussing over him, stopping him from some of his sillier activities, but that Thomas rated her highly as a literary critic. He later agreed that on no account must Louis ever publish anything without Fanny's approval.

Cynics might say, and have said, that Fanny was being clever, deliberately getting in their good books. She probably was indeed on her best behaviour, as any new member of a family would be. The anti-Fanny lobby has also suggested she was cunning from the very beginning, sending in advance a photograph of herself from America – with the warning that it was not a good one:

> Please remember that my photograph is flattering; unfortunately all photographs of me are; I can get no other. At the same time Louis thinks me, and to him I believe I am, the most beautiful creature in the world. It is because he loves me that he thinks that, so I am very glad. I do earnestly hope that you will like me, but that can only be for what I am to you after you know me, and I do not want you to be disappointed in the beginning in anything about me, even in so small a thing as my looks.

That seems a perfectly honest letter. And Thomas and Maggie quickly decided she was a perfectly honest woman. They observed and approved of qualities in Fanny as a daughter-in-law which the London literati never admitted. They saw what every parent wants to see. She had made their son happy.

Family and friends in Edinburgh came to see the happy couple, or sent them presents: no one was disagreeable about Fanny's divorce, or her son, which is quite remarkable, given the attitudes of the times. Louis's cousin Henrietta and her husband sent a pair of vases, and Louis replied, saying he had a clean tablecloth ready to display them, and that he and Fanny would visit them personally next day to thank them properly. Walter Simpson gave Fanny a Skye terrier, an ill-tempered dog by the sound of it, who clawed furniture and attacked visitors, but they loved him, dragging him everywhere. He started off being called Wattie, after Walter, then Woggs, Woggy and finally Bogue.

In the late summer, they all went for a family holiday in the Highlands, much to Thomas's pleasure. 'All goes exceedingly well with the wife and the parents,' wrote Louis to Colvin from Strathpeffer, enthusing about the heather and the birds. 'No country, no place, was ever for a moment so delightful to my soul. And I have been a Scotchman all my life, and denied my native land! Away with your gardens of roses. Give me the cool breath of Rogie waterfall, henceforth and for ever, world without end.'

From the same hotel, on what looks like the next day, he is lampooning his fellow guests in a letter to Baxter. 'I am well but have a little overtired myself which is disgusting. This is a heathenish place near delightful places, but inhabited, alas, by a wholly bestial crowd.' A rather contradictory statement, but typical of his love-hate for Scotland.

While in the Highlands, his father finally put his foot down about *The Amateur Emigrant*, which appears by now to have been at proof stage. Fanny's views on this book are not known, but Louis's action clearly shows that he felt beholden to his father, even at the age of thirty. 'My father desires me still to withdraw the Emigrant,' he wrote to Colvin. 'Whatever may be the pecuniary loss, he is willing to bear it; and the gain to my reputation will be considerable.'

What Louis gained was his father's continued financial support, enough for a stay in London, where he and Fanny ran up a bill of forty-six pounds for a week at the Grosvenor Hotel. This was partly due to Louis's treating all his London friends and partly to their own fecklessness with money. Fanny felt embarrassed by such a huge bill, telling Thomas that she was not used to London hotels. Louis, on the other hand, had always been wildly generous whenever he was in funds. As with many people who pride themselves on being able to live frugally and exist on very little when they have to, as he did in San Francisco, all frugality disappears once the money is available, especially other people's money.

In London, Fanny had another taste of what Louis's social life might be like, if he ever lived there permanently. There were long lunches at the Savile Club, then long evenings of drinking, smoking and talking with his friends. The big, bearded Henley was the noisiest, unless of course the equally voluble cousin Bob was around. Colvin sat more silently, taking it all in, his eyes and ears on the star turn. Fanny felt very out of it once again. She wanted to protect Louis from himself, stop him smoking and drinking too much and getting over-excited. Her concern for his health was genuine, and he was seriously ill at the time, but she also wanted to protect him from his friends: 'It is not good for my mind, or my body either, to sit smiling at Louis's friends until I feel like a hypocritical Cheshire cat, talking stiff nothings with one another in order to let Louis have a chance with the one he cares the most for, and all the time furtively watching the clock and thirsting for their blood because they stay so late . . . If we do not get away from London, I shall become an embittered woman.'

Fanny was jealous of Louis's friends' influence over him, and their intimacy which she could not share, though she affected not to take it seriously; and they in their turn were jealous of her hold over Louis, which they affected not to be able to understand, judging her by her squat, lumpish appearance and her lack of conversational skills.

It is easy to imagine Louis and Fanny arguing long and hard after one of these sessions, accusing each other either of showing off or of being antisocial. Louis knew which camp he preferred, and he had already made his choice, but there was part of him which enjoyed these social occasions with his literary cronies, taking him back to his student days. Fanny doubtless dismissed such an inclination as pathetic in someone of his age, while Louis explained that he did not want to live this sort of life for ever, just to have it there, to pick up and enjoy when he felt like it. That was what Fanny had to try to understand and get in proportion. Of course it was all a performance, talk for the sake of it, smart and flashy, empty and silly, he knew all that, but it was still good fun. And they were proper friends, real friends, who had helped him in the past and would in the future, so he could not let them down.

This stay in London was short. They were on the way to spend the winter in Europe for the sake of Louis's health. Not to the South of France this time, but to Davos in Switzerland, following the latest wisdom of the medical profession which recommended cold dry air and special diets for TB. It could have been worse. Another current theory was that horses were good for TB. Not eating them, or even riding them, but smelling them, breathing in their odour. So a winter stuck away in a hotel in the depths of Switzerland was probably preferable to moving into a room above a stable.

The party consisted of Louis, Fanny, Lloyd (now aged thirteen) and Bogue. Bogue at least enjoyed himself, tearing up hotel carpets and annoying other guests. In one establishment Fanny went upstairs to inspect the rooms while Louis stood talking to the landlord. 'Your mother will be down soon,' said the landlord to Louis.

None of them enjoyed Davos. Louis's health got little better and he was unable to do much work. Fanny fell ill and Lloyd was bored, stuck amidst a settlement of invalids, many of them dying, even though Louis tried hard to think of games and tricks to amuse him. There was one literary invalid already in residence for Louis to talk to, John Addington Symonds. Edmund Gosse had kindly provided an introduction, but Symonds turned out to be stiff and snobbish.

One surprise visitor did appear – Fanny Sitwell. She arrived with her son Bertie, whom Louis had played with all those years ago in Suffolk, now dying of TB. In a dramatised TV version of this winter in Davos, Mrs Sitwell would be given lots of elliptical lines and meaningful looks, and poor Fanny would not know what was going on, but alas, there are too few details to go on. Colvin unsurprisingly tells us little, and Louis reveals few details, except that he and his wife tried their best to help with poor Bertie.

Louis wrote long letters addressed to his mother, but obviously meant for his father as well. In one he gets on to the subject of Christianity again, casting a critical but not offensive eye on the Ten Commandments, saying that Christ was so affirmative, yet all the commands are 'not to do' things, which he finds strange. 'It is much more important to do right than not to do wrong . . . to blow the trumpet for good would seem the parson's business. I do not see where they get their material for their gloomy discourses.' He feels that God means us to be kind, and to be happy.

Having given his father something to think about, he then tells his mother the sort of story he knows she will enjoy: 'Lloyd heard with dismay that Fanny was not going to give me a present; F and I had to go and buy things for ourselves and go through the sensation of surprise when they were presented next morning. It gave us both quite a Santa Claus feeling on Xmas Eve to see him so excited and so hopeful. I enjoyed it hugely.'

They left Davos in April 1881 and proceeded slowly back to Edinburgh. During that summer, they all went to the Highlands again, with his parents, eventually taking a cottage in Braemar, not far from where Queen Victoria was staying at Balmoral. 'The Queen knows a thing or two,' wrote Louis to Mrs Sitwell. 'She has picked out the finest habitable spot in Britain.' He was more truthful to Gosse when he invited him to come and join them. 'If you had an uncle who was a sea captain and went to the North Pole, you had better bring his outfit.'

The weather was so bad that they were stuck inside for days. To amuse young Lloyd, Louis drew an imaginary map of an island, wrote in some suitably piratical-sounding names, like Spyglass Hill and Skeleton Island, and painted in the sea and the main features using a shilling box of watercolours. That evening, he started planning the first chapter: 'It was to be a story for boys; no need of psychology or fine writing; and I had a boy at hand to be the touchstone. Women were to be excluded. I then had an idea for John Silver from which I promised myself funds of entertainment; to take an admired friend of mine, to deprive him of all his finer qualities, to leave him nothing but his strength, his quickness. . . .'

The friend he had in mind was the bearded, burly, one-legged Henley, not a very flattering model, but it was only his physical appearance he was going to copy, or so he said. The object was to amuse, to follow the sort of boys' adventure stories which were current at the time, about pirates and brigands, the sort he himself had loved as a child – not to mock or satirise them, but to produce an equally spanking story using many of the traditional elements. Louis later admitted that he had pinched the parrot from *Robinson Crusoe*, the skeleton from Edgar Allan Poe, the stockade from *Masterman Ready* and Billy Bones and the chest from Washington Irving's *Tales of a Traveller*. 'I think little of these things, they are trifles and details, and no man can hope to have a monopoly of skeletons or make a corner in talking birds.'

Next morning he started writing. Round the fire after dinner each day he read out to the family his progress so far. 'I had counted on one boy, I found I had two in the audience. My father caught fire at once with all the romance and childishness of his original nature. His own stories, that every night of his life he put himself to sleep with, dealt perpetually with ships, roadside inns, robbers, old sailors.' When the time came for the contents of Billy Bones's chest to be ransacked, Thomas insisted on making a list of all the items inside, which Louis used, word for word.

After two chapters, he wrote off to Henley in London in a great state of excitement, apologising first of all for not finishing any of the ghost stories he was supposed to have been working on, with Fanny's help, for Henley to try to sell in London.

'Nobody, not you, nor [Andrew] Lang nor the devil will hurry me with the crawlers [as he called these stories]; but I am on another lay for the moment, purely owing to Lloyd this one, but I believe there's more coin in it than in any amount of crawlers; now see here, The Sea Cook, or The Treasure Island: a Story for Boys. If this don't fetch the kids, why, they have gone rotten since my day. The trouble is to work it off without oaths. Buccaneers without oaths – bricks without straw. But youth and the fond parent have to be consulted.'

He then refers to a project for a play which Henley has been working on, and wants Louis to share, called *Admiral Guinea*. This has a sea element, but is meant for grown-ups, and includes women. 'Your Admiral sounds like a shublime gent. Stick to him like wax – he'll do. My Trelawney is several thousand sea miles of the original of your Admiral Guinea.'

He wants Henley to send up by the fastest post any good books about buccaneers, the best he can find, for him to use as background information.

'A chapter a day I mean to do, and perhaps in a month, The Sea Cook maybe to Routledge go, yo ho ho and a bottle of

rum. It's awful fun, boys' stories, you just indulge the pleasures of
your heart, that's all; no trouble, no strain. The only stiff thing is
to get it ended. You would like my blind beggar in chapter three.
No writing, just drive along as the words and the pen will scratch!
– RLS, Author of Boys' Stories.'

He finished several chapters, with hardly a pause for breath, by
which time there had come a chance visitor called Dr Alexander
Japp. He was a minor literary figure, later the author of a biography
of De Quincey, who had criticised an essay Louis had written on
Thoreau. Louis invited him to stay for a few days, should he ever
be in the area, and continue the argument. He arrived while *The
Sea Cook* was in full flow, heard some of the chapters being read
out, declared it capital stuff and suggested it should be sent off to
a boys' magazine, *Young Folks*, where he knew the editor, James
Henderson, saying that Louis might get as much as a hundred
guineas for it.

Another visitor was Edmund Gosse:

> After breakfast, I went to Louis's bedroom where he sat up
> in bed with dark flashing eyes and ruffled hair and we played
> chess on the coverlet. Not a word passed, for he was strictly
> forbidden to speak in the early part of the day. As soon as he
> felt tired – often in the middle of a game – he would rap with
> peremptory knuckles on the board as a signal to stop, and
> then Mrs Stevenson or I would arrange his writing materials
> on his bed. Then I would see no more of him till dinner time,
> when he would appear smiling and voluble, the horrid bar of
> speechlessness having been let down.

Thanks to Dr Japp's contacts, the story was commissioned, to
appear in episodes, but the fee was not quite as much as Louis
had hoped for – only thirty-four pounds – though he was allowed
to keep the copyright. As his literary earnings were exceedingly
lean at the time, he accepted and the first episode appeared on
1 October 1881. Henderson dropped *The Sea Cook* as the title,
using *Treasure Island* instead. The author was given as Captain
George North, in the style of the time.

The first reactions were not good. At least one young reader
wrote in to say he did not like it, forcing the editor to print
a defence: 'That which you condemn is really the best story
now appearing in the paper and the impress of an able writer

is stamped on every paragraph of *The Treasure Island*. You will probably share this opinion when you have read more of it.'

Louis had in fact given up after those first fifteen or so chapters, running out of steam, which so often happened to him. In the first flush of enthusiasm he could write easily and quickly, carried away with his own excitement, then very often he would grow bored and be unable to think of what might happen next, so he would bring the work to a sudden end or more often be distracted on to a newer, more exciting topic, leaving the first one hanging. This explains why up to now so many of his books had been short, or collections of essays and short stories, none of them yet being a full-length novel. *Treasure Island* was left unfinished for some time, despite its regular appearance in serial form, but he did manage to finish it off in the winter, when again they all went to Davos.

One of the matters which distracted his attention, while still in Scotland during 1881, was an absolutely idiotic campaign to get himself elected as Professor of History and Constitutional Law at Edinburgh University. He saw it as a sinecure, requiring only summer lectures and without any teaching load, but it was a distinguished position nonetheless, paying £250 a year, which was the big attraction. Why Louis thought he had the slightest chance, given his own academic career and his total lack of interest in the law, is hard to understand, but he was aided and abetted by his father, who wrote around to eminent people, asking for their support. In Thomas's case the main attraction was not the money, as he was always willing to support his son, but the thought of Louis having another Edinburgh connection, something which would pull him back for three months every year and perhaps stop some of his wanderings.

In June 1881, Louis wrote to the previous incumbent, Professor Aeneas Mackay: 'If you are retiring, may I ask for your support? I have a great mind to try. I only wish it were a few years from now when I hope to have something more substantial to show for myself. Up to the present time, all I have published, even bordering on history, has been in occasional form.' So occasional, it is difficult to think what he had in mind, apart from the history he dragged into *Travels with a Donkey*. Professor Mackay was not fooled. His letter back reminded Louis about his own legal studies, such as they were. 'You are not the only one who has regretted my absence from your lectures,' wrote Louis in reply, 'but you were to me then only a part of a mangle through which I was slowly and unwillingly dragged – part of a course I had not chosen – part, in a word, of an organised boredom.' Not very convincing. And, at the end of his letter, Louis gives the game away: 'It is perhaps the only hope I have of a permanent income.'

He did manage to rustle up a few legal supporters, such as Charles Guthrie, his old Spec friend, and begged a few testimonials from eminent London literary friends, such as Edmund Gosse and Leslie Stephen. 'Testimonial hunting is a queer form of a sport, but has its pleasures.'

Louis, Fanny and Lloyd were in Davos, for another winter, when the news came through about the election. The winner received eighty-two votes, the runner-up fifty-one. Louis was nowhere with nine. By this time he was busily writing, which softened any disappointment, though the result can hardly have been unexpected. He was finishing off *Treasure Island*, polishing up *Silverado Squatters*, doing research for a biography of Hazlitt, and even planning a biography of Wellington. 'It must be good to live with another man from birth to death.'

The final episode of *Treasure Island* appeared in *Young Folks* on 28 January 1882. Louis then edited it into book form, and got Henley to start submitting it. Routledge were not keen, nor were Chatto, who preferred to publish his collected essays, *Familiar Studies of Men and Books*, which came out in April 1882, or his adult stories, *New Arabian Nights*, which appeared in July. 'Did you see I had joined the band of the rejected?' he wrote in a letter. Many of his London friends thought he was wasting his time anyway, knocking out stuff for children when he should be concentrating on literature.

For relaxation, he and Lloyd played at being printers and publishers, working on a little printing press they had bought in America, producing programmes and tickets for the hotels in Davos. They also turned out little books of their own, with Louis and Fanny doing the woodcuts.

Louis's health got no better, and then Fanny fell ill again. 'I wish to God anybody knew what was the matter with my wife,' he wrote. For several months he referred to her being ill, without giving any details, which has led some observers to think the cause might have been mental. By April, she was a bit better. 'I did really fear my wife was worse than ill.' Which could mean worse than physically ill, or just that she was dangerously ill. 'My wife is better again, but we take it in turns. It is the dog that is ill now.'

The news about *Treasure Island* continued to be discouraging. Henley decided to try Cassell, though Louis had very little hope. In a long, satirical letter to Henley, typically witty, he makes up a list of all the books that Cassell have so far turned down: '1 – Six undiscovered Tragedies and an unfinished autobiography by William Shakespeare. 2 – The Journals and Private Correspondence of David, King of Israel. 3 – Poetical Works of Arthur, Iron Dook of Wellington, including a Monody on Napoleon. 4 – Eight books of an unfinished novel, Solomon Crabb, by Henry Fielding. 5 – Stevenson's Moral Emblems.' He also lists some of the books which Cassell have accepted and triumphantly published: 'Brown's Handbook to Cricket, Jones's First French Readers, Robinson's Picturesque Cheshire, uniform with the same author's Stately Homes of Salop.'

He finishes with a long description of the non-existent Fielding novel, giving the plot and enthusing about the delightful characterisation, which must have amused Henley. It certainly kept Louis happy. For a while. On the whole, though, Davos was a failure. Little new writing was done. The climate did not make any significant difference to Louis's lungs; there were still signs of haemorrhaging; and Davos seemed to have a bad effect on Fanny.

In the summer, they returned to Scotland, for another family holiday, but Louis's health remained poor. There were fewer jocular letters to his literary friends. Instead he wrote a series of very solemn ones to a young art student, whom he had not met, who had written about Louis's essays, asking for advice about life, love and suchlike. Louis's reflections on sex are interesting, given what we know about his own actions.

You do not yet know how far you can trust yourself – it will not be very far, or you are more fortunate than I am. If you can keep your sexual desires in order, be glad, be very glad. Some day when you meet your fate, you will be free, and the better man. Whatever you do, see that you don't sacrifice a woman; that's where all imperfect love conducts us. At the same time, if you can't make it convenient to be chaste, for God's sake, avoid the primness of virtue; hardness to a poor harlot is a sin lower than the ugliest unchastity. I am afraid I am not so rigid on chastity: you are probably right in your view; but this seems to me a dilemma with two horns, the real curse of a man's life in society – and a woman's too, although, for many reasons, it appears somewhat differently with the enslaved sex.

In September, they decided they would try hot weather again, and look for a little house to rent in the South of France, instead of wintering in the cold and snow in an invalid community in Switzerland. Louis and Bob, being French experts, set off ahead to find something suitable. Fanny was not well enough to go with them. It must have been a holiday in itself, as life with Bob usually turned into high jinks. ('Jink' was the phrase Louis always used when remembering his Edinburgh exploits with Bob.)

This was about the first time Louis and Fanny had been apart since their wedding, so at last we have letters between them. His give some interesting clues to their relationship.

'If you think I don't want to see you, you are a great baby,' he wrote from Montpellier. 'I am going to wear beautiful rich clothes always now on condition that you do. When you come you shall have a kiss. Ever your loving husband, Louis.'

Then he added a strange postscript:

I am no good at all. Marriage does soften a person. I have neither pluck nor patience, and I must own I have wearied awful for you. But you will never understand that bit of my character. I don't want you when I am ill. At least it's only half of me that wants you, and I don't like to think of you coming back and not finding me better than when we parted. That is why I would rather be miserable than send for you.

There is also another peculiar passage.

I do not ask you to love me any more. I am too much

trouble. Beside, I thought myself all over last night; and my dear, such rubbage. You cannot put up with such a man.

In one way I see you act on these principles, for I hear from you very rarely. Indeed I suspect you of being very ill. If you are, I shall forgive you, my dear, you are provoked to it, I know. If you are not, you might write oftener, I think, to one who is devoted to silence and repose. I don't feel the least unhappy, but I don't feel the least happy either. A person who has been a good while married – (to an angel) – chafes at this position. Besides which, it is so dull.

They had been married for only two years, but had known each other for six years. The last two must have been a trifle claustrophobic, cooped up either with other invalids in Davos or with his parents in Scotland. It is hard to tell what had gone wrong between them, if anything. There is none of the dripping emotion of Louis's letters to Fanny Sitwell, apart from the angel reference (in brackets, almost as an afterthought). Louis appears self-pitying, which is unusual, blaming himself, and his health, for whatever has temporarily come between them. Fanny's own mysterious ill-health is referred to; he says he might have provoked it, which could indeed suggest mental troubles. As for 'I don't want you when I am ill', does this mean he does not want her sexually, or just does not want her there when he is ill? The latter is hard to believe, as he loved being nursed and was always grateful to her. 'If I am where I am,' he had boasted the previous year, 'it is thanks to that lady who married me when I was a mere complication of cough and bones, much fitter for an emblem of mortality than a bridegroom.'

Whatever had gone wrong, it was quickly righted. By October, he had found a house near Marseilles and Fanny joined him there. 'I vote for separation,' he wrote to Bob. 'F's arrival here, after our separation, was far better fun to me than being married by far. A separation is a most valuable property.'

On an earlier occasion, he penned some verses about Fanny.

> I am as good as deaf
> When separate from F.
>
> I am far from gay
> When separate from A.

I loathe the ways of men
When separate from N.

Life is a murky den
When separate from N.

My sorrow rages high
When separate from Y.

They had to move after a few months when there was an outbreak of typhoid in the district, brought on by bad drains. Louis
retreated to Nice, his weight down to seven stone eleven, while
Fanny remained in the house to pack up, guarding herself with a
revolver. For several days they lost touch with each other, letters
crossed, and Fanny feared the typhoid had got him. She worked
herself into a state of collapse, convinced he was dead. 'My nerves
are so shattered by the terrible suspense I endured,' she wrote to
Maggie Stevenson.

Louis eventually turned up and they found another house,
Chalet La Solitude, further along the coast at Hyères. They
moved into it in March 1883 and stayed there for the next sixteen
months.

It was at Hyères that news came through of the death of Louis's
old Spec friend, Walter Ferrier, the first of his contemporaries to
die. This produced many maudlin letters from Louis about death.
'Up to now, I had rather thought of him as a mere personal enemy of
my own; but now that I see him hunting after my friends, he looks
altogether darker. . . . I always thought I should go by myself, not
to survive.'

There was also bad news about his father's health, which was
making him more than normally depressive, but this seems to have
brought them closer, healing old wounds, with Louis trying to be
the mature comforter.

On the writing front, there was good news from home about a
play which he and Henley had written together a couple of years
earlier, in London and at their Swanston cottage: it was to be put
on at a theatre in Bradford. '*Deacon Brodie* was I suppose hissed
off the boards yesterday evening at Bradford,' he wrote to his
mother. 'But I have not heard whether bones were broken.' In fact
it received reasonable reviews, and went on to Aberdeen and other

venues in Scotland and the North of England. Henley was thrilled, hoping it would transfer to London's West End, and was eager for more collaborations.

Louis meanwhile had started on some *Nursery Verses*, based on his own childhood memories, which at first he called *Penny Whistle*. He sent them off to Henley in London as he finished each one, with notes on how he would like them illustrated: 'A good drawing of any object mentioned in the text, were it only a loaf of bread or a candlestick, is a most delightful thing to a young child. I remember this keenly. I forgot to mention I am going to dedicate 'em to Cummy. It will please her and lighten a little my burthen of ingratitude.'

Strange that at this stage in his life his thoughts should turn to childhood, but then it often takes a geographical and time gap before an experience can be pinned down. Now, aged thirty-three, living in the South of France, he started writing about lamplighters and counterpanes and other memories from his Edinburgh childhood. It was, of course, typical of him to jump around from project to project, moving between different markets, different styles. He also started a new novel, *The Black Arrow*, which he admitted was tushery, saying he had to do it for the money to pay the bills. 'When ever I think I would like to live a little, I hear the butcher's cart resounding through the neighbourhood.'

Working was living. He could not see himself ever being divorced from his pen. 'I sleep upon my art for a pillow. I awaken in my art. I am unready for death, because I hate to leave it. I love my wife, I do not know how much, nor can, nor shall, unless I lost her, but while I can conceive my being widowed, I refuse the offering of life without my art. I am not in my art. It is me.'

At the same time, he could be deeply aware that he had achieved very little so far. 'I now draw near the Middle Ages. Nearly three years ago, that fatal Thirty struck; and yet the great work is not done – not even yet conceived.'

Silverado Squatters, which had appeared first in an American magazine, *The Century*, was accepted by Chatto in London. But the best news of all came in May 1883.

'There has been offered for *Treasure Island* – how much do you suppose,' Louis wrote to his parents. 'I believe it would be an excellent jest to keep the answer till my next letter. For two cents, I would do so. Shall I? Anyway, I'll turn the page first. No – well – a Hundred Pounds, all alive O! A hundred, jingling, tingling minted quid. Is not this wonderful? Your loving and ecstatic son – Treesure Eilaan.'

In the last months of their time in Hyères there occurred two rather dramatic events. There was a visit from Bluidy Jack so severe that they were convinced Louis was going to die. It happened in the night, the haemorrhage arriving so suddenly it rendered him speechless. Taking a pencil and paper he wrote a message for Fanny: 'Don't be frightened; if this is death, it is an easy one.' But, once again, he recovered.

The other event was unprecedented, as far as is known. Fanny was pregnant. It is not mentioned anywhere by Fanny herself but is referred to in a letter Louis wrote to Walter Simpson at the end of December 1883. 'I must tell you a joke. A month or two ago, there was an alarm; it looked like a family. Prostration. I saw myself financially ruined. I saw the child born sickly, etc. Then, said I, I must look this thing on the good side; proceeded to do so studiously; and with such result that when the alarm passed off – I was inconsolable.'

Fanny was forty-three at the time, not too late to have another baby, which would have been her first by Louis. Perhaps there had been similar alarms earlier, in Davos for example, which were the reason for her ill-health, and then those curious passages in Louis's correspondence. Whether or not Fanny wanted another baby is not known. From that letter, Louis was certainly disappointed not to become a father.

At the end of his life, Louis said that his period in Hyères was the happiest he ever spent. A bit puzzling, really, when one thinks of the terrible things that happened there. On the other hand, there was that jingling, tingling *Treasure Island* news.

Hyères Today

Dear Louis,

I didn't waste any time in Nice, where you were twice very ill, but then you were pretty ill in most places. I took a train along the coast, the best way of seeing the French Riviera without actually spending anything. Life in Nice is rather costly these days, judging by the Porsches and Rolls in the airport car park, and the helicopters constantly fluttering overhead, but French train travel is a bargain. The buffet car was arranged like a self-service supermarket, stacked with little dishes, salads, puddings and wines, and it took me ages to decide what to have, especially as I kept rushing to the window to admire the views as we threaded our way along the edge of palm-fringed beaches, slicing across beautiful rocky inlets, passing through exotic places like Juan-les-Pins and Antibes.

Graham Greene, one of your Stevenson descendants, who used to live in Antibes, started a biography of you, back in the Fifties. He did six months of research, made lots of notes, but then gave it up, leaving the way clear for Furnas. I wrote to him a couple of years ago, hoping for a chat or at least a peep at his notes, and his secretary said he would dig them out, next time he was in England. Then he died.

Opposite me, in my second-class compartment, sat a French mother with her two young children, aged about eleven and thirteen. They were both wearing bomber jackets emblazoned with English slogans. That was how I knew they were French, long before they spoke.

The mother had brought her own ham and baguettes, which she sliced up on her lap. While they ate, they all read comics, including the mother, without looking out of the window, till at Cannes an elderly Frenchwoman got on and maintained one of the seats was hers. She pointed to the booking form on the window. The mother, without arguing, put one of her children on her knee, then carried on eating and reading.

I like Fanny's description of her train ride to Nice, when you were lost. She got talking to an Englishman, told him about her worries, and he asked her what she was going to do when you died. Fanny said she didn't expect you to die. 'Oh, I know all about that,' said the man, 'I've heard that talk before. He's gone for, and in this country they'll shove him underground in twenty-four hours, almost before the breath is out of his body. His mother'll never see him again. Have him embalmed, that's the thing. Have you got money enough?' At various stations, Fanny got off the train, hoping to get into another carriage and shake off the horrid man, but they were all full.

My train took two hours to reach Toulon, where I'd hoped to get a local train to Hyères and arrive the way your visitors usually arrived, but the service to Hyères had recently been drastically reduced and there wasn't a train for another four hours. I went out to look for a taxi, wondering what a twenty-five-kilometre ride would cost. I studied a poster inviting me to 'Découvrez les Dinoseurs'. Could that be a local name for some ancient form of transport? Then I saw a rather battered bus across the road, standing waiting, destination Hyères. There was no driver, but at the back sat two or three old people, looking worried, as if they'd been there for decades. I asked when the bus was due to leave and they all muttered and mumbled. I sat down and a load of German back-packers got on and asked me the same question. I muttered and mumbled, in my best French.

The driver eventually appeared and he accepted my money, telling me I should have bought a ticket in advance. The bus had its own internal video screen, very modern, but then all French transport is obsessed with computer systems. This screen continuously flashed the same words, all in English – HOLD, BEEP BEEP! OPEN, WELCOME, SCROLL UP, COVER,

PULL, SINK, FLASH, REPEAT. I became mesmerised, waiting for the sequence to come round again. I spent almost the whole of the hour's journey trying to work out the significance of the words when I should have been studying the landscape and soaking up the atmosphere. I decided in the end it was an advertisement for people who might want to advertise on this screen, demonstrating the different ways words and messages could appear. SCROLL UP, for example, rolled on to the screen. FLASH went on and off very quickly. Why it was in English was not clear. As for why anyone would want to advertise flashy, psychedelic messages on a little rural bus, filled with peasants, German students and wandering Englishmen, was an even bigger mystery.

I staggered out in Hyères, my head spinning. It seemed busy and attractive, wide-looking streets, lots of palm trees, very clean, rather affluent. I was in the bus terminus, in the middle of the town, near l'Office du Tourisme, a smart, circular building, rather impressive for a small town of only 40,000. It was very busy inside, mainly with people booking railway tickets from an SNCF desk. I walked round, looking at the displays, and noticed two neatly written quotations high up around the walls. 'Je ne sache pas d'endroit où il fut plus doux de sentir vivre – Duchesse Dino de Courland, nièce de Talleyrand.' Not much of a quote, and it doesn't even mention Hyères.

Then above me I read: 'Heureux, je ne l'ai été qu'une fois, ce fut à Hyères – R.L. Stevenson.'

That's a reasonably faithful translation of something you wrote later in life in a letter to Colvin, probably a throw-away phrase at the time, but it has given your biographers a lot of work. What you actually wrote was: 'me thought you asked me, frankly was I happy. Happy, said I; I was only happy once, that was at Hyères'.

A strange remark. Perhaps you were just being cynical about old age, and fame, and the nature of happiness. But a lucky remark for Hyères, one they can always boast about. Alas, when I asked at the desk for any booklet about RLS in Hyères, there was none. Any postcards of his house? *Rien.* Anything at all to do with RLS? *Pas du tout.* The Californians have made a little industry out of places you only passed through. Just think what they could do with Hyères.

I asked if the Hôtel des Iles d'Or was still going, the place where your visitors used to stay, but it is now closed, turned into apartments. All the grand hotels in Hyères have gone. The Park Hotel still has its name outside, but it's now council offices. The main tourist hotels are about five miles away, out on the coast. In Old Hyères, which is a few miles inland, all they have are pensions and guest-houses. I was given the names of a couple, and a town map.

I decided to find La Solitude first, before getting a bed for the night, so I got a taxi and asked for 4 Rue Victor Basch. I had made contact by letter from London with the present owner, a Monsieur Claude Gibelin, who had told me roughly what days he would be at home.

La Solitude had originally been a mock Swiss chalet, used in an *exposition* in Paris, which some mad but well-off citizen had transported to Hyères and rebuilt on a steep hillside, leading into the Old Town. I rang a bell and waited outside a metal security gate. The Swiss chalet-style wooden balcony has gone, but the house looked much as I had expected from Fanny's descriptions, a charming, overgrown doll's sort of house. Through the gate I could see a blue plaque. 'Here, during 1883–1884, lived the English author Robert Louis Stevenson. He declared, "I was only happy once: that was at Hyères."'

I rang the bell again, then jumped back when a large Dobermann came bounding out and growled at me through the metal gate. A tough-looking middle-aged man with a shaven head appeared, wearing workmen's overalls and covered in dust. I explained who I was and he stared at me for a bit, then let me in. I apologised, saying I could go away, book into a hotel and come back later, as I could see he was obviously working, but he said no, he was about to have a break anyway.

He took me round the side, up some steps and into the house. It is built on a hillside, so you enter upstairs, on the first floor. There are only two floors and the house is even smaller inside than I expected. In your day, he explained, there were no internal stairs, so the only way to get from downstairs to upstairs was to go outside, through the shuttered windows of the downstairs rooms, then up the outside steps. Claude, clearly a handyman, had built a wrought-iron spiral staircase inside, connecting his three little downstairs bedrooms to the sitting-room and kitchen upstairs. That is the only change he has made since he bought the house in 1977.

He took me into the sitting-room, with three long windows at the front, each with outside shutters, which he says were there in your time. He insisted on pouring me a whisky and then getting out the deeds of the house.

The people who erected the house lived opposite, in a much bigger house. They had their garden on this side of the road, where they plonked their Swiss folly, and then built a little metal footbridge, over the road, to connect the two. I said that the Stevensons never mentioned a footbridge, which must have been a prominent feature. He then produced a photograph I had never seen before, showing the house, with its wooden balcony, and the footbridge over the road, just a few yards down the hill. He said some neighbours had given it to him, taken by their grandfather in Stevenson's time.

In 1901, the property was sold by a Monsieur Mignon to the Jacquemaire family, Claude explained, leaning back in his chair, beaming and smiling, waiting for me to register surprise. On first meeting, he had appeared rather gruff and unfriendly, barking out his answers in a loud clipped voice. Now he was my best friend. I hadn't heard of the Jacquemaire family. Baby milk, he said, crashing down his fist on the table, they used to make the best-known baby milk in France.

In 1935, the property on this side of the road was split up, and four other houses were built on what had once been Fanny's garden. Now a fifth was going up, which he was building with his own hands, for his son, who was just about to get married.

He found the documents for when he bought the house, and pointed with a rather thick, dusty finger at a man's name, cursing him for having taken off the Swiss balcony. I said I'd heard it was bomb damage during the last war which had destroyed it, but he said rubbish, there were no bombs round here during the war. Why would anyone want to bomb a little place like Hyères?

He then took me outside, downstairs into a little dark cellar where he stores his wine and tools. He pointed with pride to some letters on the wall, 'Roux R, 1886', which he had recently found.

A mason's mark, I said, done three years after Stevenson left. We both stared at it. He waited for me to add some other exclamation, but I could think of nothing else to say, so he put the light off and we returned upstairs.

We then toured the garden, or what was left of it. It is still pretty big, arranged on six steep terraces, filled with lemon trees, mimosa, olives, roses and other sweet-smelling trees and bushes. We went up some stone steps, which he said Fanny had built, and came to the house he was building. His son was inside, working on the floor, while two women were painting.

It's quite well hidden, this new house, as are the other four, so I think that, coming back today, you would be quite pleased with the garden Fanny created. I can see why she loved it so much, and the little house. It was your first proper home, after those dreary institutional hotels in Davos, or sharing with the old folks in Scotland. Small enough to run on your own, yet large enough to have visitors for dinner, if not to sleep. It must have been like playing at house, playing at being a young married couple, on your own for once, without children or in-laws.

I asked Claude if he was an RLS fan. On a bookcase I had noticed several rows of shiny, unread-looking book-club editions of Jules Verne, A.J. Cronin and Mazo de la Roche, but nothing by you. He'd only read *Ile Trésor*, he said, as a child. What else has he written? I told him, and he still looked a bit doubtful. He couldn't understand why anyone should come all this way, just to see his little house. I was only the second person to request a visit since he bought it, though he had caught sight now and again of people reading the plaque outside. It was there when he came, put up about sixty years ago, or so he thought.

He works as a civil servant, in the social security department, handling mainly agricultural workers. The area round Hyères is covered with nurseries and little farms, specialising in flowers and vegetables, just as it did in your day. He was on holiday that week, and his wife had taken the car to work, but as soon as she came back he would drive me to my hotel. I must come back tomorrow and meet his daughter. She spoke very good English.

I booked into the Hôtel du Soleil, in the Rue du Rempart, right in the heart of the Old Town, under the walls of the old castle. You used to walk round here, according to your letters, so you must have been pretty fit, getting up here from La Solitude. I had expected the Old Town to be scruffy and run-down, now that the tourists have moved on, but it was charming, window-boxes and flowers everywhere, the walls and doors newly painted, the cobbles swept clean.

I stood at the highest point of the Old Town, in a little square outside the church of Saint Paul, seventy-five metres above sea level, and admired the panoramic view over the red-tiled roofs of the Old Town, then beyond to the coast, the Giens peninsula and the offshore islands. There are three main islands – Porquerolles, Port-Cros and the Ile du Levant, all said to have lush semi-tropical vegetation. I could see clearly why tourists had left the Old Town and moved the four or five kilometres to the seaside. In your day, tourists in the South of France were winter residents, come to escape the chills of Northern Europe, from Britain, Germany or Russia, and so the sea was not a prime attraction. Today, the mass of holidaymakers are summer visitors. They demand the seaside, with their hotels built as near as possible to the beach.

You no longer get people booking into a hotel for several months at a time, so you don't get that sort of hotel with semi-permanent residents, creating a social life of their own, which is what you experienced in Menton. I suppose today your father might have bought his own place down here, a summer retreat for the family, a nice villa somewhere inland, or perhaps in the Dordogne, so you could have used that, when you were ill.

Next day, I went back to La Villa Solitude and saw Magali Gibelen, daughter of the house, a student at Aix-en-Provence University. Her Christian name is Provençal, a variation of Marguérite. I asked her to take me to the neighbour who had given her father the old photograph of the house, hoping there might be someone still alive, with memories handed down of the Stevensons. It turned out he had acquired an old plate camera in a local junk shop. When he processed the plates, he found a photograph of La Solitude. No one knows who took it.

Magali then took me to see a schoolmistress and amateur local historian who told me about Hyères in the 1880s. I'd imagined, from your letters, that you had somehow discovered Hyères on your own, that it was off the tourist trail, without any other foreign residents. I'd got it all wrong. Hyères was the first tourist resort on the Côte d'Azur, attracting visitors from the end of the eighteenth century. In the 1820s, a deliberate tourist campaign was begun by the Deputy Mayor, Alphonse Denis. Its famous visitors included Napoleon, Queen Victoria and Tolstoy. Tolstoy's brother died in Hyères of TB. The town was particularly popular with the English, who brought golf with them and built the Golf Hotel and the Albion Hotel. From the 1890s there were two English churches catering for the resident English community. One has now gone completely and the other was recently turned into a community centre. The English stopped coming around 1937. After the war, they never returned.

'Even people in France have no idea where Hyères is,' said the schoolmistress. 'We have been forgotten by everyone, which the people like. They are happy to live simply and enjoy not being disturbed. Out on the coast, they had a holiday boom, but now with the recession it's mainly campers who don't spend much.'

So Hyères was at its height in your day, Louis, with all those grand hotels, which must have been an added attraction for your visitors, such as cousin Bob, Baxter and Henley, all of whom liked to enjoy themselves. Yet, when they departed, you returned to your insular life, working away all morning, pottering about in the afternoon. You don't appear to have made any local friends, apart from the doctor and the chemist, both of whom you kept pretty busy, *comme d'habitude*.

I asked about sanitation, which so worried Fanny. My teacher friend shook her head: 'Sanitation has always been poor in the Riviera. Everyone lets their sewage flow straight into the sea. I saw it happening last week, at a hotel in Menton. And in Toulon there's a big row now about the council needing to build a new sewage plant, but there's no land left to build on.'

She was surprised to hear about the cholera outbreak in 1883 which Fanny wrote about so vividly, perhaps over-vividly: 'According to official records, the last serious outbreak of cholera in Hyères was in 1850.'

There was no doubt you were very ill at one time, mainly the old trouble. Luckily, Fanny had her own patent medicines handy, such as a small bottle of ergotin, and managed to stop the flow of blood when you couldn't speak, sending away a clergyman who had come to pray for the supposedly dying man. 'I know Louis, and I know that he tries always to so live that he may be ready to die,' Fanny told her sister.

Henley sent out his doctor from England who seems to have helped. He pronounced that if the patient could be kept alive till he was forty, he would live to ninety. 'Between now and forty,' wrote Fanny, 'he must live as though he were walking on eggs. No matter how well he feels, he must live the life of an invalid.'

It was in Hyères that Fanny took out a subscription to the *Lancet*; she was always on the look-out for the latest medical opinion, deciding that she had to supervise the invalid herself. All those expensive doctors in Davos hadn't done much good. When Colvin came to visit, he reported that you were wearing some sort of blue goggles because of an eye inflammation – these might or might not have been Fanny's remedy, or the local quack's.

Fanny went against received wisdom of the time in that she worked out for herself that colds were infectious, caused by other people with colds, not by draughts or wet feet, as most doctors believed. She would not allow any visitor with a cold into your bedroom, and sometimes not even into the house, which was very sensible of her, if a bit awkward. I liked that time when all conversation with you had to take place through a closed door. She cut down on your drink intake, and tried to fatten you up, but she never seemed to realise that smoking – which both of you indulged in – was harmful for anyone with a lung problem.

My teacher friend said I should not leave Hyères without going out to the islands, the Iles d'Or, as they are so beautiful. 'Germans have been buying up the best sites, for luxury holiday homes, but now the rest of them are preserved as national parks.' I said they sounded lovely, but RLS never visited them.

'Oh, but the island of Porquerolles is the original of Treasure Island. That's what all the locals believe.'

I told her the prosaic truth, about Lloyd and those rainy days in Braemar, but I don't suppose it will do much good. There are today about a dozen islands round the world boasting they were the original, from San Francisco Bay to Polynesia.

Treasure Island was published by Cassell, after at least two other publishers had turned it down, in November 1883, while you were still in Hyères. You finished the year with a total income of £465.0.6d, modest enough, but your best ever, magnificent compared with those that had gone before. The first flickerings of real fame were showing, though you were not quite aware of it, stuck in Hyères. Publishers were beginning to ask you for copy, rather than you chasing publishers. It is amazing that, as early as October 1883, Lippincott in the USA was offering you £450 to go off and do a travel book about the Greek Isles – with a hundred pounds down if you agreed, which you didn't.

These early flushes of success are always the sweetest. For the first time you were making enough money from your own pen to provide for yourself and Fanny, but not too much to cause pressures and complications. I'm sure that was one factor which made you remember Hyères so happily. The other factor was health. You were in a reasonable state, except when you were supposed to be dying. Most of all, you had domestic bliss, just the two of you, on your own, without the family, enjoying each other, as the pregnancy scare would prove. 'As for my wife,' you wrote to your mother, 'that was the best investment ever made by man. She is everything to me; wife, brother, sister, daughter, and dear companion; and I would not change to get a goddess or a saint. I love her better than ever and admire her more. I cannot think what I have done to deserve so good a gift. So far, after four years of matrimony . . . the marriage recognized to be a blessing of the first water – A 1 at Lloyds.'

On reflection, Hyères is lucky to have been left with your commendation. I don't think it was really much to do with the place itself. That was where you happened to be, when circumstances happened to make you feel very happy. Especially with hindsight.

15

Bournemouth

1884—7

The next stage in what had become a regular event, trying to keep Louis alive, took them from Hyères in the summer of 1884 to Bournemouth, from the South of France to the south coast of England: not quite so exotic, though it did have its attractions. Decent sanitation, for example. It was a truth, universally remarked upon, especially by the British, that British plumbing and drainage was vastly superior to anything in Europe. This fond belief was based on the advanced industrial skills and increasingly strict health regulations of Victorian England.

Whether or not there was cholera in Hyères, which Fanny believed, there were certainly assorted fevers and diseases rife in the area, probably spread by the open drains. Someone with Louis's assorted weaknesses would obviously be best off somewhere else. Bournemouth was not chosen specifically for its superior plumbing, as that could have been found in many British towns, but because Lloyd was being taught nearby. They had sent him to Britain for his education and hoped he might attend a British university, such as Edinburgh. Bournemouth seemed a healthy sort of place, clean and spruce, with a great many pine trees, said to be very efficacious for those with respiratory problems.

There was also a family reason for the decision. Thomas Stevenson, now aged sixty-six, was in even poorer health, with periods when his speech was becoming slurred, which suggests some minor strokes. Bournemouth might be a long way from Edinburgh, but they were on the same island and within striking distance by train.

After Louis and Fanny had spent a winter in several rented establishments and guest-houses in Bournemouth, flitting from one to another, Thomas announced in the spring of 1885 that he would like them to have their own house, for which he would pay, as a sort of delayed wedding present. It would be in Fanny's name, and he would also give her £500 to furnish and equip it. A bribe? To keep them close? Possibly, but who else was he going to give his money to, if not his only son and the daughter-in-law he so admired?

The house, when they bought it, was called Sea View, but Louis changed it to Skerryvore, after the best-known of the Stevenson family lighthouses; he stuck a model lighthouse at the front door and lit it every evening. From Hyères, they brought with them the dreaded Bogue, about to turn his attention to some tasty British carpets for a change, and the intriguing Valentine Roch. She was a fair-haired Swiss-French servant whom they had acquired in Hyères; untrained at the time, she proved strong and willing, intelligent and good-tempered. By the time they arrived in Bournemouth, she was accepted more as a cousin than as a paid retainer. The most intriguing thing about her was her relationship with Louis. When she was good and behaving prettily, Louis would address her as Joe. When she was stubborn or being awkward, Louis would call her Thomassine. Valentine herself was confused, as she later described.

> When I came in to him one morning, he was busy writing and hardly looked at me. I felt then that I was in disgrace. After I had attended to his wants and was ready to leave, he handed me a scrap of newspaper wrapper on which he had written:
> 'A dearer I do not know than Joe
> A sadder girl has rarely been than Thomassine
> Joe is my friend – so may she always be.
> And for Joe's sake, that darker Thomassine
> wants a true friend in me.'

Louis's doggerel was usually rather more polished. Another example addressed to Valentine:

If I could tell, if you could know

What sweet gifts you give away
When you are kind like yesterday
I think you would be always so.

On one occasion she dressed up as a man, knocked at his bedroom door and demanded an interview with him. He sat up and asked her what she wanted.

'A contribution for a library,' she said.

'How much do you want?'

'Anything you would give.'

'Oh Joe, you are a funny fellow, why don't you ask for a pound – it is worth it.'

When Louis was very ill and Fanny happened to be away, Valentine would sleep in his room, curling up by the fireside, ready to assist should a haemorrhage occur. This appears not to have caused any scandal in the neighbourhood, so one has to accept that their relationship was beyond reproach, but to our modern, cynical eyes there is a hint of sexual sublimation at work, some erotic fantasies playing around in the mind or under the bedclothes of our poor invalid, confined to his couch, being attended to by this pretty, blonde, teasing, male-female nurse.

It was in Bournemouth that fame caught up with Louis. He soon realised that *Treasure Island*, despite its slow release and apparent minority appeal, was turning him into a major name – with adults, not just with boys. The reviews were long and favourable. Everyone was talking about it.

'I have never read it,' wrote Louis in a letter to Henley, in which he mentions that he is desperate for a good adventure story to read. 'By all that I learn, it is the very book for my complaint. I like the way I hear it opens; and they tell me John Silver is good fun. . . .' The first edition sold out very quickly, which left Gladstone searching London for a copy, and when he got one he was entranced. Not that Louis was pleased. He hated Gladstone. He was by now turning into a Conservative, more like his father, the so-called socialist leanings of his student days long forgotten. 'It appears Gladstone talks all the time about *Treasure Island*,' Louis wrote to his mother. 'He would do better to attend to the imperial affairs of England.'

In 1885, *A Child's Garden of Verses* was published, and it too was very well received. Louis had predicted it would please the public more than the publishers, which was true at the time and is now only half-true. Both public and publishers, judging by the endless reprints over the years, have loved it. It is still probably the Western world's best-known, best-loved collection of poems about childhood – as opposed to poems written for those in childhood.

In the same year, there appeared *More New Arabian Nights* and at the end of the year came *Prince Otto*, which made three hardbacks, the most so far in one year. *Prince Otto* was set in Ruritanian Europe, full of royal intrigue and sentiment. *More New Arabian Nights*, also called *The Dynamiter*, was the only book written in collaboration with Fanny. It is still a contemporary-sounding subject, as it revolves round the Irish and bombs, but one deemed a failure by most critics. It consists of a sequence of tales, all in the end connected. Fanny wrote two of them, one set in the USA and one in Cuba, both very dreary and flat. The book has some good ideas and jokes, the beginnings of some good plots and characters, but is ultimately silly and unresolved. Fanny usually gets the blame for this and it is clear she had no gift for fiction, but she was not totally ungifted as a prose writer. She later added a lengthy and well-written introduction to the book, describing their life in Hyères, explaining how the book was started there as a form of therapy when Louis was ill.

Two of the results of fame are a higher class of friend and a more devoted form of fan. The local quality, such as it was in Bournemouth, was quick to invite Louis into its social network. Louis was not keen on this, nor was Fanny, trying to conserve his strength, but he did make friends with a couple of local gentry and was quite flattered by their attention, and their titles. Sir Henry Taylor was a retired Colonial Office official. Sir Percy Shelley was the elder son of the poet. They and their wives were thrilled to find a well-known literary figure in their midst, and Louis accepted their advances. Lady Shelley took it into her head that Louis was a reincarnation of her poet father-in-law. Then she decided that Louis was in fact her own son, which did not amuse Maggie Stevenson. Lady Taylor was less ethereal, presenting Louis with a South American poncho which he enjoyed wearing in bed for many years, long after it was ink-stained and tatty.

Louis's literary and artistic friends also went up a notch or two. While in London, on a visit to the British Museum, where Colvin had become Keeper of Prints and Drawings in 1884 and had accommodation which went with the job, Louis attended several classy gatherings. 'Today I lunch with Burne-Jones,' he wrote to his mother. 'Tonight Browning dines with us. That sounds rather lofty, does it not? His path was paved with celebrities. Tomorrow we leave for Paris.' The Paris trip was a quick one, but he did manage to meet Auguste Rodin.

Henry James wrote a fan letter about *Treasure Island*, after Louis had written an article in reply to an essay by James on the nature of fiction. They had met, fleetingly, some years before in London, when Andrew Lang had introduced them, but James felt Louis was too much the Bohemian poseur. This time they began a long, intellectual correspondence which resulted in James calling at Skerryvore. They got on famously, and Fanny enjoyed his company as much as Louis did – which was not always the case. An armchair which had come from Heriot Row became the Henry James memorial chair in which he sat and listened while Louis pranced and paced about the room, being his usual amusing, dazzling, stimulating self.

Another American visitor was John Singer Sargent, who came to paint Louis's portrait. 'A very nice fellow,' reported Louis after Sargent's first attempt. 'It is a poetical but very chicken boned figurehead.'

The following year Sargent produced a much bigger canvas. 'Sargent was down again and painted a portrait of me walking about in my own dining room, in my own velveteen jacket, and twisting as I go at my moustache; at one corner a glimpse of my wife, in an Indian dress, and seated in a chair that was once my grandfather's – but since some months goes by the name of Henry James's – adds a touch of poesy and comicality. It is I think excellent, but too eccentric to be exhibited. I am at one extreme corner, my wife in this wild dress and looking like a ghost, is at the other end. Between us an open door exhibits my palatial entrance hall and part of my respected staircase. All this is touched in lovely, with that witty touch of Sargent's, but of course it looks damn queer as a whole.'

At the time, it was thought Fanny was the queer one. Not because of her Indian clothes but because of her bare feet. A rumour ran round literary London that Fanny always went barefooted, even at dinner parties.

For a while, they employed a butler – or so they called him, though he had been Thomas Stevenson's valet. 'We have a butler!' wrote Louis to Colvin. 'He doesn't buttle, but the point of the thing is the style. When Fanny gardens, he stands over her and looks genteel. He opens the door and I am told waits at table. Well, what's the odds. I shall have it on my tomb – He ran a butler.

> 'He may have been this and that,
>   A drunkard or a gutter
> He may have been bald and fat
>   At least he kept a butler.
> He may have sprung from ill or well,
>   From Emperor or sutler
> He may be burning now in Hell,
>   On Earth he kept a butler.'

Fan letters started arriving from the USA, another sign of true fame, and to the early ones Louis wrote back several long replies. To Harriet Monroe in Chicago he sent his own photograph, as she had sent him hers. He wrote to her while in bed, feeling old and ill, but pleased that 'my books were still young, my words had their good health, and could go about the world and make themselves welcome'.

At the devoted fan level the most interesting person to enter his life, for her perseverance as well as her delightful name, was Adelaide Boodle. She was a young woman, living locally, who happened to be in the middle of reading one of RLS's stories, *The Treasure of Franchard*, when lo and behold who should move into the neighbourhood but its author. (This short story, written in Scotland some years earlier, was set in France and has a well-drawn woman character, which RLS was usually not very good at. It had originally been rejected as not fit for a family magazine, presumably because there is a suggestion that the main couple are not married, but it was published in *Longman's Magazine* in April 1883.)

Adelaide decided that Louis's arrival was a sign and persuaded her mother that they should make a social call. Her mother was not so certain. On the doorstep, when at first there was no reply, Mrs Boodle burst into tears, but Adelaide hung on, and the door was eventually opened by Valentine, the French maid. She was persuaded to let them inside, where Fanny in a painting apron and Louis in his velveteen jacket were unpacking, surrounded by tea-chests and cases. They were given a cup of tea and made welcome, and Adelaide eventually became a constant if peripheral part of their Bournemouth life, an unpaid retainer, honoured with posting letters, running errands, booking hotel rooms when the Stevensons had visitors. She knew how to disappear when not wanted, or keep quiet at private moments. Perhaps they laughed at her behind her back, and probably considered her a nuisance at times, but they were amused by her naivety, her eagerness and her utter devotion. Especially to Fanny. This was the unusual part. Not many people outside her own family heroine-worshipped Fanny.

Forty years later, Adelaide produced her own book of memoirs, small and slim, but with a grandiose title, *RLS and his Sine Qua Non – Flashlights from Skerryvore by The Gamekeeper*. The main title refers to Fanny, without whom RLS would have done very little, according to Adelaide. Flashlights is a joke, while 'the Gamekeeper' was what Louis called her, when she was left to keep an eye on the house.

Adelaide came to praise Louis but stayed to admire Fanny. This might have been an intelligent move, knowing that getting on the wrong side of Fanny would limit one's welcome, but she meant it. Fanny was never in Louis's shadow, Adelaide says, despite what the Sargent portrait might suggest. Louis depended on her good opinion and only went ahead if she said so. Adelaide's admiration for Fanny's heroism and self-restraint in nursing her very demanding husband eventually grew into love. On arrival each time, 'her dear arms were held out in welcome'. Seeing Fanny asleep on the divan, 'so superbly beautiful, my attention wandered'. Watching her across a crowded room, 'I have seen her quivering with passion'. It is not clear what sort of passion is meant. It could have been fury. Adelaide does say that Fanny uttered 'disagreeable things when her conscience demanded'.

She admits that Fanny and Louis had rows, so loud and fierce a stranger might have cried murder, or called for the police, but of course these were artistic temperaments colliding, and they were always very happy afterwards. Fanny told Adelaide she could not live without Louis, and did not know what she would do if he died, but she would have to, as her task would be to see his biography through the press.

Louis and Fanny made no secret of their rows, referring to them quite openly in letters to friends. 'The Wild Woman of the West,' Louis called her after one argument. 'She is a woman, as you know, not without art,' Louis wrote to Henry James, 'the art of extracting the gloom of the eclipse from sunshine, and she has recently laboured in this field not without success. It is strange: we fell out my wife and I the other night; she tackled me savagely for being a canary bird; I replied, bleatingly, protesting that there was no use in turning into King Lear; presently it was discovered that there were two dead combatants upon the field, each slain by an arrow of the truth, and we tenderly carried off each other's corpses. Here is a little comedy for Henry James to write! The beauty was each thought the other quite unscathed at first. But we had dealt shrewd stabs.'

Out of context, these rows can be made to sound worrying or unpleasant, but read as part of their whole life they indicate an honest, affectionate, if often volatile relationship, with each partner confident enough to speak their thoughts aloud to mutual friends who will know and understand.

Adelaide also helped Louis to learn to play the piano, which he never mastered, except with one finger, and she in turn was eventually given instruction in writing. Her passion for the Stevensons was deep down a literary passion, of course, so she was thrilled when Louis began to use her as a guinea pig for a series of creative writing lectures he was going to give under Colvin's auspices at the British Museum. (They never materialised.)

Adelaide was used to repel boarders, when soon other fans arrived demanding autographs. Two women did manage to break into the house, their excuse being that they wanted to know the colour of Louis's eyes. Usually the demands were more humdrum, such as scraps of his writing, 'no matter how stupid or badly written', to sell at local bazaars. A hundred years ago, celebrities were being treated much as they are today, even when they had just arrived and published only one bestseller.

However, two new bestsellers were soon on the stocks, the first of which came to him in a dream, or at least a nightmare. Fanny wakened him from it and he complained that she had interrupted a 'fine bogey tale'. He had been writing bloodcurdling, ghostly tales for some years, one of which, *The Body Snatcher*, had been published in the *Pall Mall Gazette*, at Christmas 1884. The magazine advertised it in the streets of London by using sandwich-board men wearing skulls and carrying coffin lids, frightening passers-by, and probably the horses, till the police stepped in. Louis had been thinking for some time about goodness and evil being present in the same body, an idea he had tried in a story called 'Markheim', but not with much success.

This new story arrived while Louis was in a fever. Despite being wakened by Fanny, he remained in a fever for the next three days while he wrote it out. He let Fanny read it, as usual, and she said he had got the angle wrong. He should write it not as straight narrative but more as an allegory. She gave Louis back his manuscript and left the room. After a while, his bell rang and she returned to find Louis sitting up in bed, with a thermometer in his mouth, pointing to a large pile of ashes in the fireplace. He had burned the entire story. Then he sat up and spent the next three days writing it again. In the first version, according to his biographer, Balfour, Dr Jekyll was totally evil, with Mr Hyde being little more than a disguise. The setting in Louis's mind was originally Edinburgh, but transferred to London. There are those who think that Fanny harmed the story, by making it less explicit, as she did not want his image as a Boy's Hero ruined, but as the original does not exist we will never know. Louis himself always gave her due credit for the final version.

The Strange Case of Dr Jekyll and Mr Hyde was submitted to *Longman's*, who decided not to serialise it in their magazine. They preferred to issue it as a whole story, in book form – cloth edition one and sixpence, paperback one shilling. Alas, they were too late for the 1885 Christmas market. The bookshops would not consider it, so it was not launched till January. There was a nice review in early January in the *Saturday Review*, thought to be the work of Louis's friend Andrew Lang, which said it was like 'Edgar Allan Poe with the addition of a moral sense'; but it was an anonymous review in *The Times* on 25 January which according to *Longman's* catapulted the book into the public consciousness. This described it as the most impressive work so far from RLS's 'original genius', calling it sensational, fascinating, thrilling, written in excellent English and saying it needed to be read not once but twice. Within six months, 40,000 copies had been sold. It was quoted in newspapers and public speeches, used in church sermons and satirised in *Punch*. In the USA, its reception was even more rapturous, and it went on to sell over 250,000 copies in the next ten years. *Dr Jekyll*, for the first time, brought RLS to the attention of the man in the street, not just the readers of literary magazines and hardback books.

The other success of 1886 was a very different sort of book, which began more slowly, but over the years has also appeared in umpteen editions, as well as films and stage adaptations. Louis had started writing *Kidnapped* early in 1885 as a commission from *Young Folks*, who had published *Treasure Island* and *The Black Arrow*. He had agreed because he needed the money – the offer was three times what they had paid for *Treasure Island*.

Unlike the other two boys' stories, it was based on a real historic incident, the Appin murder of 1751. Just the sort of solid but stirring Jacobite tale his ailing father approved of. The writing did not go well at first. 'I must go on and drudge at *Kidnapped* which I hate and am unfit to do,' he told Henley in March 1885. He was then distracted by other things, returning the following year, when for no apparent reason the book practically wrote itself. 'In one of my books, and only one, the characters took the bit in their teeth; all at once, they became detached from the flat paper, they turned their backs on me and walked off bodily; and from that time my task was stenographic – it was they who spoke, they who wrote the remainder of the story.' Louis was always proud of *Kidnapped*, a real novel, he thought, of a decent length. He fell very ill before he had finished, which brought the story to a rather hurried end, though this did leave him the option of doing a sequel.

It ran in *Young Folks* in the summer of 1886, selling more copies than *Treasure Island*. It then appeared in hardback from Cassell in London and Scribner in New York.

There were some failures during the Bournemouth years, projects which drained a lot of energy and ink but brought in little satisfaction or coin, notably the plays written with Henley. Now that he was so near London, it was handy for Henley to come down, stay a few weeks, get very excited by a new idea, then spend months working on it. Fanny appears to have encouraged the play-writing at first, believing there was money in it, but she was never so keen on the unsettling presence of Henley himself.

Their first play together, *Deacon Brodie*, written in 1879, had had some degree of success in the provinces. It was performed in the West End in July 1884 at the Prince of Wales Theatre, with Henley's brother Edward in the lead. In all, they completed four plays. *Beau Austin* was a Regency comedy of manners, set in Tunbridge Wells. *Admiral Guinea*, the one Henley had been planning for some time, was the slave captain play, with Blind Pew from *Treasure Island*. *Macaire* was their version of a popular French play, meant to be smart and iconoclastic, and it was hoped Beerbohm Tree would play the lead. In the event, only *Deacon Brodie* and *Beau Austin* were performed in Louis's lifetime. The others have been performed since, but more as oddities than as serious dramas. *Deacon Brodie* has a good story, but is very hard going. *Beau Austin* has some witty literary dialogue but is basically very silly. The remaining two are shallow pot-boilers, deservedly forgotten. There were others, discussed and plotted and begun, but never completed.

It is hard to decide why Louis carried on for so long working in a genre for which he had little talent. He always liked trying different forms of writing, in different spheres, so it was in his nature to respond to any new suggestion. He also hoped to make some easy money. He kept going because he did not want to let down Henley, his old and very close friend.

Eventually, he managed to disentangle himself. 'I come unhesitatingly to the opinion that the stage is only a lottery, must not be regarded as a trade, and must never be preferred to drudgery,' he wrote to Henley in 1885. 'If money comes from any play let us

regard it as a legacy, but never count upon it in our income for
the year. These are my cold and blighting sentiments. It is bad
enough to have to live by an art – but to think to live by an art
combined with commercial speculation – that way madness lies.'

He did have one really mad idea – and that was to go off
to Ireland with Fanny and Lloyd and live with the family of
an Irish farmer who had been killed during a period of Fenian
violence. Louis was never a serious political animal but saw his
idea as a gesture against violence, which would receive publicity
in Britain and the USA, even if he himself got killed. 'I do not
love this health-tending, house keeping life of mine.'

For a number of reasons, this weird plan never materialised.
Firstly there was the death of Fleeming Jenkin, aged fifty-three,
his old friend from Edinburgh. Louis felt committed to writing
his biography. None of his planned biographies of major figures
was ever completed, but out of loyalty to the widow and gratitude
to Fleeming, he managed to write his *Memoir of Fleeming Jenkin*,
which was published in 1887. It is rather turgid at the beginning,
tracing Jenkin's family history, but becomes interesting with his
own university memories: 'I regarded any professor as a joke.'
He describes how Fleeming was hard on him, able to quell and
harness his capabilities. It is a competent piece of work, showing
he had more talent for biography than for drama.

In May 1887, Louis and Fanny were called to Edinburgh
to the bedside of his father, who was now dangerously ill. The
previous year there had been talk of a knighthood, in honour of
Thomas's engineering works and his position as President of the
Royal Society of Scotland. The rumour had cheered him, but the
title was never granted.

Thomas and Maggie had visited Louis and Fanny in Bournemouth several times, and he and Louis had gone together to
Matlock the previous year for Thomas's health, though it had not
helped their relationship. All they seemed to do was argue. 'My
father, I'm sorry to say, gave me a full dose of Hyde this morning,'
Louis wrote to his mother. 'He began about breakfast as usual; and
then to prove himself in the right and that he did well to be angry,
carried on a long time (obviously on purpose). I was very severe
with him; and refused to speak to him again until he was quiet;

after which he admitted he had been silly; and yet when I, to let him down gently, took the thing humorously, he began to start it again.' Louis was taking the brunt of intense affection, pride, concern, disappointment, anger, and now old age and illness.

Fanny had always done her best to keep Louis aware of his filial duties. 'We had a dreadful overhauling as a son the other night,' wrote Louis to his father in 1885. 'And my wife stripped me of my illusions and made me admit I had been a detestably bad one. A most unkind reticence still hangs on me now when I try to assure you that I do love you.'

By the time they got to Edinburgh, Thomas was too ill to recognise Louis. He died the next day, 8 May 1887, in his seventieth year. On his last day, he got out of bed, and on his feet smoked his last pipe, as he had always planned, despite recognising nobody around him. The funeral was said to be one of the biggest Edinburgh had ever seen. Louis was too ill himself to go to the cemetery.

Thomas left an estate of £26,000. In his will, he arranged for Maggie to have the income from it for her lifetime, plus a legacy of £2,000. Afterwards, the estate would pass to Louis, then Fanny, then Lloyd, who by this time was attending Edinburgh University and living at Heriot Row. Louis himself received the sum of £3,000. It took a year for all these arrangements to be finalised.

By this time, Louis and Fanny had moved on. Their three years at Bournemouth had been very productive, the best ever in terms of success and recognition, but had been bad for Louis's health, despite the best attentions of Dr Bodley Scott, their local doctor. Louis had hardly seen those pine trees and rarely walked the nearby cliff, living like a hermit, writing away on his couch or bed. What was there to keep him in Bournemouth, or Britain come to that, now that his father and benefactor had gone?

16

Bournemouth Today

Dear Louis,

On the train down to Bournemouth I was reading a new book by Professor Elaine Showalter called *Sexual Anarchy: Gender and Culture at the Fin de Siècle*, because I'd been told it had a chapter on *Dr Jekyll and Mr Hyde*. One does like to keep up to date with academic opinion and research. After all, Ms Showalter is head of English Studies at Princeton.

I staggered off the train, feeling slightly dizzy, brain-shocked by the mental gymnastics and critical audacity of Ms Showalter. How had I missed the fact that *Dr Jekyll* was a homosexual story? She had spotted it straight away, quoting references such as Hyde travelling through 'chocolate brown fog' to Jekyll's rear door. Then there's his continued use of the word 'queer'. Pretty conclusive, so Ms Showalter believes.

She has another interesting theory. Namely that you yourself were a repressed homosexual. This is a very fashionable assertion, so don't let it worry you too much. Sooner or later it is suggested about every famous person and is almost impossible to counter or disprove, even by the person concerned. The weasel word is, of course, 'repressed'.

Well, you did have all those very close male friends. You did marry a much older woman, which could have been a cover. You did at times address her in a letter as 'My Dear Fellow', which is very suspicious. Friends did say you had some feminine gestures, all that arm waving and hysterics. And what about dressing up in velvet?

Ms Showalter's 'evidence' is much more ingenious than that. She has carefully examined that portrait of you by John Singer Sargent, and come to a rather surprising conclusion. It's now in America, by the way, and belongs to Mrs John Hay Whitney. It is a bit blurry, which of course was Sargent's intention, trying to show you pacing up and down the room.

According to Ms Showalter, you *deliberately* turned your back on your wife, who is covered up, as if to pretend she does not exist. The door is clearly symbolic, 'opening into a dark closet'. All in all, the painting convinces her that RLS is 'the fin de siècle laureate of the double life'.

The last time I went to Bournemouth was over twenty-five years ago, to see Mimi Smith, John Lennon's aunt, the one who brought him up. She had moved into a new luxury bungalow at Canforth Cliffs, pleased to get away from all the fans who had made her life so unpleasant in Liverpool, hoping now to be anonymous. We were sitting in the sun, at the back of her bungalow, looking over the sea, when across the water we could hear a megaphone from a passing pleasure boat. 'Now, ladies and gentlemen, if you look on the shore, you can see Mimi Smith's bungalow, the home of John Lennon's aunt. . . .' Mimi was inside in seconds.

Bournemouth was totally empty until the 1830s, just a deserted seven-mile stretch of beach and heathland, with pines and heather growing in deep valleys or chines, as the shore-line gorges are known locally. The first buildings were established in the 1840s as winter residences for those with delicate constitutions. A Dr Granville, author of a book called *Spas and Principal Sea Bathing Places*, was persuaded to visit the town in 1841 and he pronounced that the local pine trees were particularly beneficial to invalids – giving off an aroma which was conducive to the alleviation of chest complaints. The population rose from nothing in 1831 to 17,000 in 1884 when you arrived, Louis, just in time to marvel at their brand-new iron pier, opened by the Lord Mayor of London.

From the beginning, Bournemouth catered for the better class of invalid or retired person, hence your titled friends. Edward VII, while Prince of Wales, even built a house in Bournemouth for his mistress, Lillie Langtry. Until 1917, the front was officially known as Invalids' Walk. Most residents appear to have been pushed along it. On reaching the sea, according to a contemporary guidebook, they were encouraged not to go on the pier itself 'except when the midday sun has dispersed all chilliness from the atmosphere'.

Today, Bournemouth is a solid retirement town of some 150,000. It has its own Symphony Orchestra, but I failed to find one antiquarian bookshop or any decent-looking restaurant. Marconi developed his ship-to-shore signals in Bournemouth in 1898. The world's first multi-storey car park was built in Bournemouth in 1920 and in 1933 came the world's first Ice Show. That seems to be the sum of its past glory.

I headed for West Cliff Road, where you and Fanny lived early on, in a guest-house called Iffley. A long road, filled with guest-houses, a garden city of guest-houses, as if they had been grown. I noted Pinehurst, Savoy, Wessex, Jennifers, but not Iffley. I then went into West Cliff Gardens, where you had two lodgings, at the Firs and at Wensleydale. No sign of either. I saw an old lady coming out of Ullswater and I asked if she had lived here long. Only twenty-six years, she said, all in the same guest-house. No, she had never heard of a Firs or Wensleydale. Names change all the time. New owners bring new images. Spanish names are popular now. She crossed the road and went into Eldorado.

I made my way to Burton Road, now technically in Poole, to look for Bonallie Towers, where you lived for almost six months and where Sargent did his first painting. No sign of it either, though I did note a Villa Menorca and one large house with mock towers.

I went into a newspaper shop to buy the local paper, as I always do, from Monterey to Hyères. The newsagent was Scottish, from Glasgow. He and his wife came to Bournemouth in 1964. 'It took us six months to meet anyone who was actually from Bournemouth. I think the first person was a dustman.' There is now a big market for European newspapers in Bournemouth, thanks to the arrival of so many language schools, teaching English to foreigners. Italians, French and Japanese are the most common. They bring good business out of season to the little guest-houses, but they have a local rule never to have all Japanese or all Italians staying in the same guest-house. One of each nationality is preferred. This is to make sure they all have to speak English. So your Bournemouth neighbours today, my dear Louis, would probably not be the titled gentry but trainee Italian waiters or Japanese computer students.

The Shelley connection is still there, but there are no live Shelleys. Sir Percy, your friend, died in 1889, not long after you left Bournemouth. His mother Mary Shelley, née Godwin, author of *Frankenstein*, had died in 1851 and had been interred in St Peter's Church, Bournemouth. Later the remains of her parents, William Godwin, the philosopher, and Mary Wollstonecraft, the early feminist writer, were transferred from St Pancras Cemetery in London to the same grave. Sir Percy was also buried there, along with his father's heart, which had supposedly been rescued on his death in Italy by Byron and Leigh Hunt, then given to Mary Shelley wrapped in a silken cloth.

I headed at last for Alum Chine Road, looking for Skerryvore. When you left in 1887, Adelaide Boodle, the Gamekeeper, was put in charge, keeping an eye on the house till you decided what to do with it. In 1890 you sold it, making yourself a handy £1,500. Up until the last war, it was used as a boarding-house.

Sadly, Skerryvore is no more. All it consists of now is a garden, hidden away behind a high hedge, a mysterious gap in a street full of very prim and proper bourgeois teeth. Bournemouth was hit by a German bomb during the night of 15 November 1940. Over fifty people died and many houses were destroyed. At number 61 Alum Chine Road – Skerryvore as was – the roof came off, most of the walls fell, and the house itself had to be pulled down.

I noticed that the house next door was a guest-house, 'Seacrest Lodge Hotel: some rooms en suite', so I rang the front-door bell. A woman opened the door, took a free newspaper out of her letter-box, said thank you, assuming I had delivered it, then closed the door. I knocked again.

Did she perhaps know anything about Skerryvore? She was not around personally in 1940, but she'd been told that it was a chance bomb which did it. That night in Bournemouth, the air-raids were elsewhere. Skerryvore was the only house in their immediate district which was affected. Her house, and the one on the other side, were totally untouched. 'It was just a fluke it got hit. The man who used to live here told me that, next morning, he was picking up slates from the roof of Skerryvore from our garden.'

You mention in your letters that you had a sea view from the upstairs rooms at Skerryvore, so I asked the woman if she could see the sea, hoping I might be invited in. She said no, the trees had now grown far too high. Would that be all? I asked if she was often bothered by people on the RLS trail. 'There doesn't seem to be much publicity for Stevenson. I don't think most people in Bournemouth know the garden exists.'

It is easy to miss, the little garden, opened in 1957, which is now on the site of Skerryvore. I opened the gate and went in and found it was more like an archaeological site than a municipal garden. A dwarf wall, about two feet high, marks out where the original walls used to stand. There's a little model of the Skerryvore lighthouse and a plaque stating that RLS lived here from April 1885 till August 1887. Naturally, now that it's in council control, there are standard-issue wooden seats and a neat little litter-bin.

The rooms, where Sargent once painted you and Henry James once sat, are now little flower-beds, filled that day with pansies and primulas. I worked out which must have been the main living-room, then stood on the site of Henry James's chair and stared out of the window, now open for ever. The long, rectangular garden ends in a little wood, with pine, birch and holly trees. I estimated the site to be a hundred yards in length and about thirty yards wide, a much bigger property than I had expected. No sign of any tomatoes. According to Adelaide Boodle, Fanny was the first to grow them in Bournemouth.

At the very end of the garden, there is an iron railing, stopping anyone descending or perhaps falling by accident into Alum Chine itself, a deep, dank, mysterious pine-covered gorge. In your day, you had your own entrance; you could get from your garden, unseen by anyone, down into the chine and follow it directly to the sea.

I went back into the road, looking up and down at all the other houses, many of them now little hotels. You did well for yourself, or at least your father did well for you. There are contemporary sketches of Skerryvore, so I know the shape and style, very like so many others in the area, but until now I had not been aware of its impressive size. But, my dear Louis, what were you doing here? Silverado I can understand, and Hyères was charming and idiosyncratic, ideal for a young, arty couple. But this sort of house, in Bournemouth . . . No wonder you changed the house's name, trying to disguise what you had done, fetching up amongst the new villa-owning class, the solid Tories, the bourgeois class you'd always mocked. In Hyères, you were still travelling, still finding yourself. By settling yourself here, you were apparently someone who had made it, who had joined the provincial establishment. In Bournemouth you arrived as a successful writer. But did you really need to have a butler?

You were certainly proud of that butler and your new status, but at other times ashamed, despising your new values and new situation in life, worried that you might be here permanently, sucked in for ever to the gentrified suburban life. Standing in the road, I decided that your father's death was only the excuse to uproot yourself, one you had been looking for. That madcap Irish idea was only its odder manifestation. Bournemouth was not for you, Louis, and you knew it. But you must have wondered where your real home would be.

As I was standing and pondering, I noticed for the first time that the street opposite was called Robert Louis Stevenson Avenue. Apart from the garden, it is Bournemouth's only public sign or mark of interest in RLS.

RLS-searchers must not however miss the town's library. Not quite on the scale of Yale's or Edinburgh's when it comes to RLS material, but I amused myself for a few hours looking up old cuttings and pamphlets for any Stevenson references. In the *Bournemouth Echo* of 22 November 1941, a year after the air-raid destroyed Skerryvore, it was reported that all that survived of the Stevenson occupation were three relics – a bell from a lighthouse and two tablets on a wall which commemorated the deaths of two of your dogs, Bogue and Coolin, both inscribed in Latin.

I found a little booklet, produced in Bournemouth in 1924, to commemorate the life of your doctor, Thomas Bodley Scott, who became a good friend. I discovered he had been born on 8 March 1851, so he was almost exactly your age, which must have helped your friendship. The Bodley part of his name came from his ancestor Sir Thomas Bodley, founder of the Bodleian Library in Oxford. When he retired from medicine, aged seventy-two, he became a local councillor and in November 1923 was elected Mayor of Bournemouth. He did not see out his mayoral year, dying on 26 January 1924.

'Among the friends and patients of his younger days,' says the booklet, 'was Robert Louis Stevenson who lived at Skerryvore on the West Cliff, and ever afterwards treasured the remembrance of his doctor's kindness, sympathy and skill.' This was certainly true. After all, you did give a lavish dedication to Dr Scott in your first book of adult poems, *Underwoods*, published in 1887, just as you were leaving Bournemouth.

In a 1934 copy of *Chambers's Journal* I found a first-person memoir of Stevenson in Bournemouth by Clive Holland which has a description of you being carried downstairs by Fanny. I knew you were a seven-stone weakling most of your life, but hadn't realised Fanny was so strong. I also found a faded type-written list, compiled by some former librarian, which catalogued all the portraits done while you lived in Bournemouth. The list was surprisingly extensive for a four-year stay. More proof of your sudden fame. There were three Sargent portraits – one done at Bonallie Towers (but destroyed), plus the two at Skerryvore. Sir William Richmond, RA, in London did an unfinished portrait, and William Strang, RA, did an etching in Bournemouth. Many of your best-known photographs were taken in Bournemouth. Lloyd was a keen photographer, and so was Sir Percy Shelley. You also sat for a local portrait photographer, W.J. Hawker, who had a studio at 1 Old Christchurch Road. I tried but failed to find out what had happened to his studio and old plates.

I also came across an interesting note in connection with the Sargent painting, which said that Fanny had put on the Indian dress to lighten the colour scheme. It also explains that she was sitting by the door because she was getting ready to close it, worried that you might be in a draught, pacing up and down the room in your normal manner. That sounds caring to me, not a sign of sexual deviation.

17

America and the South Seas
1887–90

Robert Louis Stevenson's party of five people boarded the good ship *Ludgate Hill* at London docks on 27 August 1887, bound for New York. There was RLS, aged thirty-six, man of letters, man of the moment, judging by the sales and coverage of his recent books, heading for healthier climes and taking with him a crate of champagne, a present from Henry James for consumption during the journey. Accompanying him was his dear wife Fanny, aged forty-seven, quite pleased to be leaving England and some of her husband's more annoying, cloying, supercilious friends, and returning to her homeland, though sad to give up her Bournemouth garden on which she had worked so hard. With her was her son Lloyd, aged nineteen, rather studious-looking in his rimless spectacles. He had by now abandoned his Edinburgh University studies, for ever he hoped, as he much preferred the idea of buying one of the new-fangled typewriters and becoming a writer like his stepfather, possibly in the Wild West or somewhere similar. It seemed easy enough, this writing business, and was now paying surprisingly well.

There was one servant, Valentine Roch, about to undergo another culture shock. She had managed the switch from the South of France to Bournemouth. How would she stand the New World?

Completing the party was Margaret Stevenson, aged fifty-eight, widow, mother of RLS. Quite a surprise, when you consider her sheltered background, ill for so much of her early and middle years, used to a big house, fine clothes, servants, comfortable life, social status, but here she was, as bright and lively as any of them, ready to enjoy a long sea voyage and unknown adventures ahead. A good omen, perhaps, for Louis? Perhaps he would throw off his long-term illness, as the Balfours often did (and in physique and temperament he was more a Balfour than a Stevenson), and would blossom in his middle years and live to a reasonable age.

Sidney Colvin, who came to see them off, had less sanguine thoughts. He feared he would never see his friend again. Not through illness or early death, but because the wanderer would never wander back. On the other hand, he had thought that eight years ago, when he had bid Louis farewell in London.

Louis wrote to Colvin almost immediately, denigrating the passengers, making his usual jokes. 'Our fellow voyagers divide into two classes – the better sort consisting of the baser kind of Bagmen, and the worser of undisguised Beasts of the Field. . . . Havre is a city of some show. It is for-ti-fied. It is sit-uated in France, a country of Europe. You always complain there are no facts in my letters.'

For the sake of economy, and to add a bit of variety to the voyage, Louis had decided not to travel on one of the new luxurious transatlantic liners which sailed direct from Liverpool or Southampton, but on a semi-cargo boat. At Le Havre, they were all surprised when the boat proceeded to pick up some horses and monkeys, bound for a zoo in America, which at least provided Louis with material for a good letter to Henry James. 'I enjoyed myself more than I could have hoped on our strange floating menagerie; the stallions stood hypnotised by the motion, looking through the ports at our dining table, and winked when the crockery was broken; and the monkeys stared at each other in their cages.'

In New York, Louis found he was a Celebrity, and was given the appropriate treatment, with reporters clamouring to interview him. The pilot who led their boat into harbour revealed that his nickname was Hyde while his jollier co-pilot was called Dr Jekyll: out of the book and into the language, all in a matter of months. Mr and Mrs

Charles Fairchild, the wealthy couple who had commissioned the Sargent portrait, had booked Louis's party into a top hotel, at their expense, and then invited them to their home in Newport, to get away from the attentions of the New York press. Louis sat for a sculptor, Augustus St Gaudens, who produced the wall plaque of him sitting up in bed, cigarette in hand. 'America is a fine place to eat in, and a great place for kindness,' wrote Louis to Henry James, 'but Lord, what a silly thing is popularity. I envy the cool obscurity of Skerryvore.'

Big sums were being offered to him the moment he landed, for almost anything he cared to write. *Scribner's* bid $3,500 for twelve monthly articles, on any subject, while the thrusting Sam McClure, who was building up a coast-to-coast syndicated agency, offered $10,000 a year for a weekly column, plus $8,000 for the serial rights to his next book, *The Black Arrow*. Louis was never quite sure how to translate these massive figures into pounds, but the rate then was about five dollars to the pound. So, whatever he chose, he could easily make himself around £2,000 a year, about ten times what he had been used to.

He wrote warily to Henley about the money – 'huge as it is, the slavery may overweigh me' – but with more delight to cousin Bob. 'What fun! Wealth is only useful for two things: a yacht and a string quartette, for these I will sell my soul.'

They had thought of going to Colorado for the winter for Louis's health, but instead went up-state in New York to the Adirondack Mountains where a Dr Trudeau had a TB centre on Saranac Lake. Fanny hated it, and during the winter managed several expeditions elsewhere in the States, visiting relations. Maggie took a trip on her own to look at Niagara Falls. Louis, Lloyd and Valentine somehow managed to survive the winter, despite the cold which made clothes stick to the floors, ink go solid and Valentine's handkerchief freeze under her pillow. Lloyd had bought a typewriter in London, taught himself to use it and co-operated with Louis on a story called *The Wrong Box*. Louis himself had started *The Master of Ballantrae*.

'I am likely to be a millionaire if this goes on,' he wrote to a young English critic and fan, William Archer, 'and be publicly hanged at the social revolution; well I would prefer that to dying in my bed, and it would be a godsend to my biographer, if ever I have one.' In an earlier letter to Archer, he had thanked him for sending a novel called *Cashel Byron's Profession* by a new author, G.B. Shaw, enquiring how old he was. 'I say Archer, my God, what women. It is HORRID FUN. Tell me more about this inimitable author.'

The bold McClure came up to Saranac to see Louis, offering more deals. They discussed a tour of the South Seas, expense no object, yacht no problem. Apart from writing his wonderful essays, Louis would be able to take a phonograph with him to record the sea noises and the natives singing, jolly useful when he gave a lecture tour afterwards. McClure produced a South Seas Directory which Louis pored over, imagining the white beaches and palm trees, as one would, stuck in a freezing log cabin. He should really have been listening more carefully to McClure, for he forgot he had already signed away the rights in his travel essays to *Scribner's*. This led to a most embarrassing situation and a grovelling letter to *Scribner's*, explaining his mistake. Agents do have their uses.

McClure was one of those scores of people who passed through Louis's life and later shared their memories with the world. He went the next year to London, carrying introductions from Louis, and he signed up the young Conan Doyle and the even younger Rudyard Kipling. 'In London I found that most of Stevenson's set was very much annoyed by the attention he was receiving in America; a most extraordinary spirit of hostility and jealousy. They were resentful of the fact that Stevenson was recognized more fully, more immediately and more understandingly in America than in England at that time. Some of Stevenson's London friends agreed that he was a much overrated man. And personally I was the very essence of what was most hated in Americanism . . . they all hated and despised me, made fun of me, and [they thought] I didn't seem to know it. . . .'

McClure does not name the so-called friends, but Louis soon found out. In March 1888, while Fanny was in California, visiting relations and checking the possibility of hiring a sea-going yacht, Louis received a letter which began one of the nineteenth century's more complicated literary quarrels.

The argument was with William Ernest Henley, Louis's big, burly, bearded, one-legged Long John Silver of a friend, not a great name today, remembered only for one or two lines from his stirring Victorian poem, 'Invictus'.

> I am the master of my fate;
> I am the captain of my soul.

In his time, though, he was an important literary figure, editor of *London*, the *Magazine of Art*, then later the *Scots Observer*. He had been one of Louis's closest and most intimate friends since they had first met when Henley was in hospital in Edinburgh. They had struggled together over four plays, and prided themselves on their honesty with each other. Henley had done sterling work for Louis as his informal London agent, contacting publishers, sending round manuscripts, arranging proofs. Henley, though just a year older, had usually addressed him as 'My dear lad', but now Louis was the international star, keen to send Henley payments for services rendered, as Henley had fallen on thin times.

The letter from Henley which caused all the trouble needs to be read carefully, so that the context of the offending paragraph can be seen.

> Dear Boy, If you will wash dishes and haunt back-kitchens in the lovely climate of the Eastern States, you must put up with the consequences . . . I am out of key today. The Spring, sir, is not what it used to be . . . *Enfin!* Life is uncommon like rot. *C'est convenu.* If it weren't that I am a sort of centre of strength for a number of feebler folk, I think I'd be shut of it dam soon . . .
>
> I read *The Nixie* with considerable amazement. It's Katharine's; surely it's Katharine's? There are even reminiscences of phrasery and imagery, parallel incidents – *que sais-je*? It is also better focused, no doubt; but I don't think it has lost as much (at least) as it has gained; and why there wasn't a double signature is what I've not been able to understand . . .
>
> Louis, dear lad, I am dam tired. The Chatelaine's away. The Spring is spring no more. I am thirty-nine this year. I am dam, dam tired. What I want is the wings of a dove – a soiled dove even! – that I might flee away and be at rest.
>
> Don't show this to *anybody*, and when you write, don't do more than note it in a general way – By the time you *do* write, you will have forgotten all about it, no doubt. But if you haven't, deal vaguely with my malady. Why the devil do you go and bury yourself in that country of dollars and

spew? . . . However, I suppose you must be forgiven, for you
have loved me much. Let us go on so to the end . . . We have
lived, we have loved, we have suffered; and the end is the best
of all . . . Forgive this babble, and take care of yourself and
burn this letter. Your friend, W.E.H.

The bit that hurt was that second paragraph, apparently slipped
in as a side-thought, before Henley goes on with his smart French
phrases and old pals teasing. Louis took this paragraph as the
whole point of the letter, and the instruction to burn it, supposedly
because of Henley's malady, was a trick, forcing Louis to keep the
subject quiet.

The innuendo was aimed at Fanny, accusing her of plagiarism.
The Nixie was a short story which that month had appeared
in *Scribner's*, but had been an original idea by Katharine de
Mattos, Louis's cousin, sister of Bob Stevenson. She had married
a Cambridge atheist, then divorced, leaving her with children and
no money. Thomas Stevenson, on his death, had instructed that
she should receive help from his estate. She had been a welcome
visitor at Skerryvore and Louis had dedicated *Jekyll and Hyde* to
her, not, as it transpired, a very appropriate gesture.

While staying at Skerryvore, she had told a story about a
couple meeting on a train, with the woman turning out to be
mentally deranged. Fanny had offered the suggestion that the
woman should be a watersprite, a Nixie, not mad. Louis had
encouraged Katharine to write it out and Henley had then tried
to get it published, but with no success.

Later, according to Louis's account, and Fanny's, Katharine
had agreed that Fanny could take the story over, as she had failed
with it. Fanny had then re-written it, and had it published with her
name on – Fanny Van de Grift Stevenson. The Stevenson part no
doubt encouraged *Scribner's* to be interested in it.

Louis thought long about his reply, but then blasted off the
following to Henley:

My dear Henley,
    I write with indescribable difficulty; and if not with per-
fect temper, you are to remember how very rarely a husband
is expected to receive such accusations against his wife. I can
only direct you to apply to Katharine and ask her to remind you
of that part of the business which took place in your presence

and which you seem to have forgotten; she will doubtless add the particulars which you may not have heard . . .

I am sorry I must ask you to take these steps; I might take them for myself had you not tied my hands by the strange step of marking your letter 'private and confidential' . . . I wish I could stop here. I cannot. When you have refreshed your mind as to the facts, you will, I know, withdraw what you said to me; but I must go farther and remind you, if you have spoken of this to others, a proper explanation and retraction of what you shall have said or implied to any person so addressed, will be necessary.

From the bottom of my soul I believe what you wrote to have been merely reckless words . . . but it is hard to think that anyone – and least of all my friend – should have been so careless of dealing agony . . . This is the sixth or seventh attempt that I make to write to you; . . . You will pardon me if I can find no form of signature; I pray God such a blank will not be of long endurance.

ROBERT LOUIS STEVENSON

Katharine then became embroiled in the row, much to her distress. She denied she knew what Henley was doing, saying she had not put him up to it, but alas for Louis and Fanny she did not on the other hand agree she had officially handed her story over to Fanny. Nor did she say the opposite. Instead she said she 'was sick to death of the matter' and the whole quarrel was making her ill. More letters flowed from Louis, still steaming with rage, unable to work, complaining to Baxter that his enemies had ganged up against him. 'The bottom wish of my heart is that I had died at Hyères; the happy part of my life ended there.'

Fanny joined in the row, even more hysterically. 'In my heart I shall never forgive those who have borne false witness against me. While they eat their bread from my hand – and oh they will do that – I shall smile and wish it were poison that wither their bodies as they have my heart.'

Louis began to have some doubts about the conversation he thought he remembered, in which Katharine had handed over her property. 'Suppose that I am insane and have dreamt all I seemed to remember, and that my wife has shamefully stolen a story from my cousin?' All the same, he would still blame Henley for his dreadful accusations. 'Was this the class of matter that a friend should write to me?' As the storm raged and the argument moved on, with Fanny and Louis becoming more self-righteous and paranoid, they began to blame Katharine, who had done and said nothing, for starting it.

Henley did apologise – but only for upsetting Louis, causing him such distress and heartache, denying it was done out of unfriendliness. He never took back his accusation that Fanny had stolen Katharine's story.

There were various undercurrents to the storm. The money being given to Katharine was one, which doubtless made it hard for her to come out and directly criticise the Stevensons. There were also money matters between them and Henley, hence Louis's rather pathetic harping back to Hyères, before money had brought responsibilities and complications.

Louis had recently been furious with Henley's actor brother Teddy, touring the States with a production of *Deacon Brodie*, who had got involved in a drunken brawl in Philadelphia, then fled to New York, booking himself into a grand hotel, far better than the one which had been agreed, leaving Louis to pay the bill. 'The drunken whoreson bugger and bully living himself in the best hotels, and smashing inoffensive strangers in the bar!' wrote Louis to Baxter. 'It is too sickening . . . all I try to do for WE, in the best way, by writing these plays, is burked by this inopportune lad. Can nothing be done? In the meanwhile I add another £20 to WE's credit.'

The relationship between Louis and Henley had always been a bit complicated. Louis had been upset that Henley had not liked *Travels with a Donkey*, yet had said nothing at the time. Basing John Silver on him had not been exactly complimentary. It is hard to work out the time-scale, but it would appear that bits of *Treasure Island* might have been planned for their joint play, before Louis had completed his novel. That must have hurt Henley, when the project he was not associated with became a big success. They had had other recent rows: these are referred to in their letters, but details are not known. Perhaps Louis jumped upon this supposed transgression, to cut the cords with Henley. In the end, none of them came well out of the row. Louis and Fanny over-reacted, kept it going too long, became petty and then hysterical, which could indicate that deep down they did feel some guilt. Whatever had been agreed with Katharine, Fanny should still have given her joint credit for the story.

Henley exacerbated the situation, knowingly. He did have a genuine point to make, but his motives included envy at Louis's success and personal dislike of Fanny. Katharine walked into it, being mealy-mouthed when the subject first came up and not making her desires clear. Her polite, non-committal middle-class British mumbles were not understood by the forthright Fanny. Then later she opted out, hoping to escape any blame, but ended up losing Louis's love and friendship. As for Louis's friendship with Henley, that was ruined, for ever.

What better way to escape such human squalls and raging temperaments than to go to sea, fight the wind and waves rather than outraged egos? Fanny had found a yacht in California which seemed to suit their purposes, and after a stay in New York, during which he spent an afternoon in Washington Square with Mark Twain, talking shop, Louis joined Fanny in San Francisco.

The yacht they had in mind, the ninety-four-feet-long *Casco*, was lean and sporty, very fast, luxuriously equipped with the best of Victorian good taste, but its owner, a Dr Merritt, was not all that keen on hiring it out to some arty Scotch author and his strange-sounding party, one of whom was an elderly woman of fifty-eight, who might well die en route. He interviewed Louis and to his surprise found him sensible and serious, but he insisted that his own Captain Otis must be in charge. The deal was that Louis would rent the yacht for $500 a month, plus all running costs and any repairs. For a six-month cruise, Louis estimated it would cost him £2,000, taking a hefty lump out of his inheritance, but he hoped to recoup this by writing a regular letter from the South Seas for McClure, at the rate of $10,000 dollars for fifty letters; in addition there would be money from *Scribner's* for the serialisation of *The Master of Ballantrae*. So by his pen he should easily cover all expenses, for his party of five plus a crew of seven. A huge commitment, nonetheless. It depended on his continuing health and a continuing acceptance of his writings. At Hyères, his main responsibility had been to two people, himself and his wife, in a cheaply rented, modest house. Now he was responsible for twelve people, either feeding or paying them, his extended family complete with staff, a cross between Grand Tourists and New Age Travellers, sailing first class and carrying enormous overheads.

No wonder that Louis, as he approached thirty-eight, began at last to display a more serious, mature side, showing signs of middle-aged irritability, occasionally becoming pompous, as in his row with Henley, less carefree, more conservative. Henley maintained there were two Stevensons – the one who went to America in 1887, and the one who never came back. Fanny, in his eyes, had changed Louis, ruining the free spirit, the boy of immense promise and talent he had once loved.

All the same, hiring the *Casco* for six months and going off cruising into the unknown was just as mad and adolescent as anything he had done in the past. His letters were still full of good jokes, silly remarks, light-hearted banter, but naturally the self-imposed weight he had taken upon himself began to get him down from time to time – being responsible for so many people, having to keep at it, filling up the pages, regardless of how he felt. He had always worked hard, always pushed himself, but increasingly he felt trapped. Success did not change his personality, making him conceited and unpleasant, as Henley alleged, but the trappings of success tended to make him depressed rather than happy. It was not surprising that his mind often wandered back to the carefree days in Hyères.

However, once at sea, all worries seemed to leave him. The real purpose of the voyage was health and self-indulgence, to get himself fit again. He had followed the advice of doctors over the years, now he was listening to his body. It told him that, in his life, he had always felt best when on water. Ergo, take to the sea.

This was hard luck on Fanny. She was sea-sick the moment they set sail, and Lloyd and Valentine did not feel well either. Only Louis and his mother truly enjoyed themselves. 'I will never leave the sea,' wrote Louis. 'The sea is the highest form of gambling.' Having escaped his landlocked illnesses, he was willing to take his chance on a watery grave. He raved to Adelaide Boodle about the good the sea was doing him, compared with 'the wretched house plant of Skerryvore'. He felt that for ten years his health had been declining, but now the sea was restoring him. 'Voyages passed like a day in fairyland.'

They left San Francisco on 28 June 1888, with Captain Otis in command. He was aware of having a famous author on board, but was not over-impressed. He considered that *Treasure Island* was good enough as a story, but very poor when it came to seamanship. When asked what he would do in an emergency, such as old Mrs Stevenson being swept overboard, he thought for a few moments before giving his reply: 'Put it in the log.'

After a month, they reached the Marquesas Islands. Some native women came on board, one of whom lifted up her dress and tried out the velvet cushions with her bare bottom. She also kissed the portrait of Queen Victoria they had hanging on the cabin wall, and a photograph of Andrew Lang. Louis loved all the natives he met on every island, their enthusiasm and beauty, their language and customs, and identified with them in their struggles against colonial oppression and exploitation, whether British, American or German, the three powers who were currently trying to carve up chunks of Polynesia between them. In the South Seas, Louis made a point of calling himself Scottish, not English, identifying with the native situation, comparing the persecution of the Highlanders, who were not allowed to retain their culture or their tartans, with that of the Polynesians, not allowed to retain their religion or their tattoos.

They moved on to Tahiti, where Fanny wrote to Colvin that Louis was swimming in the sea every day, living almost entirely in the open air and going around in skimpy clothes which looked like pyjamas. Louis and Lloyd both wore floral wreaths round their necks. As for Maggie, she was going around barefoot, never wearing stockings. She did not, however, forget her widow's hat, which appears perched on her head in all photographs of her in the South Seas. This gives her a starchy, stiff look, from which some commentators have deduced she was a stiff and starchy person, not enjoying herself in her travels. In a later memoir, Maggie said that she only ever grabbed her widow's cap when a photographer was around, for the sake of appearances. There usually was a camera not far away. Lloyd took one with him, and from the sound of it they also took dark-room equipment, along with a typewriter. In one gale they lost a whole set of photographic plates.

Six months after they left San Francisco, on 24 January 1889, they arrived in Hawaii, where they paid off the *Casco* and sent her home. Valentine also left them. 'The usual tale of the maid on board the yacht,' wrote Louis. This appears to mean a shipboard romance with one of the crew. Valentine went off with her wages to California and got married, becoming Mrs Valentine A. Brown. Years later, she was still devoted to Louis, and was grateful for her years with him, but there is a suggestion that she had not got on quite as well with Fanny.

In Hawaii, they were met by Fanny's daughter Belle who had been living in Honolulu with her husband Joe Strong and their eight-year-old son Austin. Joe was doing well as a painter and they were both in with the royal set. Louis and Fanny soon met the king of Hawaii, Kalakaua, and became good friends, admiring his many talents. 'His Majesty is a very fine intelligent fellow,' wrote Louis to Baxter, 'but O Charles, what a crop for the drink! We calculated five bottles of champagne in three and half hours, and the sovereign quite presentable, although perceptively more dignified at the end. . . .'

They also became close friends with the young Princess Kaiulani, heiress to the throne, who was half-Hawaiian and half-Scottish. (Her father, A.S. Cleghorn, had married a princess.)

The Stevensons took a house outside Honolulu on Waikiki Beach, then practically empty, except for the palm trees and a handful of summer cottages. Louis got down to some writing, finishing off *The Master of Ballantrae*. He also took a trip on his own to a nearby island, Molokai, which contained a leper colony, where Father Damien, the controversial priest, had once been in charge. The Catholics considered him a hero, but rival Protestant missionaries were muttering that he was corrupt and sleeping with the women lepers. Louis took his side and later wrote a letter in his defence.

They stayed six months in Hawaii, with their future plans never quite clear. Louis told one correspondent that he would be back in England in the summer, then wrote to Baxter about meeting him in Madeira. In May, Maggie departed for Scotland, to visit an ailing sister, presuming that Louis would follow her the next year. Louis found Hawaii not as warm as some of the other islands he had visited, his health was not as good as it had been at sea, and he was becoming appalled by the 'awful whites'. Honolulu was too civilised and commercialised for his tastes. There were horse-drawn cabs, dusty streets, constant steamer arrivals, rival newspapers, electricity, and the King even had a telephone. The solution seemed to be another voyage. It says much for Fanny's forbearance that she agreed to it, despite her experiences so far.

'I hate the sea,' she said in a letter to Mrs Sitwell, 'and am afraid of it, but I love the tropic weather, and the wild people, and to see my two boys so happy. To keep house on a yacht is no easy thing. When Louis and I broke loose from the ship and lived alone amongst the natives I got on very well. It was when I was deathly sea-sick, and the question was put to me by the cook, "What shall we have for the cabin dinner, what for tomorrow's breakfast, what for lunch? and what about the sailors' food? Please come and look at the biscuits, for the weevils have got into them, and show me how to make yeast that will rise of itself, and smell the pork which seems pretty high, and give me directions about making a pudding with molasses – and what is to be done about the bugs?" – etc. etc. In the midst of heavy dangerous weather, when I was lying on the floor clutching a basin, down comes the mate with a cracked head, and I must needs cut off the hair matted with blood, wash and dress the wound, and administer restoratives. I do not like being "the lady of the yacht," but ashore! O, then I felt I was repaid for all.'

They hired another yacht, the *Equator*, a trading schooner this time, not quite as luxurious – which did copra trading round the islands. Under the command of its young Scottish master, Captain Reid, they left Hawaii in June 1889, heading first towards the Gilbert Islands. Now that Maggie and Valentine had gone, Fanny was the only woman on board. 'Fanny, in the midst of fifteen males, bearing up wonderfully,' wrote Louis to Colvin. Perhaps resolutely would be a better description.

During this voyage, or it might have been during the previous one, Fanny thought she had fallen pregnant once again, according to a later remark in a letter about her South Sea cruising to an American friend, Mrs Low. Nothing came of it, it was another false alarm. Most biographers have assumed she imagined it, as by now she was approaching fifty.

Near Christmas they reached Samoa, landing at Apia on the
island of Upolu. By chance or subconscious intent Louis had
arrived on one of the islands which that New Zealand visitor had
recommended to him, all those years ago in Heriot Row. His first
impression of Samoa was that it was not as beautiful as Tahiti or
the Marquesas; nor were the people as attractive as elsewhere, he
told Baxter. 'But they are courteous; the women very attractive
and dress lovely; the men purpose like and well set up, tall, lean
and dignified.'

On the waterfront at Apia they fell in with a local trader,
Harry Moors, who offered them accommodation and any help
while they looked around. As they explored the island they found
that, just a couple of miles inland, above the town, the heat was
not as oppressive and there was always a gentle wind. They also
discovered that the island, though far less civilised than Hawaii,
had good communications, with regular mail steamers going from
Apia to Sydney and San Francisco, vital if Louis was to keep
sending copy and manuscripts out into the world.

As he got to know the Samoans better, he became interested in
their political problems and fascinated by their history and culture,
songs and tattoos, legends and traditions. This was a development
which Fanny had already noted. She saw him becoming more
obsessed by the past than by the present. It was a trend she
feared, creatively and commercially. She wrote to Colvin, warning
him about what was happening.

> Louis has the most enchanting material that any one ever
> had in the whole world for his book, and I am afraid he
> is going to spoil it all. He has taken it into his Scotch
> Stevenson head that a stern duty lies before him, and that
> his book must be a sort of scientific and historical impersonal
> thing, comparing the different languages (of which he knows
> nothing, really) and the different peoples . . . leaving out all
> he knows of the people themselves. And I believe there is no
> one living who has got so near to them or who understands
> them as he does. I am so sure that you will agree with me that
> I am going to ask you to throw the weight of your influence
> as heavily as possible in the scales with me. What a thing it is
> to have a 'man of genius' to deal with. It is like managing an
> overbred horse. Why with my own feeble hand I could write
> a book that the whole world would jump at. . . .

Furnas, whose 1952 biography of RLS is still the best, disagreed with Fanny. He believed she was wrong to try to dissuade Louis away from history, saying that Western readers needed to know and understand the background. In Louis's letters, I personally skip the bits where he tries to explain the Samoan language, giving endless examples, and in his book *In the South Seas*, published posthumously, I fear boredom sets in when I come to yet another mystical Polynesian legend and quaint tradition. What I love are his first-hand accounts and reflections, with the minimum of historical research dragged in, which was what slowed up *Travels with a Donkey* and was mercifully absent in *The Amateur Emigrant* and *Silverado Squatters*. An observer of the human race, who can write with such wit, wisdom and polish as RLS, comes along very rarely.

In February 1890, Louis wrote to Baxter, telling him he had bought an estate, two or three miles above Apia, with five streams, waterfalls, fifty head of cattle and a great view of forests, mountains and warships in the harbour. To Dr Scott, his old doctor in Bournemouth, he said it was around 400 acres in area. 'I shall only return next summer to wind up my affairs in England; thenceforth I mean to be a subject of the High Commissioner.'

Harry Moors had found the land for him, and no doubt made himself a decent percentage on the sale, and was instructed to get work started on a dwelling. It was to be called Vailima, meaning five streams.

Louis had made an important decision, unexpected in some ways, as he seemed to have got into the habit of endless voyages, living most of each year at sea. But now he was going to build, not rent, a proper home for himself and his family in Samoa. A place to stay for ever? He was certainly planning never to live permanently in Britain again.

With the building work started, Louis set out for Sydney, intending to go on from there to London to settle his affairs, but he fell ill once again. He took another cruise in another trading vessel, and then returned to Samoa in October 1890. This time he was ready to settle down, after three years of Pacific wanderings. Or forty years of wandering, if you consider that all his life he had been travelling, and so far never arriving.

Samoa Today – Arrival

Dear Boy,

A few months before I left for Samoa there was a spate of stories in the newspapers which shocked every RLS fan in the country, if not the world. Members of the RLS Club in Edinburgh were most upset and were quoted as saying it should not be allowed, what was happening out there. Vailima, it was reported, was going to be made into a tourist attraction. Some Americans were behind a plan to turn it into a Disneyland, with cable-cars up to Mount Vaea. Even worse, it appeared the Americans were Mormons. What would your father have thought? The good, stern Presbyterians of present-day Edinburgh naturally had visions of some bizarre religious order, trying to convert everyone.

I wrote to the Mormon Church, Western Samoa, asking for the latest information, but got no reply. I wrote to the Tourist Department, Government of Western Samoa, hoping there must be some such body, but got no reply either.

Then the stories stopped. Your beloved Samoa was out of the news again, probably for another few decades. Only once before in recent memory has Samoa made the British press and that was in 1991 when, to the amazement of the sporting world, they beat Wales in the Rugby World Cup. Everyone then tried to find Western Samoa on the map, which is very hard, as it is worth only a dot on even the largest map, usually tucked into a crease between the hemispheres. The population is 160,000, about the size of Swansea, which led to endless jokes at the expense of Wales.

It's halfway round the globe, from where I sit in the UK. I couldn't decide whether going east or going west would be better. My travel agent advised going west, via California and Hawaii, something to do with world flight paths, more options, better bargains, which is exactly the way you went, though for different reasons.

I was exhausted by the time we got over Upolu, not having slept properly for twenty-seven hours, and found myself blinking in amazement when I looked down and saw this turquoise marble sea all round the island, kept in by a jagged string of coral reef, totally unreal, and such a violent shade of turquoise.

'KEEP SAMOA SAFE FROM AIDS.' That did rather bring one down to earth. It's the first thing you see, landing at Faleoloa airport in the western corner of Upolu. The airport is small and unworldly, the locals standing around gaping as if they have never seen planes before, or Westerners. My taxi-driver told me, repeatedly, that no Samoan had so far died of Aids. The sign was a warning to all foreigners.

The drive along the west coast road to Apia takes about forty minutes and must be the nicest drive from any airport to any capital in the world. No modern buildings, no ugly building sites, no unattractive dwellings, just a gentle glide, passing native villages which have hardly changed for centuries, still dominated by *fales*, the traditional Samoan houses, built like bandstands, with roofs propped up on poles, standing open to the elements.

In your day, the roofs were mostly thatch. Today, a lot of them are made of corrugated tin, but the shape, style and purpose are the same. Whole families live in them, with no separate rooms, no privacy. As I slid past, I could clearly see inside, able to inspect the beds, tables, dressers, lined up as if they had cleared the floor for a dance. All human *fale* life is also visible, going about its domestic business, eating, talking, watching videos, undressing, going to bed. In each village, there is still a large *fale*, kept empty, waiting not for the band to arrive but for meetings, where the chiefs can hold court or the women's committee get together.

My first impression of Apia was of a charming if run-down colonial town which the modern world had forgotten, with wooden shops lined up along the front, old churches gently leaning, small banks and low offices, unmade pavements, no fast-food outlets, no flashy window displays, very much as you last saw it – except for the Monster. This is a new building right on the waterfront, dominating the landscape, completely out of scale with the town, completely out of character. My taxi-driver said it was a gift from the Chinese. Hong Kong? No, Communist China. It's their bit of aid, to help Samoa. It will house all the government departments, bringing them together in one place. The catch is that the Chinese imported all their own labour, plus the concrete, wood and all materials. What Samoa gets is an empty building, and some local politicians will get their moment of glory, when this giant is finally opened, a monument to the concrete age.

I'd booked into Aggie Grey's hotel, a legend in the Pacific, so all the guidebooks say. Aggie was the daughter of William Swan, a chemist who emigrated from Lincoln to Samoa in 1889 and married a Samoan woman. Do you remember him? You usually made friends with every local chemist and doctor. Aggie, born in 1897, married twice, each time to Scotch-sounding men – Gordon Hay-Mackenzie and Charlie Grey. During the last war, she sold hamburgers and coffee to American soldiers, moving on to booze, of which she managed to get ample supplies, despite New Zealand's ban on alcohol.

Yes, New Zealand. That will surprise you. All those colonial clashes you had to live through, as Britain, Germany and the USA jostled for control of Samoa, and which caused all that bloodshed and civil strife, were fought in vain. Germany and the USA did appear to win at first, when in 1899 Samoa was split between them. Western Samoa became German, while the eastern islands became American, which they still are. However, in 1914, on the outbreak of the First World War, New Zealand took control of Western Samoa. That lasted till 1962 when the country became fully independent. It was during this long New Zealand rule that the Samoans took up rugby. The New Zealand connection is still strong, with many Samoans emigrating to New Zealand to work – or to play rugby. The All Blacks usually have a few Samoan-born players.

Aggie Grey's little bar became well known throughout the Pacific, especially with Allied troops, and she is said to have been the model for Bloody Mary in *South Pacific*. James Michener did stay at Aggie's, but says he only based the good bits on her. Her snack bar developed into a hotel, and numerous celebrities have stayed there. She died in 1988, aged ninety-one, by which time she had helped put Samoa on the tourist map. In return, her hotel has appeared on Samoan postage stamps.

The hotel has recently been revamped, and some think it's now too modernised, but it looked nicely colonial to me, especially the large wooden veranda area at the back, the tropical gardens and the *fale*-style lodges in the grounds. My room was in the new modern bit at the front and I felt disappointed at first, in case I was missing out on ambience, till I walked out of the front door. Louis, how did you stand it? Why did you not leave Samoa the moment you landed?

I walked only a hundred yards before collapsing. The humidity was totally oppressive. I felt my body melting, my clothes wringing wet, all energy sapping away. Throughout the next two weeks, I hardly ever felt comfortable, except in my beautifully air-conditioned bedroom, or in the hills, very early in the morning. I don't know how you lasted those first few months in Harry Moors's shack on the waterfront. Up in Vailima, admittedly, you did have a bit of breeze, but you still had to move around, come down to Apia sometimes. Where did you get the energy for all those books? Reading your letters, it is clear that many of your visitors did find it too hot. 'We like the climate, but it doesn't suit everyone.' You got very upset when someone went back to London and said Samoa was an awful place.

The hotel is still run by Aggie Grey's family – under the managership of her son, Alan Grey, chairman of the Samoan Rugby Federation. On the reception desk was young Aggie Grey, her granddaughter, with flowers in her hair. Most of the staff, male and female, sported flowers, and bare feet. The men were in skirts, of course, in the Samoan fashion.

I'm not sure how to pass on to you my next observation. In your day, it was easy. Now we have to be careful when describing people, lest we be accused of sexism, ageism, any other ism. *Samoans are incredibly attractive.* Such fine bodies, noble features, smooth, light brown skin, marvellous complexions, forever smiling. Unlike most Pacific islanders, they are pure Polynesian, with no outside mixtures of European, Chinese or Indian. Even purer than in your day, which is unusual. The 'blacks' whom you often mentioned were African slaves, bought in for the plantations, but they later left.

You, of course, raved about the lovely bodies of the girls and their beautiful, naked breasts. They went topless in your day, which must have been a bit distracting. You clearly did not avert your eyes, or your cameras. Even your maids are sitting around bare-breasted in some of your photographs, carefully posed. Taken by Lloyd or by you? It's not always clear. Lloyd was only twenty-two when you settled in Samoa, a very impressionable age.

I think you did a lot to suggest the idea in our stiff Western minds that Samoa was some sort of sexual paradise. Then along came Margaret Mead in 1928 and her book *Coming of Age in Samoa*, a huge bestseller. She described these beautiful people in much more scientific detail, and recorded their happy, casual attitude to their sexuality. She claimed this was the reason they were so stress-free. The myth of their sexual availability suddenly made Polynesia very attractive to scores of painters, writers and assorted hedonists. Until, in 1983, another anthropologist, Derek Freeman, accused Mead of doctoring her figures and denounced her conclusions. Most experts today have turned against Margaret Mead. So are present-day Samoans stressed, are they sexually available? Don't ask me – I'm just here on the RLS trail.

Next morning, I asked at reception for information about Vailima, if I could get in, what were the opening hours. I knew that, after your death, it had been sold to a Gustav Kunst, who lived there for some years. During the New Zealand administration it became a government building. Since Independence, it has been the official residence of the Head of State. What I didn't know was that the cyclones of 1991 and 1992 had done so much damage that the house was now boarded up and empty. No one could get in, until the Mormons had done their work. They were expected soon, I was told. How soon? No one seemed to know.

Bright and early, to avoid the worst of the heat, I turned left out of the hotel and set off to explore, keeping well into any shade. Now that I examined the sea-front carefully, I could see how dirty and dusty the pavements were, several shops were derelict and the pretty leaning church was in fact about to fall down. The sea looked scummy and uninviting, the harbour empty, except for a couple of dirty tankers.

I went into a craft shop and bought some postcards. The Samoan in charge spoke excellent English, with a New Zealand accent. He turned out to be called Harry – grandson of Harry Moors, your agent friend, who helped you find Vailima. He offered to take me into the little guest-house next door, where you first lived, which is now empty and disused. How kind, I said, but you have your shop to run. No problem, he said, getting ready to leave, there aren't any other customers around. At that moment, a car drove up outside, and a noisy family got out. It was his own wife and children, come to see him. Another time, I said.

I found myself outside the public library, so I went in, wondering if they had an RLS collection. There was no one at the desk, so I stood for a while, coughing, till a woman appeared and said there was a staff meeting, could I wait. I wandered round, looking for my own books, as one does, as you did, as all authors do. I found only one of mine, on Wordsworth, but three of my wife's novels, early ones, which she now hates.

When the meeting was over, the Head Librarian came out to ask what I wanted. Yes, they did have a Pacific Room, which included an RLS collection, but it was not open to the general public. She seemed at first loath to let me in, someone straight off the street, but she softened.

The RLS collection was on three shelves, all printed material, with no original letters or manuscripts. Most of the books I had already read, but there were several small publications which were new to me. I sat reading a booklet called *RLS as I Found Him in His Island Home* by Captain Hiram Morse, published privately in 1902. He said that, despite your poor health, you were 'capable of greater exertions than many men who were apparently superior physically. . . . He gave a dozen orders to many different persons without changing his tone. He would sit quietly in his boat, appearing as unconscious as a native, but once upon his feet, he was all action.'

He has a long description of attending one of your parties at

Vailima with 'naked men and half clad women, European band boys and natives, all mixed up'. Sounds fun.

I had a drink in a bar and found myself sitting beside a group of Samoan women. Or so I thought. Then I realised they were all men, despite their painted nails, make-up and jewellery. Had I wandered into a gay bar? In Samoa? I noticed that two were clutching briefcases. After several drinks, and many high-pitched giggles, they left and went into a nearby bank, their place of work, so it appeared.

At the end of the sea-front I came to a circular thatched building called the Western Samoa Visitors' Bureau. I explained I was on the RLS trail, and was told I must speak with Fuimaono Feretoi Tupua, Chief of Samoan Cultural Affairs at the Bureau. And also a chief, or *matai*, in his own right.

He was aged about fifty, married with four sons and one daughter, a large, well-built, military-moustached, very distinguished-looking gentleman, as befits a chief. He went to a local missionary school and then to theological college, but never finished. 'Six months before the end, I began to doubt if I did have the calling to be a priest. Instead I decided to do useful work for the government and my people.' He then told me something that will interest you, Louis. You saved his grandfather from prison – Tupuola i Lotofago. Do you remember the name? One of the chiefs who later built your road? I'd brought a copy of your Samoan letters with me, but they were in my hotel bedroom. (Sure enough, his grandfather's name is mentioned. I photocopied the relevant pages, as he'd never seen the letters, and later gave them to Fui. I was allowed to call him that by then, but he always addressed me as Davies. Very Victorian.)

'Your Louis Stevenson was a great friend to Samoa. We are still grateful for what he did for us. He fought for our cause, the only one who supported Mataafa.'

I asked what the chances were of seeing the present King Mataafa, one of the four Paramount Chiefs of Western Samoa. Fui is a member of his tribe, but doubted it would be possible. The king did not give interviews. Anyway he was always very busy. And, if not busy, he would be playing golf.

I remarked on Fui's skirt, which was heavy and formal. He

said it was actually a Fijian skirt, which he found better for office use, as it was properly tailored, with belt and pockets, not just a simple wrap-around which most men wore. I asked if under their skirts Samoans went naked, like kilted Scotsmen are supposed to be.

'I have a tattoo,' he said. 'That is the Samoan underwear.' He lifted up his skirt to reveal an amazing tattoo, dark blue and dense, starting from just above his knees and going right up to his waist. It did look like underpants, or at least very dark long johns. The size and design of his tattoo indicated his chief status. He had it done aged twenty-six, on becoming a chief.

Tattoos are still very popular in Samoa, with men and women. In your day, it was a very painful process, done by someone in each village using wood splinters, natural dyes, then you were wrapped in leaves. 'That art has died out now, which is a shame. I don't like to see the old crafts disappearing. Now it is done with proper medical instruments and is less painful. Tattoos are symbolic, showing you are proud of your Samoan heritage and your *fa'amatai*, or family tribe. All the four tribes are still very strong. The paramount chiefs and the lesser chiefs have huge powers to discipline and control their family members. This is why Samoa today still has only 200 policemen. They are not needed. The chiefs control their people. We want all our traditions to continue. We don't want to end up like Hawaiians. We want to remain unique.'

As a *matai*, Fui is responsible for an extended family of some 4,000. These days they are allowed to marry whom they like, though some will still ask for his approval. The chief's main duty is to look after the family's property and rights and help members get jobs. 'I could be deposed if the tribe thinks I'm a bad chief and not doing enough to help.'

I asked about Margaret Mead. Had she got it all wrong, about the happy, fun-loving Samoans? 'Not totally wrong, but people told her things, not knowing they were going into a book. Some told her things to make fun of her, for amusement. Some told her things they thought she wanted to hear.'

That morning, at breakfast, I had read in the *Samoan Observer* about the appallingly high suicide rate in Samoa, one of the worst in the world. In the ten years from 1979 to 1989 there had been

588 suicide attempts, over half of them fatal, the rest resulting in permanent damage. Most were fifteen- to twenty-five-year-olds, killing themselves with a weed-killer called Paraquat, causing a slow, lingering, horrible death. The implication being that they were making their own family suffer. So much for happy, smiling Samoans? So much for the strength of tribal families?

'Ah,' sighed Fui, 'the power of the *matai* system is not quite as strong as it was. When I was young, I was given a good whack if I did anything wrong. You can't do that today. Young people are under so many pressures. They hear about life in the West, and their freedoms, and resent our traditions. We need to go back to the old ways, and have more discipline.'

I asked about the gay bar and he explained that the men were *fa'afafine*. I'd seen a mention of them in an American guidebook, which suggested it stemmed from an old tradition in certain families where, if they had too many boys, some were brought up to do female jobs, and dressed accordingly. Fui said this was all wrong. He knew of no such tradition. 'There were none when I was a boy.' But perhaps you never noticed, or there were none in your circle? 'No, it's only happened in the last twenty years. It's Western influence that's done it, people going abroad and picking up these habits. There's a couple of hundred of them in Apia, who go around in two main groups.'

Are they ridiculed or attacked? 'No, they are accepted. They have good jobs, in government and in banks, and do good work. If you want help with a project, you can rely on the *fa'afafine*. A group of them recently did some gardening work along the front. They are our people. In fact my son is one of them. . . .'

I later asked several other Samoans about the *fa'afafine* and was told they covered a spectrum of sexual orientation. Some were boys, dressing up for fun, who would eventually get married and settle down. Some were gay. Some were transvestites. But it is true they are all accepted. They have their own 'female voice' choir who sing with the real women's choir in church. They have their own netball team, which plays in the women's league. They turn up at big rugby matches in full female gear, leading the cheers and the chants, like majorettes.

One of the biggest social occasions of the year is their drag show, to pick Miss Fa'afafine. All their families turn up and the hall is always full, though it is feared this event is becoming too popular, attracting gay groups from Australia and America who are likely, the Samoans fear, to bring in some undesirable habits and infections.

19

Samoa
1889–90

One day in December 1889, the Reverend W.E. Clarke of the London Missionary Society was walking along the front at Apia, when he chanced upon some people, coming towards him.

> I met a little group of three European strangers – two men and a woman. The latter wore a print gown, large gold crescent earrings, a Gilbert-Island hat of plaited straw, encircled by a wreath of small shells, a scarlet silk scarf round her neck, and a brilliant plaid shawl across her shoulders; her bare feet were encased in white canvas shoes, and across her back was slung a guitar. . . . The younger of her two companions was dressed in a striped pyjama suit – the undress costume of most European traders in these seas – a slouch hat of native make, dark blue sun-spectacles, and over his shoulders a banjo. The other man was dressed in a shabby suit of white flannels that had seen many better days, a white drill yachting cap with a prominent peak, a cigarette in his mouth, a photographic camera in his hand. Both the men were bare-footed. They had, evidently, just landed from the little schooner now lying placidly at anchor, and my first thought was that, probably, they were wandering players en route to New Zealand, compelled by their poverty to take the cheap conveyance of a trading vessel.

Louis, complete with wife, and stepson Lloyd, often looked like that, especially in their early days at Vailima, when they were little more than camping, knocking their little wooden shack into shape and wondering what to do with their large plantation. Lloyd in his dark blue sunglasses must have looked rather unusual, but no doubt it was a legitimate aid for his poor eyesight, not a fashion statement.

Vailima had only four rooms at first, two up and two down, when Louis returned to Samoa in October 1890, and settled in permanently, but they were soon creating a new building. They even built a fireplace, the only one in Samoa, not exactly necessary in a round-the-year tropical climate. Most commentators have assumed that, because of humidity, it was used for airing Louis's clothes, to help with his chest problems.

White staff were hired for indoor work, as they had been told that the native Samoans were not up to these duties; but the German cook proved drunken, clumsy and hopeless, and they soon moved on to training their own Samoan staff, both indoors and out. In the early days, all they had to eat between them for dinner one night was an avocado. When guests came for breakfast, they were told to bring their own food. But soon they were getting supplies sorted out, with Louis going up and down to Apia on his horse Jack, and Fanny beginning to experiment with local produce. On Tuesday 3 November 1890, Louis boasted to Colvin in a long letter, they enjoyed a rather delicious dinner: 'Stewed beef and potatoes, baked bananas, new loaf-bread hot from the oven, pineapple in claret. These are great days. We have been low in the past, but now we are belly-gods, enjoying all this.'

Fanny was in charge of outdoors, gardener-in-chief, with Louis helping, after a fashion. She consulted the experts at Kew Gardens on what plants to try and took advice from someone in Washington DC on the best type of grass. For the front lawn, she had the ground cleared and the soil sifted to eighteen inches, levelling it herself with a spirit level and string.

The climate at Vailima proved excellent for Louis's health and he took his turn with a bush knife and a machete, clearing away the undergrowth, feeling virtuous and fit, if not achieving very much, commenting on the satisfaction to be got from an afternoon's weeding, for which a manual labourer would have been paid a few pennies, compared with earning an easy ten pounds from an afternoon spent writing.

Louis's normal day, according to a letter to Colvin in March

1891, began at 5.45, just before sunrise, when a houseboy brought him tea, bread and a couple of eggs. By six o'clock he was at work, sitting up in his bed – consisting of mats, pillows and a blanket, but no mattress or sheets – writing away for the next three hours. He was finishing off *The Wrecker* (written in collaboration with Lloyd) and *In the South Seas* (his syndicated letters which later became a book), and starting *The Beach of Falesa*, a tale set in a South Sea island. Around nine o'clock he wandered outside and did a spot of weeding till lunch at eleven. After that, some more writing, then perhaps another spot of weeding in the afternoon. He might then have a swim in his own pool, a natural one nearby in one of his streams, beneath a waterfall. Dinner was early, at 5.30. After that some reading, or perhaps a game of cards, a few tunes on his flageolet. Bedtime was at sunset, usually around eight o'cock.

Fanny, by her own account, written in a diary she kept till 1893, seemed to spend the whole day out of doors in the first couple of years, struggling with the elements and the staff. Her object was to make the plantation self-sufficient, or at least to produce enough to feed themselves, which she saw as a necessity, living in such a remote place. She brought chickens from Sydney, but they caused a lot of trouble before she could get them to lay eggs for Louis's breakfast. They had three piglets which were stolen, a horse which ran loose and disappeared. More horses came, and a wagon for them to pull, but the horses ate their own stable and the wagon turned out to be the wrong type, too light for heavy work on the plantation. The weeds seemed to spring up again as soon as any clearing was made. Then there was the problem of getting proper implements. In Apia, she moaned, one could buy champagne, but not spades.

Her Samoan workers were big and strong enough, but they had to be taught Western ways. Fanny instructed one of them to take a pail of water upstairs, only to see him grip the handle of the pail in his teeth, then shin up a pole to the veranda. Living his life in a one-storey *fale*, he had no experience of a staircase. In the gardens, there were plants that the Samoans would not touch, trees they would not go near for fear of disturbing the spirits. Fanny had to resort to her own magic, to persuade them her spirits were more powerful. In one trick she put a finger of each hand on to the closed eyes of a labourer who was scared to work in a distant part of the garden. She then shifted her hands, touching his eyes with two fingers of the same hand, giving him a sudden slap with the free hand, saying that was her spirit at work. He need now have no fear, as her spirit would be protecting him. Naturally, they thought she was a witch.

Eventually, by trial and error, she managed to get things growing, such as tomatoes, peppers, aubergines, oranges, celery, avocado, asparagus, pineapples, mangoes, bananas and cabbages. She more or less successfully kept cows, pigs, hens, horses, cats and bees. She experimented with some of the more interesting large leaves from the local trees, cooking them for Louis's dinner. He refused to eat them. She did, and was very sick. She also tried making beer from bananas, but that was a total failure.

Heriot Row was sold, and many of the better bits of furniture and paintings were eventually shipped out to Vailima. Maggie returned in 1891, throwing in her lot with them, as a permanent member of the family. She brought her own maid, Mary Carter, and a sofa for her own use. 'Which showed plainly that she meant to stay,' remarked Fanny, rather tartly in her diary. One of the more muscular Samoans specialised in washing and ironing Maggie's widow's caps, and also delighted in wearing the caps himself.

Around the same time, Belle and Joe Strong also took up residence, with ten-year-old Austin. They had lost a second son, Hervey, the same name as the son Fanny herself had lost. Joe was soon wearing a Samoan skirt (over his trousers, by the look of the photographs), and liked to pose with a white cockatoo on his shoulder. They were both smokers, like Louis and Fanny, which meant the whole household was puffing away, except Maggie. She did not approve of such a disagreeable habit, however fashionable.

Louis, ever mindful of Austin's education, gave him some lessons, including French and English Literature, or at least Scottish Literature, judging by the fact that, on Christmas Day, 1891, young Austin delighted the family throng with a rendition of 'Young Lochinvar'.

By the end of the first year of permanent residence, the Vailima household had therefore grown to seven assorted Stevensons –

Louis, Fanny, Lloyd, Maggie, Belle, Joe and Austin – and nineteen Samoan staff. There was talk of Lloyd going back to finish his university education, at Cambridge this time, but nothing happened. Instead, he was allowed his own bachelor quarters, a little house built for him nearby.

By April 1891, Louis estimated that so far he had spent around £2,500 on Vailima, which included £400 or so for the land itself, then another £2,000 in buildings, paddocks, roads, labour. No sign yet of the plantation paying for itself. Luckily, Louis's income continued to remain high – by now around £4,000 a year, enough to cover the running costs of his estate and extended family, which were soon reaching £1,300 a year.

Their social life expanded, too, once their house was in order, and Louis made friends with several of the local missionaries, such as Mr Clarke, despite being very critical of the work of most missionaries who he felt were destroying local culture. He also made friends with American and German officials on the island, although he blamed them for fomenting rivalry amongst the tribes. This is typical of colonial life for any exile. You start by disliking the very idea of the other ex-pats, hating their opinions and values, but in the end you are thrown up against them, for want of other social contacts. You find that, after all, some of them are really perfectly decent people.

Close friends included Rider Haggard's brother, who arrived to be the British Land Commissioner, and his opposite number from the USA, H.C. Ide, later Samoa's Chief Justice. When Louis heard that Ide's daughter Annie had been born on Christmas Day, thus denying her the chance for ever of a proper birthday, he sent her a letter, handing over to her his own birthday. It was done as a legal document, clause by clause, with appropriate legal phrases, Latin quotations – so let no one say that Louis had wasted his legal training – with little jokes thrown in: 'And considering that I, the said Robert Louis Stevenson, have attained an age when O, we never mention it, and that I have now no further use for a birthday of any description.' There was a penalty clause, should Annie ever break, neglect or contravene the conditions in the document: 'I hereby revoke the donation and transfer my rights of the said birthday to the President of the United States.' (In Monterey, at the Stevenson House, there are a photograph and a letter from Annie, as a grown woman.)

The Stevensons were soon giving grand dinner parties, showing off their elegant home and fine cuisine. The solid mahogany furniture from Heriot Row might have seemed a strange choice for a tropical house, but it fitted in well with all their other furnishings – the best china and glass from Europe, redwood from California for the walls, silks and satins from the East. Almost everything had to be imported, from the smallest nail to glass for the windows. Lloyd ordered an ice-making machine from Scotland, but never got it to work. Other choice items included a Chippendale sideboard, a piece of sculpture by Rodin, a piano, six Colt rifles in a display case and one of Sargent's portraits of Louis.

Their most splendid room was a new one downstairs, measuring sixty feet by forty, with a grand staircase, perfect for big parties, whether they were entertaining Samoan friends, such as the Mataafa and the other chiefs, local colonial officials or visiting Europeans.

From the upstairs window, Louis could see boats arriving in the harbour – though not the harbour itself – and was always on the look-out for a British man-of-war. He loved entertaining their officers and crews, especially if they had a band on board. An evening which ended with music and dancing was his greatest delight; he was a poor dancer and not much good at music, but he prided himself on his flageolet playing and his attempts at composing.

There are many photographs of the social gatherings which took place at Vailima, and you can see what large numbers were entertained and how large a staff was needed to look after them. They had now progressed from roughing it in a wooden barricade, as Louis had called it, to throwing lavish parties in a tropical mansion, the grandest house on the island. On special occasions, the indoor staff wore their best skirts, which Louis had created for them – made out of Stuart tartan.

Louis had in a sense created his own clan, with himself as chief. In the early days, some of the Samoan staff left without giving any reason, or proved lazy and uncooperative, but gradually they began to think of Louis as a white *matai*, the head of their tribe, who would look after them, care for their needs, in health and in sickness. In return, they would always be loyal. Louis could reduce their wages, tell them off, yet meet with no objection. Whatever Tusitala did was right. That became Louis's name in Samoan, teller of tales. The process of living by tale-telling was considered the biggest magic of all, which of course it is. They could never understand how such enormous wealth, which clearly he must have to maintain such a large establishment, could come from his pen. They were forever trying to catch sight of the Bottle Imp.

Fanny never tried to learn Samoan, being bad at all foreign languages – even stuck on her own in Paris, with her children, she could not manage a word of French. Louis however fancied himself as a linguist and spent a lot of time learning the native tongue, taking lessons from a missionary, as well as studying Samoan customs and legends. He took the Samoan side in most political arguments against the colonial powers, sending off letters to *The Times* in London on their behalf, using his influence where he could. He might easily have found himself deported, despite the fact that Lord Rosebery, the Foreign Secretary, was a fan of his writings.

Louis always kept contact with England. Christmas presents, for the family and staff, were ordered from the Army and Navy Stores in London and literary gossip came through Colvin. The latest books were sent out and news of the rising stars passed on to him. 'Kipling is by far the most promising young man who has appeared since – ahem – I appeared,' he wrote to Henry James. He then sent a fan letter direct to Kipling, and started a correspondence with him, inviting him out to visit them in Samoa: an easy enough invitation to issue, living at the other side of the world, but Kipling at once started making travel plans, although the visit never took place. Later, in 1892, Louis began a correspondence with a bright young Scottish writer, J.M. Barrie, ten years his junior, but with whom he felt a great affinity, having Edinburgh connections in common.

Meanwhile, in London, Colvin was worried that Louis was becoming bogged down by Samoan culture and history. He agreed with Fanny that it would eventually have an adverse effect on his writing. He found a lot of Louis's letters hard to follow, and boring whenever he went into detail about local political rows. George Meredith, whose prose Louis admired more than that of almost any other living author, felt that Louis's self-banishment meant that he was cutting himself off from contemporary social developments, which would therefore be a disadvantage to him as a writer. Louis, for his part, liked to believe that being removed from London influences was a good thing. 'Human nature is always the same, and you see and understand it better when you are standing outside the crowd.'

It is true that many new and exciting literary developments were happening in London in the early 1890s, leading to a new openness in discussing sexual relationships, thanks to the activities of Oscar Wilde and then his trial, to Thomas Hardy's *Tess of the D'Urbervilles*, and to the influence of Zola, said to be obscene, and of Ibsen, said to be a revolutionary. Louis might have been a long way geographically from some of these more avant-garde influences, but *The Beach of Falesa* was proving that he was not out of touch with modern thinking and preoccupations. 'It is very strange, very extravagant, I dare say, but it's varied and picturesque, and has a pretty love affair, and ends well.' That is what he told Colvin about his new story in late 1890, without going into detail. The initial idea had come into his head in the rain forest, 'and shot through me like a bullet in one of my moments of awe in that tragic jungle'. Returning to it the following year he was clearly excited by its progress. 'Golly it's good, but the story is craziness. Miss Uma is pretty. All my other women have been as ugly as sin.'

It turned out to be a contemporary tale, not some Polynesian legend, which is what Colvin and others feared, though there are some spirit devils in it. 'The first realistic South Sea story, with real South Sea characters and details of life,' Louis boasted. 'You will know more about the South Seas after you have read my little tale than if you had read a library.'

Alas, when it was submitted to publishers, they thought it disgusting and demanded changes. 'It seems it's immoral and there's a to-do, and financially it may prove a heavy disappointment,' wrote Louis. What upset people was that the hero, Wiltshire, a white trader, picked up a native girl and slept with her, enticing her into

sex with a fake one-night marriage certificate, a very common trick
used in the islands by disreputable white traders. The writing itself
is sexy, not just the plot, with an exciting beginning where we see
the lovely half-naked girl, her chemise wet, her breasts bare, and
naturally young Wiltshire, who is telling the tale, falls for her. 'The
want of her took and shook all through me, like the wind in the luff
of a sail.' It was steamy stuff, for the 1890s.

It first appeared in the *Illustrated London News* in July 1892,
but with the marriage contract omitted. It then came out in book
version from Cassell in 1893, one of three stories in *Island Nights
Entertainments*. The contract was mentioned this time, but 'one
night' altered to 'one week', which seems silly. It made Louis very
cynical about ever trying to treat adult love in an acceptable way.
'With all my romance, I am a realist and most fanatical lover of
plain physical sensation, plainly and expressly rendered, hence my
perils.'

Louis himself always considered *The Beach of Falesa* one of
his best works, and many modern critics believe it is his finest
short story, but it seems to me unsatisfactory. It is told in the first
person, by a non-literary hero, which makes the writing tedious,
and in the middle the plot becomes confused and ridiculous, full of
blood and thunder, but the beginning and the ending are good.
You can, of course, search for deep psychological insight into
Louis, if you think Wiltshire is based on him, which I do not. At
the time, Wiltshire's character, and his sex life, were a revelation,
as the bad side of South Sea traders had been concealed from the
public; but the male-female relationship is not really explored.

Would he even have started on such a topic if his father
had still been alive? Probably not. Fanny appears to have made
no objections, though she was against certain other stories. It is
a pity that he did not persevere with further present-day, realistic
tales, but the problems with the publishers and public put him
off. Or so he said. Deep down, whatever his boasts about being a
realistic writer, he did feel happier with 'romance'. That does not
mean sentimental love stories but romance in the sense of strong,
stirring narrative, with real emotions and real people, which just
happen to be set in the past. Was he frightened to expose himself,
to reveal his true feelings and emotions, by avoiding contemporary

situations? He would deny this. His defence would be that real people are in the past, just as much as in the present. He never cared much for Dickens's social obsessions and characters, finding them decidedly exaggerated.

However, the writing of *The Beach of Falesa* was one of his happiest experiences. He was pleased with the idea, and thrilled by how it was going. In fact the whole of the first year of permanent settlement in Samoa appears to have been a happy and rewarding period, creating his lovely house, developing the plantation, surrounding himself with his own folk, winning over the Samoans, entertaining visitors, storing up some pleasurable memories and scenes.

'Yesterday all my boys were got up for their work in moustaches and side-whiskers of some sort of blacking,' he told Colvin in December 1890. 'It was a sight of joy to see them return at night, axe on shoulder, feigning to march like soldiers, a choaragus with a loud voice singing out "March – Step! March – Step!" in imperfect recollection of some drill.'

His health was excellent and he was able to ride and swim and take part in some of the rough work. 'I am a mere farmer. My hands are covered with blisters and full of thorns. Letters are doubtless a fine thing, so are beer and skittles, but give me farming in the tropics for real interest. Life goes in enchantment.'

How then to explain that remark, quoted already, about being happiest in Hyères? He was living in Vailima at the time he wrote it, on 19 March 1891. He had been out in the garden working. While weeding, he told Colvin, he had been having an imaginary conversation with him, as he very often did:

> Today, for instance, we had a great talk. I was toiling, the sweat dipping from my nose, in the hot fit after a squall of rain; me thought you asked me, frankly was I happy. Happy, said I; I was only happy once, that was at Hyères; it came to an end from a variety of reasons, decline of health, changes of place, increase of money, age with his stealing steps; since then, as before then, I know not what it means.

He goes on to say that he still has many pleasures, such as the delight of weeding, and that he does not want to change his circumstances. All the same, the thought for some reason has struck him, that he was happiest at Hyères. What people or things, conditions or events, could possibly be making him unhappy, in such an ideal, romantic, tropical paradise of a place like Vailima?

Samoa Today – Consul and King

Dear Louis,
Here I am outside the gates of Vailima, happy to see it, but not happy that so far I have been unable to get inside. You would probably be horrified at the huge noticeboard which has been erected beside the front gates. In lurid blue and yellow lettering it announces that restoration work on the Robert Louis Stevenson Museum will be completed by December 1994. Then there's a line which reads: 'The only property Stevenson ever owned.'

Our mini-bus had stopped to give us all a photo opportunity, so we'd poured out to study the notice, take snaps, activate the camcorders and try to get a glimpse of your house. No luck. It's too far up the driveway, obscured by trees. I thought of jumping over the wall, trespassing on the grounds, just to get a proper view, but I was still waiting for permission to have an official look round, or for the Mormons, whichever would be quicker. For a very small island, things take a very long time to happen. As you know.

So I'd joined a tourist trip along with ten other people. Our Samoan guide was an exotic creature who told us to call him Tommy. He was large and hefty, built like a rugby player, but totally feminine in his mannerisms, fluttering his eye-lashes, studying his long and beautifully painted nails, forever arranging the flowers in his hair. He was a great guide, who kept up an amusing running commentary all the way. 'That's where Stevenson and his wife

Fanny are buried,' he said, as we drove off, pointing to Mount
Vaea. 'They now have a good time together. Now we're approaching
what we call Beverly Hills Drive.' He raised his eyebrows, pouted
his lips, pretending to be a Hollywood star. Everyone smiled. A
camcorder whirled.

Just above Vailima, there are indeed some very smart villas,
with lush gardens, secure gates. You chose well. It is now the
smartest area to live in Samoa.

'That's McKenzie's house,' said Tommy. 'He owns our biggest
supermarket. I wish I'm related to him.'

I was sitting beside a blonde German girl, aged eighteen, who
was missing most of Tommy's jokes as her English was not up
to his English. She was on her own, doing a world tour, before
going to university to study science. She'd been in New Zealand
for a month, working in a bar, and had saved enough for a week in
Samoa. I asked if she wasn't scared, travelling on her own. 'During
the day it is fine, everyone is very helpful, very nice. But at night I
stay in my guest-house. Every night, I am sitting reading. If I go
to a bar or disco, everyone wants to dance with me.'

Six of the other passengers, half American, half British, had that
morning stepped off a rather dirty-looking cargo boat, *Clydebank*,
a good Scottish name, which was why I had noted its arrival in
Apia harbour. It was the sort of cargo-plus-passengers boat you
sailed on from Le Havre, not very common today, but romantic
and dreadfully expensive. They'd paid £8,000 each for a 120-day
round-the-world chug, across the Atlantic, through the Panama
Canal, to Tahiti and now Samoa, then back via Suez. 'The storms
on the Atlantic were so bad that four containers were swept straight
off the deck.'

Samoa doesn't have much of a tourist industry. In 1992, there
were only twenty-three places to stay, with Aggie's Hotel at the
top, then the Tusitala, followed by a handful of little guest-houses,
offering in all 489 bedrooms. The total number of visitors arriving
on the island came to 41,000 – but two-thirds of these were either
Samoans, back from New Zealand to stay with their families, or
visiting businessmen. That means there were only 14,000 real
tourists. The recent cyclones have put people off, and the lack of
decent beach accommodation. You can't swim in Apia, for either

9a: Skerryvore,
Bournemouth: their
home 1884–87, bought
by his father

9b: Lloyd Osbourne,
RLS's step son:
Treasure Island was
written to amuse him

10a: South Sea Island feast, RLS top left: in 1888, he set sail
with his family, plus mother, hoping to improve his health

10b: Lloyd, Fanny and RLS, plus his mother, right,
meet King Kalakaua of Hawaii

11a: RLS settled in Samoa in 1890 and built a house
and plantation called Vailima with around 400 acres

11b: Vailima today: rebuilt after cyclone damage,
thanks to American Mormons

12a: RLS and Fanny entertain a sailors' band,
plus locals, at Vailima

12b: RLS at Vailima, in one of his many velvet jackets

13a: RLS and family, photographed in Sydney, 1893:
Fanny, left, her daughter Belle, and Maggie, RLS's mother

13b: RLS inside Vailima, with Lloyd, left

14: RLS writing

15a: RLS dictating to Belle at Vailima

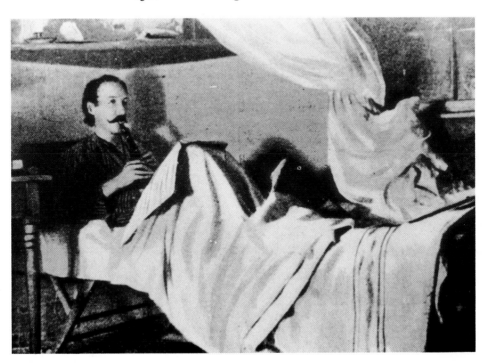

15b: RLS in bed, playing his flageolet

16a: RLS's grave on Mt Vaea, Samoa,
where he died, Dec 3, 1894

16b: Bas relief medallion of RLS,
with cigarette in hand

rocks or sewage. Even Aggie's hasn't got a beach. Best to go to the northern coast. However, if you are thinking of returning in another life and hoping to find things much as you left them, let me recommend Samoa. California would be too much of a shock.

Back at the hotel, still no answers to my calls, but Aggie's was in a state of great excitement, the staff running around in fancy clothes, the reception girls all giggly, brushing each other's hair, trying out new styles. I'd forgotten it was the night of the *fiafia*.

Fiafia is the Samoan name for a village play or musical, the sort which you witnessed many times, so I felt I had to see it. Originally, they had warriors doing war dances and half-naked girls performing erotic fertility dances, their bodies suitably oiled. The missionaries finally put a stop to most of the naked nonsense, but there was still a lot of flesh around in your day.

I took my place in the outdoor restaurant, beside the swimming pool. A stage had been set up and most seats were already filled. They were mainly local people, by the look of them, not hotel guests, families in their best clothes, out for an island's night entertainment. As I listened to the chatter, I could hear Samoan being spoken by the older members, then they'd switch to fluent English, with a New Zealand accent, when addressing their children. It was clearly the exile's treat – the son or daughter made good in New Zealand, home for Christmas, was taking out the family.

The show began with loud drum music, then suddenly a horde of warriors in loincloths and palm leaves jumped up from behind the stage and went into a wild war dance. It was very impressive. Then I began to think, isn't that my waiter, I'm sure I've seen him behind the bar, and that's surely one of the gardeners. Then the exotic dancing girls came on – last seen at the reception desk or making the beds. They were all Aggie workers, thus totally amateur performers, which meant there was none of that phoney professional gloss, sickly smiles and empty thank-yous, but people taking pride in performing their own traditional Samoan dances.

Aggie Grey junior took part, plus her own daughter and nieces, all dressed up in Samoan costumes. At one point, about to introduce another song, she announced she had something special she wanted us to know: 'All the girls are virgins.' They were aged from sixteen to fifty, all sizes, all shapes, sitting demurely on stage, smiling nicely, totally unembarrassed by this personal but totally irrelevant information. I tried to imagine how such news might be greeted in Britain. Loud cheers or jeers from the lads, loud protests from the feminists. None of the watching Samoans was sniggering, nobody seemed surprised, apart from a Canadian couple, guests in the hotel, whose eyes I caught for a moment, as we exchanged silent amusement. Sex amongst the Samoans is clearly worth a study today. Innocence and purity at one end. Transvestism at the other. Suicides scattered along the way.

The music was provided by five drummers, five guitarists and someone on a ukulele – all of them hotel staff. The ukulele sounded strange, in such a tropical setting, then I remembered in several of your letters you mention a banjo being played at these sorts of gatherings, and of course the missionary described Lloyd as carrying a banjo. It was obviously a ukulele. When I got home, I looked up its origin – and it turns out to be a Pacific instrument, first recorded in Hawaii.

Next morning, some good news. Two people I'd been trying to contact said they'd see me, both counterparts from your life in the 1890s. Firstly, the Hon. British Consul, Bob Barlow, had returned from a trip to New Zealand. That's where he's from. He's not British at all. He's lived in Samoa for seventeen years, coming first on an assignment in the Attorney General's office. 'Then I went troppo and decided I'd rather stay here than go back and compete on the gin and tonic circuit.' He's a lawyer, in private partnership, who'd helped out the previous British representative, then took over three years ago when he retired. 'The job's normally not very arduous. There's only forty British citizens on the island, including nuns and businessmen in transit. I know the exact figure because I had to compile a list when we had a royal visit last year from Prince Edward.'

He's also Secretary of the Western Samoan Rugby Union while his wife helps run the netball league. He says there's no ex-pat community, in the old Somerset Maugham sense, with all the whites congregating in some colonial club. 'That all went out twenty years ago.'

I told him I'd been up to Vailima and asked if there was any local resentment about the Mormons. Their proposed development had received some poor publicity in the West. 'I think it's partly the fault of the Mormons themselves. They haven't issued enough information so far about what their plans are.' He too had heard they were expected soon.

As I was studying the consul, noting his lean thin frame, his drooping moustache, I thought that he looked very like you, Louis. 'You're not the first person to say that.' The most recent was an Australian TV crew, doing an RLS documentary in Samoa, who persuaded him to play the title role. He had only a few words to say, all in Samoan, addressing some chiefs. 'I'll probably get teased to blazes when my Samoan friends hear it. I'm sure I've got the nuances all wrong. They made me ride a horse, which I haven't done since I was twelve, and then the horse bolted. This time the saddle slipped, and I ended up under the bloody horse.'

They dressed him up in period clothes, complete with your style of boots and jacket, as seen in all your photographs, and made him dye his hair, as they said his was too grey. 'That was the biggest insult. After all, I'm only forty-six. What an insult. Stevenson was younger than me.'

My next appointment was with King Mataafa. My friend Fui had finally fixed it, saying he would pick me up and take me to the king's office. It wasn't far away, just along the front, in a small, rather run-down office block which also houses the US Embassy, the Dutch Consul, the accountants Coopers and Lybrand, Apia Fast Photos and the HQ of the Congregational Church. About fifty per cent of Samoans are Congregationalists, thanks to the work of the London Missionary Society, still referred to in Samoa as the LMS. About one-quarter are Catholics. The rest are Methodists and Mormons.

The king is a commissioner of the Congregational Church, and thus has use of one of their offices, though he doesn't work there full-time. Fui said I should call him His Highness, at least at first. He stressed that it was an audience, not an interview. The king does not give interviews. I was not to make notes or ask him questions.

We walked down a long corridor, with offices partitioned up into smaller offices, all a bit churchy and dusty. The king was at a desk in a little office on his own. Aged about fifty, well built, grey hair parted severely on one side in the old English fashion, dressed in a linen skirt, short-sleeved white shirt with a striped club tie, bare legs and leather sandals.

Fui introduced us, then he left. The king had stood up to greet me, then sat down again. Silence. Does one wait, or what? I hate silence, so I burbled away, telling him how much I liked Samoa, how I was on the RLS trail, and naturally wanted very much to meet the descendant of the King Mataafa who had been a close friend of RLS's. As I rambled on, the king picked up a briefcase from the floor, opened it on his desk and took out a copy of a genealogical table which he handed to me. The names were in Samoan, but some of the symbols were explained in English – a triangle equalled male, a circle female, a triangle with a line through meant deceased. It covered his family over the last 200 years.

I asked him to point out King Mataafa IV, your friend in the 1890s. If I understood correctly, the present king is his great-great-nephew. He assumed the royal title in 1977 – Mata'afa Fa'asuamaleau Patu. Technically he is not a king any more, just a paramount chief, though his followers often refer to him as their king. As in your day, there are four Paramount Chiefs, one of whom is chosen as Head of State. The present one is His Highness Malietoa Tunumafili II. I'm sure you'll recognise that name from the political struggles you got caught up in, back in the 1890s.

I asked if he had children. He has eight – three sons and five daughters. Two sons are working in New Zealand – one of them a Congregational Minister, ministering to the Samoan community. The other, formerly in the Samoan police, is dead. One of his daughters was at that moment in New Zealand – touring with a Samoan women's soccer team. The king himself used to play a lot of sport, especially boxing and cricket. 'Every morning I still go to the gym – before I come to the office.' Every afternoon, he plays golf, his main passion in life. 'My handicap is fifteen, but it has been eleven.'

He gave me a copy of the genealogical table and I asked him to autograph it, with his title, which he did. I asked if I could take his photograph, thinking of all the wonderful ones you took. He agreed, but not with much enthusiasm. His English was a bit hard to understand. Or perhaps he wasn't used to pushy foreigners, bossing him around. As I left, the audience over, he said that his family was still grateful for the help you gave in their battles, all those years ago. There are, fortunately, no battles for him today. Only on the golf course.

Back in the hotel, I heard American voices from the dining-room. Had the Mormons arrived at last? I glanced inside and saw a distinguished-looking couple in their sixties, sitting having lunch. I introduced myself and they immediately asked me to join them. No, they were not Mormons, but they too were here on RLS business – researching for a musical.

Jack and Carolyn Fleming from Florida, so I discovered when Jack gave me his card, which also announced 'SEAPLANE – An All American Musical'. I think I must have missed that one, I said. Well, it's been on at the Kennedy Center in Washington, said Carolyn, and in Florida, and they had hopes of a Broadway production one day. Yes, it is about seaplanes, the story of the first Atlantic seaplane crossing of 1919. They'd written the book and lyrics together while Allen Pote had done the music. Their next production will be all about RLS. The title will be *Tusitala Story-Teller*. 'I see *Child's Garden of Verses* as a ballet sequence,' said Jack. 'We'll have RLS, Cummy and choruses of singing and acting children.' 'It will be very whimsical,' said Carolyn.

That morning they'd been to the library, the one I'd visited, and been charmed to find in the files an old Australian TV drama about RLS, which I'd missed. They still had some major decisions to make about their musical, such as whether to do the whole of your life, or just the Samoan years. What did I think? Oh, stick to Samoa, I said, more than enough material here. By the way, how many musicals had they done, and how long had they been in show business? I didn't catch the answer, as they were more interested in hearing my theories about your marriage, which of course fas-cinates all RLS-lovers. I asked again about their musical careers, and it emerged that they are not in fact full-time playwrights. Jack was a cardiologist, but he's always been very keen on the theatre, singing and writing songs.

A doctor, and one who knows about RLS! Just the person I wanted to talk to, to ask exactly what was wrong with Louis.

'There was never a positive diagnosis of TB. X-ray diagnosis had not yet been invented. No positive smear for the TB bacillus was reported,' he said. 'So I'm convinced that TB is in question for two reasons. If he had had it all his life as assumed, and if all the episodes of fever and severe illness and hemoptysis were directly due to the TB infection, then more than likely it would have spread through his body as he got older and probably would have gotten much worse. It didn't do that. Secondly, TB is infectious, yet while he was coughing up blood frequently, no one in his family or the people around him – and don't forget there were a lot of those in Samoa – not one of them was reported to have contracted TB, to my knowledge.'

If it wasn't TB, what was it? 'Probably bronchiectasis. The bronchial tubes deteriorate with a series of infections, perhaps beginning after an episode of childhood pneumonia in RLS's case. You can have chronic bronchitis and bronchiectasis all your life and periodically it may be exacerbated with acute bacterial infections.

'Fanny was right with her colds theory – keeping him away from germs was good for him. It wasn't the cold in Davos or the heat in Samoa that helped – just the fact of being withdrawn from the main sources of pollution.

'But all his life he did the very worst thing anyone with a bronchial infection can do – he smoked. That was terrible for him. You used to see a lot of bronchiectasis about thirty years ago when I was a young doctor, but not so much today. Antibiotics have changed the course. If Louis were here now, multiple antibiotic therapy would immediately have increased the quality of his life.'

A tragic thought, Louis. In a weekend with us, you could have been as good as cured.

21

Samoa
1892—4

Back in England, people thought it was all a bit mad, Louis cutting himself off from the mainstream of literary and civilised life. But if it improved his health, and he clearly loved what he said was a tropical paradise, and he was writing away as hard as ever, then what could they say? He issued invitations to visit Samoa, to old and new friends. Rudyard Kipling had said yes and Conan Doyle, another of Louis's new correspondents, was also invited. Baxter was certainly going and started making definite plans. Then it began to emerge in Louis's letters home during 1892 and '93 that perhaps Samoa was not such an ideal holiday destination for literary gentlemen, whatever the attractions of staying with one of the world's best-known writers.

He had indeed become exceedingly well known, in fact his fame seemed to increase with his remoteness. The magazine-reading public had fallen in love with the idea of this romantic invalid, exiled in his romantic home. 'Is fame all it's cracked up to be?' Belle once asked him. 'Yes, when I see my mother's face.' Maggie had moved on from childhood photograph albums to endless scrapbooks, sticking in every review or mention of her beloved son, whether they were favourable or not. On the front page of each scrapbook she wrote the same inscription: 'Speak well of my love, speak ill of my love, but aye come o'er his name.'

It was on a visit to Australia in March 1893 that Louis realised just how celebrated he had become. 'I found my fame much grown on this return to civilisation,' he told Colvin. 'People all looked at me in the streets of Sydney; and it was very queer. Here of course [Vailima] I am only the white chief in the Great House to the natives; and to the whites, either an ally or a foe. It is a much healthier state of matters. If I lived in an atmosphere of adulation, I should end up by kicking against the pricks. No chance of taking myself too seriously here.'

In Sydney he bought three topaz rings (his birth stone), inscribing two of them to Fanny and Belle – and agreed to give some interviews, one of which, at great length, appeared in the *Westminster Budget* on 5 May 1893, complete with photographs, touched up by the look of them, of Louis, his lovely family and dusky servants. It is an excellent interview, with good quotes from Louis, about art, his books, his life in Samoa. 'You have no white servants then?' asks the interviewer. 'To have a white servant would be simply to sow dissension. The white man is always grumbling, and he thinks a deuce of a lot of himself.'

The interviewer happens to ask Lloyd's age – all the members of the Stevenson family had become household names – and Louis affects not to know, suggesting he asks Fanny, which he does. This was quite a scoop, as Fanny never gave interviews, or even denied stories about her in the press. She graciously reveals Lloyd's age – twenty-four – but then talks only about her plants and flowers at Vailima, and her struggles with them.

What people back home did not properly realise, either reading about Louis in the public prints or from his private letters to friends, was that he had gradually walked and talked himself into a dangerous situation. Very soon he was in the middle of real violence. Civil war is not exactly what one wants when visiting a tropical paradise, even if one's host is a literary lion.

Was this therefore one of the elements in Samoan life which made Louis think such happy thoughts of Hyères? If anything, thoughts of war encouraged and excited him. 'As for wars and rumours of wars,' he told Colvin, 'you must surely know enough of me to be aware that I like that a thousand times better than decrepit peace in Middlesex.'

Samoan politics of the 1890s were confused and complicated,

made worse by the 1889 Treaty of Berlin, which gave the three powers – Britain, USA and Germany – joint administrative control over things like land and justice. As ever, money and economics were behind the struggle for political power, with Germany in control at the time Louis arrived in Samoa. Germany owned most of the plantations, producing copra from coconuts, and had imported black labourers to work them. They had their own puppet king, Laupepa, brought back from exile, which did not please the other two chiefs, notably Mataafa. Britain and the USA, while backing the official king, were involved in various devious arrangements with the chiefs to lessen German power.

Louis supported Mataafa's claim to be king from the beginning, not just because all the Samoans employed at Vailima were his supporters, but because he considered him the better man, a good, decent, honest, God-loving leader (a Roman Catholic, not Congregational, like his successor). Louis had a large stake in Samoa, having sunk his capital and most of his income into the island, and considered he was there to stay, so it was natural he should follow closely what was happening, but if he had been wiser and more sensible he would have stayed his hand, kept his opinions to himself. Instead, encouraged by Fanny, he was immediately publicly proclaiming himself on Mataafa's side. He chaired a political meeting and wrote outraged letters to *The Times* about the behaviour of officials.

Mataafa then broke away and set himself up as a quasi-independent but illegal king, guarded by armed sentries. Louis made a great show of going to visit him, riding twenty miles across rough land on his rather scraggy horse Jack, most of it in pouring rain, then taking part in six hours of political discussions. On that occasion Fanny and Belle came with him, which made Mataafa's men presume they must be Louis's two wives.

On another visit to Mataafa, he took his mother, the redoubtable Maggie, and then the Countess of Jersey. She was the wife of the Governor of New South Wales, in Samoa on a visit to see Bazett Haggard, and became very friendly with Louis. She could not of course visit the rebel Mataafa officially, because of diplomatic protocol, so Louis took her there under cover, using the name Amelia Balfour. Shades of *Kidnapped*. In London, a Foreign Office official

noted on a dispatch that 'Mr Stevenson would do better if he stuck
to novel writing and left politics alone'.

In July 1893, the posing and politicking turned serious. Mataafa
moved into armed rebellion and civil war broke out. The public
hall in Apia was turned into a hospital and Louis observed opera-
tions and helped the wounded. There were headless bodies around
Vailima and the Stevensons themselves prepared for a siege, knowing that rival tribes might exert revenge on the whites as well as on
Samoans. Out came the Colt rifles, ready for action.

'I suppose if our house should be attacked, Belle and I must
retire to a back apartment with some crochet work and not ask
what is going on,' wrote Fanny in her diary. 'A strange thing that
would be for a person of my spirit. I was never a coward in my
life and never lost my presence of mind in an emergency, and I
have met some very serious ones.'

Haggard, the British Land Commissioner, implored Fanny
and Belle to stay in town, not at Vailima, and he would protect
them. 'He said we would lie under a table and hand cartridges to
him. "No," I said, "I do not wish to be found dead, lying under
a table, shot through the stomach." "Well then," he rejoined,
"I'll go under the table and hand cartridges to you, and you can
shoot." His scheme was not attractive and I steadily refused. His
last word was, "You are going to sell your life for a few banana
trees." '

Fanny totally identified with Mataafa's cause, and kept Louis
up to the mark:

> I intend to do everything in my power to save Mataafa,
> and if Louis turns his face from him by the fraction of an
> inch, I shall wear black in public if they murder him, or
> if he is brought into Apia a prisoner I shall go down alone
> and kiss his hand as my king. Louis says this is arrant mad
> quixotism. I suppose it is; when I look at the white men at
> the head of the government and cannot make up my mind
> which is the greater coward, my woman's heart burns with
> shame and fury and I am ready for any madness. . . . Were
> I a Samoan I would, and I believe successfully, agitate for a
> massacre of the whites.

Mataafa's rebellion was nevertheless defeated. He was sent into
exile and the lesser chiefs were put in gaol. Louis went to visit

them, with Fanny, Belle and Lloyd, taking gifts of kava, the ceremonial drink, and tobacco. During 1894, the chiefs were slowly released. In September, as a gesture of gratitude to Louis, the chiefs announced they would build him a new road at Vailima, the Road of the Loving Heart. They did it themselves, as a mark of esteem, chiefs not normally engaging in such work, and Louis gave a great feast for its opening, writing himself a suitably stirring speech.

Throughout these years of political turmoil, in the background and sometimes the foreground, Louis continued to work as hard as ever, give or take the odd holiday and outbreaks of real war. Furnas estimates that he produced 700,000 words of printed copy in four years in Samoa, an enormous amount. *Catriona*, a sequel to *Kidnapped*, was written quickly, in four months in 1892, a pleasure for him to write, and still a pleasure to read. Like *The Beach of Falesa*, it had a successful woman character, as well as a few erotic undertones.

But then he reverted to his old habit of jumping back and forth between projects, starting a new one when he ran out of inspiration for the old. *The Wrecker* was another collaboration with Lloyd, begun at sea during their voyage on the *Equator*, then finished in Samoa. It is Louis's longest book, meant to be a sort of thriller about confidence men and tricksters; the action moves through Paris, Grez, Edinburgh, San Francisco, Napa, California, Honolulu, Sydney, Samoa – in other words places they knew well. It is all action and little heart, and betrays its main purpose, which was to make them some money. *Scribner's* paid $15,000 to serialise it. As a novel, it is no more memorable than *The Ebb-Tide*, another saga, again written with Lloyd.

St Ives, begun in January 1893, was meant more as a romantic comedy, with a Scottish setting, but it suffered from being written at the height of the war and also, which was a new and worrying sign, during bouts of depression. For once, Louis began to fear that he had worked himself out. 'The truth is, I have a little lost my way, and stand bemused at the cross roads,' he wrote to Edmund Gosse in June 1893. 'I have at least four novels begun, they are none good enough. *The Ebb-Tide* deserves to be torn to pieces.' Instead, he left *St Ives* and returned to an old project, *Weir of Hermiston*, hoping that would go better.

He did worry a great deal about his work: about taking on too many projects, about his failing creative energy, about new young writers coming up. 'A new writer, if he is any good, will be acclaimed generally with more noise than he deserves.' He felt at times that he had taken on too big an economic burden and that Vailima would eventually bring him down, the way that Abbotsford had proved a millstone for Walter Scott. It was a neat analogy, a mansion created for similar romantic grandiose reasons.

There was some substance to his worries about his creative work – Colvin in London was beginning to fear he had lost form – but there was little basis for his financial anxieties, real though they sometimes appeared to him. By 1894, he could see that, all things being equal, he would soon have £1,000 a year in unearned income – thanks to the capital he was amassing, now that the main work of Vailima was over, and the healthy royalties flooding in from his previous books. Even more encouraging was the first appearance of a collected edition of his works. This is what all authors yearn for, uniform reprints of old books, which bring in new money but do not require any new work, apart from perhaps the odd introduction. Few achieve this in their lifetime, and very few indeed in their early forties. In the autumn of 1894, when Baxter set out from Scotland, bound for Samoa via Suez, he was clutching the first two volumes of the Edinburgh Edition, proof that financially the Stevenson lifestyle, to which they had all become accustomed, could be supported for several years to come.

Domestically, there were other tensions at Vailima, which had not been apparent in the first couple of years. Being a cheerful and normally an ever-singing canary, Louis either chose to ignore them or did not care to pass them on to his friends back home. Fanny, in her diary, is less reticent. Maggie Stevenson, for example, was, hardly surprisingly, beginning to get on her nerves. It was a situation liable to lead to irritations, if not explosions. Charming her in-laws at Heriot Row, especially old Thomas, when the visits were only temporary, was rather different from living together permanently under one roof. Fanny could not really object when Maggie returned to live with her only son, as she had brought enough of her own relations to the marriage, but who was the Woman of the House, who was in charge domestically, either of Louis's health or of ordering the servants around?

Maggie was clearly a good sport, game for everything, even in her sixties, as her letters from the Pacific show. She boasted about how capable she had been on those voyages, always managing to be at the table for meals when the rest of them were down with sea-sickness, giving up her cardigans and bodices, swimming in the ocean for the first time in twenty-six years, wading from the boat to shore without help, walking the beaches in bare feet, putting up with mosquitoes ('one can't expect perfection'), mixing with the natives and eating their peculiar food, including raw fish. People were always telling her she was amazing, having lasted at sea for so long. 'No French woman would have endured it.'

Yet she was still a woman of her period and background, not really willing to slum it like Fanny, or to throw all convention away. When the political battles began over Mataafa she did not like being on the side of a rebel. 'She has been worried lest we should lower our "social status",' wrote Fanny, 'by quarrelling on political subjects with the government officials.'

She brought her religion, not just her sofa, with her from Edinburgh, and insisted on evening prayers, attended by the whole household. Louis agreed to all this, and took some pride and pleasure in thinking up little homilies, devising his own prayers, addressing the family and staff in his role as clan chief. Maggie loved it but, should the whole household not turn up, she became most upset.

'There is a big row on hand concerning – prayer!' wrote Fanny on 23 September 1891, the dash and exclamation mark indicating she did not consider prayer a big subject. 'Joe, having scalded his hand very badly, took Austin away to help with the fowls. Unfortunately, Belle was caught prowling like a cat, with no ostensible business on hand, and then there was an explosion. Mrs S considers that she has received a personal insult. A fight about prayers is really enough to bring a cynical smile to the lips of a bishop. Mrs S says she will not be left to pray with only servants.'

Fanny also took against Maggie's maid Mary, whom she consid-

ered impertinent and silly. Mary lent thirty dollars to an ex-servant
from Vailima, who departed without paying it back. Fanny felt it
was Mary's own fault, for having lent money to anyone without
consulting her first. But it was Mrs Stevenson who received most
of her more scathing remarks:

> She dislikes the life here which we find so enchanting and
> is disappointed and soured that she is not able to persuade us
> to throw it all up and go to the colonies. We have given the
> colonies [Australia] a fair trial and they mean death to Louis
> whereas this is life and reasonable health. I think she could
> be happier if she had some occupation, but I can't think of
> anything she would like. All the rest of us have every moment
> accounted for and are all enthusiastic in our different depart-
> ments. It is very difficult for me to understand that anyone
> can prefer a life of calls, leaving and receiving cards, with a
> proper church and invested meals and a nap on Sundays, to
> this open air paradise where one feels so near to heaven.

What, one wonders, were the occupations which her son and
son-in-law followed with such enthusiasm, with not a moment
unaccounted for? Little did Fanny herself know what exactly was
going on. Her diary, which she filled in most days, gives us a few
clues, even before the inevitable happened.

'Today, Lloyd and I leaned over the balcony to look at a
couple of pretty women,' she wrote on Christmas Day, 1891.
'One of them took that moment to change her lava lava. A
pull and she was naked as she was born. Some instinct made
her look up, and I must say she was somewhat startled. I was
rather startled myself.' She does not record the twenty-three-year-
old Lloyd's reaction, startled or otherwise. Then she repeats an
equally touching story, on a similar theme, which Joe had told
her.

> When Joe first arrived in Samoa, he was invited to a picnic by
> a native lady. Arrived at the spot, he found himself the only
> man present amidst a bevy of native beauties, all of them very
> handsomely and correctly dressed for the occasion. A sudden
> shower came up and what was Joe's surprise to behold all
> these elegant ladies pulling their garments over their heads and
> handing them one by one to an old dame. Satisfied that their
> finery was safe, the ladies then proceeded to clothe themselves
> after the fashion of Mother Eve, that is, with leaves.

It is some time before Fanny appears to learn the truth about Joe, although there are clues in Louis's letters when he describes Belle going to a great many balls without her husband, in the company only of Lloyd, where she dances enthusiastically with various handsome sailors.

A year later, at Christmas 1892, after a gap in her diary of about a month, Fanny reveals something of what happened:

> *December 23rd, 1892.*
> My diary has been long neglected. About the time I stopped writing we found Joe Strong out in various misdeeds: robbing the cellar and store-room at night with false keys. In revenge, when he found that he was discovered, he went round to all our friends in Apia and spread slanders about Belle. We turned him away and applied for a divorce for Belle, which was got with no difficulty, as he had been living with a native woman of Apia as his wife ever since he came here – an old affair begun when he was here before. Also, he had been engaged in an intrigue with Faauma. He came up here late one night to beg forgiveness and ask to be taken back. I was so shocked at seeing him that I had an attack of angina, which seems to remain with me. Louis was made sole guardian of the child, who has been sent to Nelly to school.

Faauma was a maid, a very pretty one, on whom Louis often commented in his letters, and with whom Joe was also conducting some sort of affair. He had managed to keep the other wife in Apia hidden for a long time by pretending he was going to the dentist, which often meant he had to come home very late at night. Louis had always tried hard to think the best of Joe, finding him good company and a reasonable artist, but in his letters he had moaned about his laziness, drunkenness and money-grubbing.

Was Belle blameless? In the family memoirs she is, but there was a strange incident in Hawaii, recounted by Belle herself, in which Fanny and Louis ordered her to Australia, just her and Austin, because 'my friends were altogether too lively and I'd be much better away from their influence'. On the voyage, she is told to 'discourage any attempts at intimacy from strange young men'. Joe himself was taken with the Stevensons, which would suggest they still had hopes for him, despite his behaviour.

As for Lloyd, he too is known to have had several affairs with Samoan women, but as a bachelor, given his own bachelor

quarters, his behaviour was viewed in a different light. Whether
or not he had any children is not known, but there were rumours.

With Joe banished, and young Austin sent to school in California,
Belle began to take a greater role in Louis's life. Originally they had
not got on too well, perhaps going back to her conduct in France,
her marriage to Joe, some of her dubious friends, plus her loyalty
to her father, Sam, whom she had adored. (He gave her twenty
gold dollars when she ran away and married Joe.)

Belle now assumed the job of Louis's secretary and amanuensis,
taking dictation if he was tired of writing or suffering from writer's
cramp. When he was forced to rest his voice on one occasion, she
taught him some basic deaf-and-dumb signs, so that he could
dictate without speaking. As his secretary, she was in charge of
answering all the fan letters which flooded in. They devised a
system for dealing with the public's requests. Any letter which
addressed him as Steph Henson or Stephenson went straight in the
wastepaper basket. So did any rude or unreasonable demands, such
as 'Sir, I think you are the greatest living author, please send me
a complete set of Samoan stamps'. For nicer fan letters, or polite
requests for his autograph, Louis had a two-tier system of printed
cards. What he called a Penny Plain Reply was a card on which
he simply wrote his name and date. A Tuppence Coloured reply
was reserved for those who took the trouble to send an addressed
envelope. In this case they might get a whole sentence, such as
'Smoking is a pernicious habit' (a joke, as of course the whole
household was smoking) or some atrocious verse:

> How jolly tis to sit and laugh
> In gay green-wood
> And write the merry autograph
> For other people's good.

Louis gave a good thumbnail sketch of Belle, and the rest of
his family, in a letter to J.M. Barrie, another of those who was
invited to come out and visit them at Vailima, telling him about
the people he would meet.

> Belle: Runs me like a baby in a perambulator, sees I'm
>   properly dressed, bought me silk socks, and made me wear
>   them, takes care of me when I'm well, from writing my

books to trimming my nails . . . manages the house and the boys, who are very fond of her. Does all the hair-cutting of the family. Will cut yours and doubtless object to the way you part it. Mine has been re-organized twice.

Lloyd: Six foot, blond, eye-glasses – British eye-glasses, too. Address varying from an elaborate civility to a freezing haughtiness. Decidedly witty. Has seen an enormous amount of the world. Keeps nothing of youth, but some of its intolerance. Unexpected soft streak for the forlorn. When he is good he is very, very good, but when he is cross he is horrid. Of Dutch ancestry, and has spells known in the family as 'cold blasts from Holland'. Exacting with the boys, and yet they like him. Rather stiff with his equals, but apt to be very kindly with his inferiors – the only undemonstrative member of the family, which otherwise wears its heart upon both sleeves; and except for my purple patches the only mannered one.

Fanny: She runs the show. Infinitely little, extraordinary wig of grey curls, handsome waxen face like Napoleon's, insane black eyes, boy's hands, tiny bare feet, a cigarette, wild blue native dress, usually spotted with garden mould. In company manners presents the appearance of a little timid and precise old maid of the days of prunes and prisms – you look for the reticule. Hellish energy; relieved by fortnights of entire hibernation. Can make anything from a house to a row, all fine and large of their kind. Doctors everybody, will doctor you, cannot be doctored herself. . . . A violent friend, a brimstone enemy. . . . Is always either loathed or slavishly adored – indifference impossible. . . . Dreams dreams and sees visions.

Louis: Exceedingly lean, rather ruddy, black eyes, crows-footed, beginning to be grizzled, general appearance of a blasted boy – or blighted youth. . . . Past eccentric – obscure and oh we never mention it – present industrious, respectable and fatuously contented. . . . Really knows a good deal but has lived so long with aforesaid family and foremast hands, that you might talk a week to him and never guess it. . . . Name in family, The Tame Celebrity. Cigarettes without intermission, except when coughing or kissing. Hopelessly entangled in apron-strings. Drinks plenty. Curses some. Temper unstable. Manners purple on an emergency, but liable to trances. Essentially the common old copy-book gentleman of commerce; if accused of cheating at cards, would feel bound to blow out brains, little as he would like the job. Has been an invalid for ten years, but can boldly claim you can't tell it on him. Given to explaining the Universe – Scotch, sir, Scotch.

The description of Fanny is far from flattering. Bits of it can easily be quoted out of context, ignoring the fact that Louis's descriptions are meant to be wittily scathing, and used in evidence against Fanny, which many people have done over the years. From the very beginning of Fanny's arrival in Louis's life, she had enemies. This has continued over the past hundred years, with biographers and commentators taking sides, usually against her.

So, the matter of Fanny cannot be ignored any longer. Up to now I have given her the benefit of the doubt, refusing to damn her the moment she appeared on the scene, as so many have done, but something changed in the relationship between Louis and Fanny in Samoa. Things were not as once they were. Would that explain the real reason why Louis felt happier in Hyères? If so, what exactly happened between them, and who or what caused it?

Fanny records in her diary various arguments with Louis from their early days in Samoa, bits of which were crossed out by hands unknown, to give the impression that Fanny and Louis's marriage was one continued ray of sunshine. In 1956, an American scholar, Charles Neider, analysed the original handwritten diary with infra-red photographic equipment and found eighteen pages where passages had been deleted. For example, the following two bits were cut out.

'Louis says that I have the soul of a peasant,' wrote Fanny on 23 October 1890, 'not so much that I love working in the earth and with the earth, because I like to know that it is my own earth that I am delving in. Had I the soul of an artist, the stupidity of possessions would have no power over me. He may be right.'

On 5 November she returned to the same theme: 'I am feeling very depressed for my vanity, like a newly felled tree, lies prone and bleeding. Louis tells me that I am not an artist but a born, natural, peasant. I have often thought that the happiest life and not one for criticism. I feel most embittered when I am assured that I am really what I had wished to be. Of course I meant a peasant without aspirations. Perhaps if I had known in time I should have had none of it! I have been brooding on my feelings and holding my head before a glass and now I am ashamed. Louis assures me that the peasant class is a most interesting one, and he admires it hugely.'

Not exactly true confessions, but I suppose one could see this as a sign of serious divisions between them, picking up the words 'depressed, embittered, brooding', proof that she is suffering from being a failed artist and therefore jealous of Louis. On the other hand, you could read it as a harmless argument, the sort all couples have, where someone has been irritated by a certain remark. Not everyone likes being called a peasant.

All the suppressed remarks in the diary are roughly at this level, recording two or three petty rows with Louis, plus some of Fanny's more catty remarks, such as the ones about Maggie Stevenson's snobbery (already mentioned) or about Lady Jersey, whom Fanny described as being 'very selfish and greedy of admiration, sensual mouth, a touch of vulgarity, courageous as a man, and reckless as a woman'.

This is Fanny writing frankly in her personal diary, bits of which were later crossed out, perhaps by Belle, to protect other people or the romance of the perfect marriage. Louis in his letters is rarely horrible about anyone, keeping up his witty, charming public face, never revealing any intimate or worrying details of his marriage. Until April 1893. That is when he tells Colvin Fanny has been ill. They have all been very worried, but said nothing. Fortunately, she is now over it:

At first she annoyed me dreadfully, now of course that one understands, it is more anxious and pitiful. The dr has been. 'There is no danger to life,' he said twice. 'Is there danger to

mind?' I asked. 'That is not excluded,' said he. Since then I
have had a scene with which I need not harrow you; and
now and again she is quiet and seems without illusions. It
is a beastly business.

Frank McLynn, in his recent biography of Stevenson, reports
an allegation that Fanny had a mental breakdown. It began in
1891 and lasted eighteen months, taking her into 'total insanity' in
1893. He asserts she had always been a hypochondriac, paranoid,
a manic depressive, and traces it back to the death of Hervey, the
baby son she lost. The reasons for the total breakdown in 1893,
he surmises, included the strain of Vailima, jealousy of Louis's
success as a writer, especially now that he was in better health and
less under her influence, and jealousy of Belle, her own daughter,
who had become so close to Louis, and of other women such as
Lady Jersey.

I find it hard to be so definite, either about a total mental
breakdown or the alleged reasons. Fanny clearly did have serious
mental problems some time around April 1893, but I am inclined
to suggest other causes. Until then, her diary has been perfectly
sane, give or take a few wild opinions, the sort we all commit to
our diaries. Alas, the diary is empty for the first half of 1893,
beginning again in July. Over the years, she did have periods of
physical illness, but not as many as Louis. As for her temperament,
her likes and dislikes were more violently expressed than Louis's,
but in many ways they were very similar, given to moments of
passion, fury and often hysteria.

A case could equally be made out for Louis being the manic
depressive, which was what Harry Moors alleged. There are
enough examples of Louis being hysterical, having to be bitten to
calm him down, given to throwing things. With Fanny in Paris he
threw that bottle against the wall while Mrs Sitwell, not given to
nasty tittle-tattle, remembers him throwing a book across a room.
(It was a book of poems by Robert Bridges which he was reading
out to her, saying how brilliant they were, while she remained
impassive. Louis was so furious 'he leapt in the air, crying, flung
the book across the room and himself out of the house in a paroxysm
of disappointment'.

In Samoa, Fanny suffered from several physical complaints,

such as gallstones, which were later operated on, and an aneurism, a permanent swelling of an artery, in this case in her brain. 'I am in a horrid state from the drug given me by Uncle George's advice [Louis's doctor uncle] for what is supposed to be an aneurism inside my head,' she wrote in her diary on 28 October 1891. 'The beating in my head is already much less distressing, but my eyes and nose are swollen and I have continual brow ache and not much sleep. Uncle George recommended chlorydine. Lloyd gave me a dose, as he thought, but it turned out to be something else, tasting like an embrocation, unless possibly the stuff has gone bad, and in so doing, changed its taste and smell.'

Another possible reason for Fanny's problems, which may or may not have created signs of mental instability, was the menopause. Fanny was fifty-four at the height of her supposed insanity in April 1894, and many of her aches and pains, fears and depressions, anxiety and irritability, lack of confidence and sleeping difficulties, are classic symptoms. Once of course you decide she has had a total mental breakdown, then naturally you can look back into her past, examine all her actions, and come to almost any conclusion. Fanny was ill and severely depressed in early 1893, and would appear to have been suffering some sort of 'illusions', according to Louis's letter, but there is no evidence that this had happened before, unless you are of the opinion that she was always unbalanced; afterwards, she appears to have recovered totally.

There is another element to their life in Samoa which has to be examined: sex. Here again we must conjecture, as not even Fanny in her diary or Louis to his most intimate friends spells out just what happened. They appeared to have stopped sleeping in the same bed during the Pacific voyages, at least for a great deal of the time, judging by references to cabins and sleeping arrangements made by Fanny, Louis and his mother. No doubt sexual relations would have been difficult or embarrassing on a yacht, with his mother in the next cabin, sailors on watch, and one or other of the participants being sea-sick, though they must have managed it if the story of the false alarm is true.

Once permanently on shore in Samoa, Louis and Fanny began to have their own bedrooms, referred to as such in their letters and diaries. 'My bedroom presents a most extraordinary aspect,' wrote Fanny in 1891. 'Whenever a thing is twice lost downstairs, I order it up to my room, so that it cannot be taken out without my knowledge. Amongst my dresses are hanging bridles, straps, and horse ropes. On the camphor wood trunk which serves as my dressing table, besides my comb and toothbrush, is a collection of tools, chisels, pincers, a pistol and boxes of cartridges, strings of teeth (fish, human and beast), necklaces of shells, fine mats and tapas piled up in heaps. My little cot bed seems to have got into its place by mistake.'

This is clearly her own bedroom, dressing-room and general junk-room. Louis's references to his bedroom are a bit more confusing, as he changed his room several times and often had a bed in different places, using one to work on and one to sleep in. It seems obvious he is mostly sleeping alone when in various letters he describes his daily routine, starting at 5.45 when he is wakened by a servant. In a hot climate, it might have been a personal preference to sleep alone, or a sign of consideration for the other's ill-health, and have no sexual significance.

Earlier on, in their Bournemouth years, there is a reference to Fanny finding it easier to sleep when she is on her own. 'I am just the reverse,' wrote Louis to Colvin, 'and sleep better when I am with you.'

The separate rooms in Samoa might also have been connected to Fanny's menopause, plus the fear of becoming pregnant at her late stage in life. Or because she did not fancy sex any more. The age gap of eleven years, which did not seem to matter when they married, could now be causing problems, with Louis still a relatively young man, in reasonable health for once, while Fanny was beginning to feel washed out.

If Fanny was losing her desire, and Louis was retaining his, then Samoa was not quite the place to be, with all that unsettling naked flesh around, and other men like Joe and Lloyd taking advantage of it. Louis had always had an eye for the women, by his own confessions, and pretty girls are always being mentioned in his letters. Then there is the sudden surge of sexual explicitness in his work, like *The Beach of Falesa*. Could that indicate longings or sublimations? He was very fond of going off on his own to Apia, riding down the hill on his horse, visiting bars and having jolly times with Harry Moors. No hint of impropriety has ever been mentioned, nor is there the slightest evidence, apart from Fanny's jealousy of Lady Jersey.

During this period, 1892–4, in which much has been made of Fanny's depression and mental troubles, Louis was betraying just as many worrying signs. He feared his art was drying up and that he could go on no longer. 'I am tired out and intend to work no more for six months at least,' he wrote on New Year's Day 1894 – a vow of course he did not keep. In October, he wrote to Colvin half-regretting he had ever taken up full-time writing:

> The truth is I am pretty near useless in literature. Were it not for my health which made it impossible, I could not find it in my heart to forgive myself that I did not stick to an honest commonplace trade when I was young, which might now have supported me during these ill years. My skill deserts me, such as it was or is. It was a very little dose of inspiration and a pretty little trick of style, long lost, improved by the most heroic industry. . . . I am a fictitious article, and have long known it. I am read by journalists, by my fellow novelists and by boys. I did take myself seriously as a workman of old, but my practice has fallen off. I am now an idler and cucberer [*sic*] of the ground. . . .

He was also worried about his health. In the main it was fine in Samoa, and only deteriorated when he went to Australia or Hawaii, but in February 1893 he did have a couple of visits from Bluidy Jack. His stomach gave him trouble from time to time, for which he took drops of laudanum. Then there were some strange new problems, not mentioned before in his letters, such as violent headaches. Fanny encouraged him to give up smoking and drinking, which he did for a while, only to find that made his headaches worse, so he gave up giving them up. His writing wrist became increasingly painful, leading him to use a sling and to start dictating to Belle, but her story of him having to use deaf-and-dumb language is mystifying. Writer's cramp could not cause that. Some sort of minor stroke, perhaps?

Louis mentions his physical ailments in passing, being more concerned by general feelings of gloom and impending mortality.

He had first made remarks about an early death some twenty years before – he had always expected to die young, given his state of health – but they had faded in recent years. Now his letters became full of it again.

'If I could die just now, or say in half a year, I should have had a splendid time on the whole,' he wrote on 30 January 1894. 'But it gets a little stale and my work will begin to senesce; and parties to shy bricks at me; and now it looks as if I should survive to see myself impotent and forgotten. It's a pity suicide is not thought the ticket in the best circles. My father lived to think that I had been wiser than he. But the cream of the jest is that I have lived to change my mind; and think that he was wiser than I. Had I been an engineer, and literature my amusement, it would have been perhaps better. I pulled it off, of course, I won the wager, and it is pleasant while it lasts, but how long will it last? I don't know, say the Bells of Old Bow.'

In September, he told Baxter that he was looking forward to dying: 'I have been so long waiting for death, I have unwrapped my thoughts from about life so long, that I have not a filament left to hold by.' In November, in a letter to Colvin, he appeared to fear growing old more than death. 'I do not like the consolations of age. I was born a young man.'

In the middle of all these morbid thoughts about death and old age, which no doubt his friends largely ignored, coming from a forty-three-year-old who had been contemplating death most of his life and was now supposedly enjoying the best health he had ever had, there was a strange passage about sex. On the surface, it was just another of the regrets he was pouring out to his friends, along with making literature his full-time task and not having any children. It occurs in September 1894, in a letter to his cousin Bob.

> If I had to begin again, I know not – si jeunesse savait, si vieillesse pouvait – I know not at all – I believe I should try to honour Sex more religiously. The worst of our education is that Christianity does not recognize and hallow Sex. It looks askance at it, over its shoulder, oppressed as it is by reminiscences of hermits and Asiatic self tortures. It is a terrible hiatus in our modern religions that they cannot see and make venerable that which they ought to see first and hallow most. Well, it is so. I cannot be wiser than my generation.

It is not clear if he is talking about his own life, wishing he had had more sexual experiences or had valued what he had more highly, a not uncommon feeling in the middle-aged, which the French tag might suggest; or thinking purely about his own writings, wishing he had treated the subject better; or just looking at the attitude of society as a whole. Interesting, all the same, and well ahead of his time.

The year 1894 was not, however, one long round of misery and regret. It was the year in which the chiefs built him his road, much to his delight. Fanny appears to have been back to good health and many splendid parties were held at Vailima, especially when there was a visiting British ship in harbour.

'It is hard for an outsider to realise the life and animation there is in Samoa,' wrote Lloyd. 'There were usually visitors in the house and the cool of the 'noon often brought callers from the "beach", missionaries, officials, blue jackets, local residents, priests, Mormon elders, passing tourists – all the flotsam and jetsam of a petty port lying in one of the great thoroughfares of the world. The American conjures up a picture of a frontier post; the Englishman harks to Kipling and station life in India; and both are wrong. Samoa is very cosmopolitan for all its significance on the map and its white population four hundred souls: balls, picnics, parties are of common occurrence.'

We know Lloyd managed to have a good time, but so did Louis. On special occasions, he had the servants powder their hair with lime – and put on their tartan skirts, of course – while he wore his best rings and his best velvet jacket with a little bronze thistle in the lapel, a present from the Caledonian Society of Hawaii. Louis had established better relations with the German community, once the Mataafa revolt was over. 'We are getting up a paper chase with some of the young German clerks,' he wrote to Colvin in July 1894, 'and have in view a sort of child's party for the grown ups with kissing games, etc, here at Vailima.'

Louis loved dancing, but like Dickens he was no expert. He could do a passable polka but was terrible at waltzing. This did not stop him trying and, according to Belle, he would often jump out of bed in the night to practise a new step. He loved birthdays and Christmas and giving surprise presents, usually with one of his verses attached. And he was a devil for silly, childish jokes, such as unravelling his mother's knitting or pinching hairpins from Fanny's or Belle's hair. Belle described these as his Idiot Boy moods, when he would go round the house 'interfering in whatever his women-kind are engaged in'.

Was he homesick? Loyal Scots like to think he was, pointing to the sudden run of Scottish-based books – *Catriona*, *St Ives*, *Weir of Hermiston* – and his interest in his own ancestry; he wrote home to relations for family trees, perhaps because he knew he would never see Scotland again. 'Here I am until I die, and here I will be buried.' It is mainly in writing to his Scottish friends, like Baxter, that he goes on about the heather and the glens or the old days in Lothian Road. Like so many exiles, he enjoyed having familiar objects from home – not just the tartan and Glenlivet whisky, but Crosse and Blackwell's pickles, or when looking forward to putting 'myself outside a pint of Guinness'.

I do not think he had any intention of leaving Vailima, not even to visit literary London, though he was looking forward to his writer friends coming to visit him. Rudyard Kipling never made it, nor did Barrie. He received several visits from a well-known Italian painter, Count Nerli, who did his portrait, and several much longer and greatly enjoyed stays from a young cousin, Graham Balfour, whom Belle rather fancied.

On 14 November the whole household, together with guests from two ships, celebrated Louis's forty-fourth birthday with the killing of a fatted cow, twenty pigs, fifty chickens, seventeen pigeons, plus 804 pineapples and twenty large bunches of bananas. Tinned salmon was also opened. Maggie noted the numbers exactly in her diary. 'Dear Lou, what cause for thankfulnesss that he has been spared to see his 44th birthday in so much health and comfort.'

One of his comforts was a return to form in his writing; he fairly whizzed along with *Weir of Hermiston*, now that he was back into it, convinced it was going well. It is a story set in eighteenth-century Scotland, about a hanging judge and his son who is totally opposed to capital punishment, strong on female characters and timeless in the handling of the clash between father and son. Most people think this would have been his masterpiece, if only he had finished it.

On 3 December, Fanny woke with a foreboding that something dreadful was going to happen, perhaps to one of the family, possibly Graham Balfour, who at the time had gone off to see some other islands. Louis assured her it was just her imagination. There was nothing to worry about.

After working on *Weir of Hermiston*, he later changed for dinner. He came downstairs and found Fanny still rather gloomy, so he went to the cellar to get out a bottle of his best Burgundy. He was mixing mayonnaise for the evening meal, standing chatting to Fanny on the downstairs veranda, when he put his hand to his head and cried out in agony, 'Oh, what a pain. Do I look strange?'

Fanny and a servant helped him to a chair where he quickly lost consciousness. She tried to revive him with brandy, assisted by Maggie and Belle, who together pulled off his boots. Lloyd protested, saying that Louis always wanted to die with his boots on, then he saddled a horse and rode down to Apia to get a doctor. A cerebral haemorrhage was diagnosed. Shortly after eight o'clock, on 3 December 1894, Louis passed away, without regaining consciousness.

That evening, officials and friends from all over the island came to pay homage to Louis, laid out in the hall, his body covered with the Union Jack, the little thistle in his velvet jacket. Mataafa's chiefs, who so recently had built his Loving Road, cleared a path up to Mount Vaea, Louis's chosen resting-place, and on the afternoon of the next day, 4 December, Louis's body, covered with the flag from the *Casco*, was taken up the mountain on the shoulders of his Samoan friends and laid to rest.

22

Visiting Vailima, Climbing Mount Vaea

Dear Louis,

I could hear some loud American voices from the dining-room, so I popped my head in, and there were three Americans, in bright Hawaiian shirts, entertaining several Samoan officials in their best skirts and most formal jackets and ties. I asked one of the waiters, and part-time war dancer, if they were the Mormons, and he nodded. Now, I thought, should I barge over and say look here, you guys, I'm a paid-up member of the RLS Society of Edinburgh, Scottish born myself, and we're all a bit cheesed off, not to say alarmed, by reports that you Yanks are going to turn the home of our Blessed Louis into some sort of Disneyland or a Mormon Mission Station. Take that, you blighters.

Or, should I just keep quiet for the moment, gently ingratiate myself, find out what was happening, and get invited to look at Vailima and their plans? Yes, you can guess what I did. Carefully, I closed the dining-room door and withdrew.

That evening, at dinner, the three of them were on their own, talking much more quietly, so I went over and introduced myself. By a coincidence, one of them, Jim Winegar, had read something I'd once written, so I was invited to sit down and join them. The other two were called Dan Wakefield and Rex Maughan. Dan and Jim were from Provo, Utah, and Rex, who appeared to be the leader, was from Phoenix, Arizona. All three seemed charming and sincere, and extremely interested in me and my project. They'd been researching RLS for the last two years, but had not found many people to discuss him with.

Yes, they were indeed Mormons, but their project has nothing whatsoever to do with the Mormon Church, either in Samoa or in the USA. It all goes back thirty years, when they were in their twenties, and were sent out for two years to work as Mormon missionaries in Western Samoa. They met each other here, became friends, then returned to the USA, went their separate ways, each apparently doing well in their respective careers.

Six years ago, Dan heard by chance that a rain forest was in danger of extinction on the island of Savaii. (Today's Western Samoa consists of two islands, Upolu, where Apia is situated, and Savaii.) The local *matai* had decided to let a Japanese firm cut down and cart away the trees in return for money to build a village school. 'Once a rain forest is cut down, the land will die,' said Dan. He contacted his old missionary friends, Rex and Jim, and together they got enough money to build the school for the village. At the same time, they acquired the rain forest, handing over 30,000 acres of it to the government to be a national park, safe for ever. That was their first contact with Samoa since they'd left in the 1960s.

Two years ago, they were contacted again, this time to help save Vailima, and once again they decided to come to the rescue. It has proved a more complicated venture. For most of these two years they have been in long-drawn-out legal discussions, getting bills through Parliament, acquiring all the relevant permissions, so that they can develop Vailima, the gardens and Mount Vaea. They had only recently received final consent, giving them a twenty-year lease on the site, with an option of another twenty years. They had not wanted to talk about their plans till everything was settled, but bits of news had crept out, most of it wrong, so they said, hence the bad publicity. They certainly were not going to install a cable-car up Mount Vaea. That had only been a suggestion, by a Samoan, which they personally had never favoured.

'We are doing it to help Samoa,' said Rex, fixing me with his open blue eyes. 'We love Samoa and the people. We have great memories of living here, and we can still speak the language. We didn't know much about Stevenson, until all this began, but now we love him as well.'

It turned out that, in three days' time, they were going to have a formal reception at Vailima, which was their reason for coming from the States. They would then officially announce their plans and mark the beginning of the work. 'We'd like to invite you,' said Rex. I asked if there was a chance of seeing the house now, before work commenced. They weren't sure. Work was going on at present, clearing up the garden and driveway for the reception. Rex said he'd let me know tomorrow.

I had a post-dinner swim in the pool to celebrate meeting my new friends, which was a mistake. The water was like soup. Even at ten at night, the heat was oppressive. So I went to bed early, cool in my air-conditioned room, excited at the prospect of seeing your home at last. I fell asleep wondering what was in it for the Mormons. Were they really so altruistic? Where did their money come from anyway? And, if you had had air-conditioning at Vailima, would you have slept with Fanny?

I waited all morning for word from Rex, swimming in the pool, hanging around the hotel lobby. I rang his room, then Dan's, then Jim's, to find they'd all gone, up to Vailima without me. However, just before lunch, Rex returned to Aggie's and said he was now ready to show me Vailima.

I must have been rubbing my lips, trying to get rid of the taste of the chlorine, because Rex insisted on giving me a tube of some lip-balm. Made out of aloe, he said. That would help me. Did I know what aloe was? A plant, I think. My mother used to buy something called flowers of aloe. Rex smiled, produced some leaflets from a pocket in the car, and explained he was the world's largest grower of aloe, controlling thousands of acres in the USA, Mexico, the Dominican Republic and elsewhere. He also manufactures and sells cosmetics and medicines, using aloe, and has a world-wide sales force. So, he's done pretty well.

He took out a coloured postcard of a ranch and asked me if I recognised it. It did look vaguely familiar.

'Southfork,' he said. 'Ever heard of it?'

Of course. The *Dallas* ranch, as seen in the TV series.

'I've just bought it.'

Dan and Jim had also done fairly well for themselves, one in agriculture and one in marketing, but not quite on a level with Rex. Most of the Vailima money, at the moment, was apparently coming through Rex, but the plan was to get as many people involved as possible. That was why they'd set up the Robert Louis Stevenson Museum – Preservation Foundation Inc. That'll be the new owner of your old house, presumably for the next forty years. It's a non-profit-making charity, to which anyone can contribute. 'Fortunately, I've been able to find the money so far, but I'd like others to have a chance to contribute, so it is a public project.'

At the gate to Vailima I couldn't help commenting on the Stevensons' 'only property' line. 'Yes,' said Rex, 'that is perhaps badly worded. We should have said the only property he ever *built*.'

There were several fallen trees on the driveway, so we left the car and walked the last hundred yards or so towards the house, where Jim and Dan were standing waiting on the lawns.

Louis, I must congratulate you on choosing such a splendid site. I knew about the views, but hadn't realised Vailima was on its own little sylvan plateau, sheltered by Mount Vaea behind, with the sea in front. The main view is a 180-degree seascape, very dramatic, still with nothing man-made to be seen. As in your day, the town and harbour of Apia are obscured, somewhere below the trees, but I could see what I presumed must be the funnels of that cargo ship, *Clydebank*, and the outlines of further ships, out at sea. What fun to watch ships approaching Apia, miles and miles away at sea, before the townspeople were aware of them. You could easily dash down the hill on a good horse, or even old Jack, with an invitation for the captain of any interesting ship, and be there to hand it over the moment he landed. And yes, it did feel marginally cooler up here, though Vailima is just three miles out of Apia, and only 200 metres above sea level.

Alas for the house itself. I could see it was in very poor condition, the tin roof broken, windows smashed, walls with holes in. The cyclones of 1991 and '92 had made it uninhabitable.

Inside, I stood looking at the crumbling walls, bare floors and sagging ceilings. 'Do we go back to the original house or not?' asked Rex. They had been discussing that problem for months, during the drawing up of the architectural plans for the re-building. You yourself made endless changes, during your five years of ownership, then the German to whom Fanny sold the house added another wing, at least he transplanted Bachelor Hall, where Lloyd had lived, and added another entrance hall at the front. In the end, they have decided to stick with the present shape and size of the house, but try to rearrange the rooms as you used them, although some of them have been partitioned or altered over the years.

I was impressed by how well they had studied your letters and Fanny's, looking for clues to how you arranged the house. A shame you never did any drawings, the way you often did, such as of your room at Heriot Row. They are now convinced they know which was your bedroom, which was Fanny's, which was your mother's and where the smoking-room was.

I stood in front of the upstairs fireplace, still the only one in Samoa, I was told. Brick surrounds, quite large. I think you were trying to capture the atmosphere of Heriot Row, not to use it for airing. That would have been a bit common, having clothes hanging up in a formal room. Rex thought that no, it was for airing clothes and sheets, very necessary for someone with a bad chest.

Downstairs, they want to create an office and some private quarters for use by the Head of State, which is how Vailima has been used, these last fifty years. Upstairs, they are going to run a Stevenson museum, filling it with as many Stevenson mementoes as they can get. Rex has already started collecting and says he has promises of some furniture, paintings, letters, books and other objects. I wished him well, but didn't fancy his chances. Stevenson stuff is now hard to find, even if you are a multi-millionaire. He said he had contacts working on it.

Dan has a grandiose plan to bring a real ship to Vailima and put it on display – the *Equator*, he says, the ship on which you arrived in Samoa. 'It later became a cargo boat, then it sank off Washington. It's recently been found and renovated. I hope I might get the US Navy to stick it on the deck of a battleship and bring it out to Samoa. Well, why not? Could be a nice goodwill mission, and great PR for the Navy.'

The museum will have a curator, and a small entrance fee will be charged. 'We need to do that, to contribute to the running costs.

But we won't make any money out of it. We're doing it because if we hadn't done it no one else would. The Samoan government has got no money for such restoration work.'

It's hard to see how they could make any profit anyway. Tales of Disneyland were silly, now that I was here. Samoa, if not quite tourist-free, is almost tourist-proof. They expect a small flurry of visitors in December 1994 for the centenary, then a trickle afterwards. The Samoan government, and the people, want to stay as they are, not be Westernised, commercialised, overrun. For the present, anyway.

I became convinced, Louis, that the Mormons' hearts were in the right place. They are saving and restoring your house out of love. Their rewards will no doubt be in Heaven.

My tour finished in your bedroom, where we stood discussing your sex life. Then the Mormons asked me what I thought about Fanny, as a person. Was she a good thing or a bad thing? I explained that the present-day mood appears to have swung against Fanny, judging by McLynn's merciless descriptions of her as a fantasist, money-grubbing, coarse, unscrupulous, jealous woman, apart from being insane. His main theory is that it was sex that attracted you to her, and you had to marry her as you'd slept with her, being a man of honour, while she went for you for your money.

My opinion is that she was to be admired, all things considered, but then I like tough, outspoken, intelligent, strong-minded women. I admire her for putting up with those three years of sailing round the Pacific, which she hated, just to please you. I like the way she cared for your health, studying your medical condition, doing what she thought was best. I like the fact that she was involved in your work, giving her opinion, even when not asked. We have to thank her for the final version of *Dr Jekyll*. I don't think the marriage was based on sex, not after the first year or so. She was your soul-mate, a kindred spirit, with a stimulating, dynamic, unusual personality you had not encountered before. I think it's particularly unfair to say she married you for your money. Marriage had been agreed at a time when you were cut off from your family, without a penny, without any prospects. No one could have relied on your father coming round, nor, if you had died early and Fanny been left a widow, on your parents ever giving any money to her. The marriage lasted. I think you always loved her, even when you felt saddened or disturbed by changes that had taken place. You could have done a lot worse.

Yes, she was jealous of your friends, but I can understand that. She was possessive, and wanted to protect you, and then later her image of you and her. Her hatreds of people were certainly a trifle intense, and she went beyond the bounds now and again. So did you. It was asking a lot, having those Osbournes in her wake for you to support, but that's the way with families. You did not complain about Lloyd, whom you always loved, or Belle, treating them both as your real children. As for Fanny's illnesses, which I don't think led to total insanity, I feel sorry, for her and for you, rather than critical.

What I would like to know is the contents of the letters you wrote to each other during that time you were apart. You told Colvin you never wrote, but I don't believe it. I would like to have read your love letters, of any sort, just to know what was there between you.

I felt sad somehow, reading Fanny's Samoan diary, and your own letters in the later years, at the lack of evidence of any great moments of affection between you. Yes, I know you left her charming verses pinned to her mosquito net beside her bed, and wrote amusing poems about her, but they were not totally complimentary. In 'Mother and Daughter', about Fanny and Belle, you called them 'my pair of fairies plump and dark, the dryads of my cattle park', and said that 'one apes the shrew, one the coquette'.

There's one very small scene, which I like, nothing really, just a scrap of conversation between you, when you are telling Colvin about coming home one evening: 'Fanny and I rode home, and I moralised by the way. Could we ever stand Europe again? Did she appreciate that if we were in London, we should be *actually jostled* in the street? And there was nobody in the whole of Britain who knew how to take kava like a gentleman?' I can see your smiles, sharing the joke together. I can't think of many other times when you describe being alone. They must have happened, but you've left us little evidence.

The Mormons, to a man, were in favour of Fanny. But then

they are Americans, like Henry James. He was one of the very few of your friends who always defended her.

The reception was held at Vailima on the covered terrace at the end of the building. It had looked like a bomb-site only two days earlier, but now the walls and floors had been scrubbed, garlands hung from the walls and pillars, chairs and tables laid out. A fascinating display of old photographs and drawings was set up on a table, showing the house as it was. Outside, the lawns had been cut and the gardens spruced up. Not quite as splendid as when you gave your grand parties, but impressive all the same. There were over a hundred people present, including the Prime Minister, Cabinet members, judges, chiefs, church ministers, foreign consuls. While we waited for the Head of State to arrive, we were entertained by the Samoan police band who were sitting on a raised dais, performing Western tunes from popular musicals, but not very well. I'm sure the band from one of your British gun-boats would have done a lot better.

The assorted Samoan dignitaries were in their best suits – ties and heavy serge jackets, with matching skirts. From the waist up, they looked stiff and formal, while below, with their skirts, bare feet and sandals, they looked totally informal, like mismatched cut-out uniforms from a children's book. No alcohol was served. I assumed this must be due to the Mormon influence, but when I was complaining to a government official he said no, it's government policy. Some people had been drinking rather too much at public receptions recently.

There was some milling around, table-hopping and gossiping while we waited. I met by chance Ellen Shaffer, one of the few Western women amongst the guests, aged eighty-nine, formerly Curator of the Silverado Museum and a renowned RLS expert. Not in the best of health, but still a sharp, formidable American woman. Perhaps a bit like Fanny. 'What do *you* think of her then?'

'Fanny was the best possible wife for Louis. She was shrewd and practical, doing things which were good for him, when he didn't realise it, such as keeping away people with colds. She was very good in her handling of Mrs Stevenson, knowing her strong Scotch mind, but she stood up to her. She originally wanted family prayers in the mornings, the coolest time of the day, and the best for Louis's work, but Fanny didn't want him distracted.

'Lloyd was not an ardent worker. His biggest job in life was being RLS's stepson. He produced eighteen books and collections in all, but he missed his co-author. He was what we call a "chaser", going after the girls. I wouldn't be surprised if he had several children in Samoa we don't know about. . . .'

I looked around, examining faces, observing tattoos, till at last word came through that the Head of State was indisposed, so we could start without him. A Master of Ceremonies stood up on the dais and welcomed everyone, in Samoan and then in English, apologising first for the lack of lavatories, as of course the house was still semi-derelict. 'But there are lots of bushes you can use, if you have to.' Smiles all round. A cleric blessed us all, then we started the buffet lunch, provided by Aggie Grey's hotel, whose staff had had to cart every item, the food, soft drinks, crockery and linen, up from Apia, there being no facilities in the house.

After the meal came the speeches. The official engineer and then the three Mormons, in turn, explained what the plans were for Vailima. I moved my chair to get the best of the breeze and catch a glimpse of the view across the lawns, breathing in the smells, memorising the sights and faces, trying to forget the lack of alcohol. I wondered if there was any of your Burgundy still lurking in the cellar. At least we had not been served kava.

It was Dan Wakefield's turn to tell us about the plans and as I watched him I realised he was shedding a few tears, the emotion of the moment being too much for him. Finally, the Prime Minister planted a tree to mark the beginning of the restoration work. Every guest, on leaving, was given a beautifully printed copy of your *Prayers Written at Vailima*, with a new introduction by Ellen Shaffer. I shall treasure it.

I awoke at 5.45 to climb Mount Vaea, knowing that a really early start would be the only way I could manage it. I'd ordered a taxi for six o'clock and was at the bottom of the hill by 6.30. There was some low cloud, a good sign. The first stretch was rocky, a typical Lakeland climb, over volcanic-like boulders, but easy enough. Then it turned into a decent grassy path. I'll be up this in no time, I thought.

I came to a sign saying 'Rainforest Foothills'. A welcome or a warning? The foliage all around had now become jungly, but the path itself was still clear enough, so I walked on, whistling the while. Then I came to another sign, pointing round the hill, which said 'One hour – long trail'. There was also a path which appeared to go straight up, probably more direct, but bound to be steeper, harder, so I plumped for the circular route.

Almost immediately I realised my mistake. No one appeared to have walked this way for years. Massive trees had fallen, no doubt in the cyclones, totally blocking the path. I wasn't walking any more, but clambering up and over these dead giants, not all that high, but very dangerous as they were so slippery. Very slowly, I fought my way forward, over the bodies, then down through the undergrowth, pulling creepers apart, slashing at palm leaves. My clothes, my whole body, were wringing wet. All I had on was a T-shirt, shorts and trainers, plus a notebook and camera, so I was travelling light. After half an hour of endless slipping and sliding, making no apparent progress, I began to think I was totally lost. If I fell, I would slide straight down the hill, disappear into the undergrowth, gone for ever. How would anyone find me? Was this your final joke, Louis, insisting on being buried on top of this hill, just to confuse and confound the pilgrims?

Then I realised something unusual. Despite bare legs and arms and a flimsy T-shirt, despite battling through dense undergrowth, despite the tropical heat, I wasn't being eaten alive. Now in Lakeland, or even worse in Scotland, clambering through dense vegetation like this, I would be black and blue by now, bitten by insects, scratched by brambles, thistles, gorse, thorns, nettles. This rain forest was benign. I could have walked totally naked and come out unscathed, as long as I didn't fall. The palm leaves were cool and smooth and felt refreshing to the touch. No one in their right mind would crash through an English landscape in bare legs, yet we think of our nature as soft and gentle, while foreign, tropical nature seems wild in tooth and claw.

That must have been another attraction for you, dear Louis. Perfect for a poorly person. It would explain twenty-mile gallops without ill-effects. No chance of bites and infections. Hardly anything in Samoa has either teeth or claws. Samoa is such a remote island that very few species have managed to get this far. No monkeys or snakes, elephants or crocodiles. The only mammals are a Polynesian rat, which I never saw, and a bat, which I did see once, round the hotel pool one evening. Very few native birds, and those they did have the Samoans have eaten almost to extinction. The forest was silent, apart from my moans and curses, bangs and crashes. The only life I came across was a flock of tiny white moths, hovering low over the base of a banyan tree, newly born, ready to newly die. I tried to catch one in my hand, but it melted into nothing.

There was a clearing at last, and a signpost, again containing useless information – 'Rest Area'. Fifteen minutes later, another sign, equally stupid – 'View Point'. Below, I could just make out the corner of Vailima.

Suddenly I emerged into fresh air, blue sky, light and greenery, catapulted out of my dark tunnel, and there in a little clearing, on the brow of the hill, was your grave. Long and low, painted white, bigger than I expected. I walked round it, reading the various inscriptions. On the side facing Vailima is your own verse. It includes a common mistake, 'home from the sea', instead of 'home from sea', which upsets all pedants, but I quite like. It's such a good epitaph, and very hard to ruin.

> Under the wide and starry sky,
> Dig the grave and let me lie
> Glad did I live and gladly die,
> And laid me down with a will.
>
> This be the verse you grave for me
> Here he lies where he longed to be
> Home is the sailor, home from the sea
> And the hunter home from the hill.

At the other end is a memorial to Fanny, added twenty years after your death, intertwined with a tiger lily, which was her nickname, and some lines you once wrote for her.

> Teacher, tender, comrade wife,
> A fellow-farer true through life.
> Heart whole and soul-free,
> The august father gave to me.

On another side is a thistle, representing Scotland, and a plant which I took to be a hibiscus, representing Samoa.

I looked out towards Apia, to the lonely sea and the sky. I hadn't seen anyone all morning, but then I had got lost and taken the wrong route. I thought about those Samoan chiefs, carrying you up. The direct way, presumably, being locals, which was the way I took going down. So easy, no obstacles whatsoever. I was down in half an hour.

At the bottom, I dived straight into your pool, leaving my camera and T-shirt beside a red hibiscus. You used to swim here most days. So cool and clear and refreshing, getting ready for the end you didn't know was coming.

23

Post Louis

1894–1994

Louis's will was quite complicated, but then he had had some time to think about it, doing the earliest draft when he first went abroad, bringing it up to date whenever he was convinced he was about to die, or when there had been family ructions, as with cousin Katharine. Like all successful writers, he left future riches as well as hard cash, royalties yet to come if people continued to buy his books, which might well be far more than his supposed worth on the day he died.

In Britain, he left estate worth £15,525, mainly the earnings from his writings which Baxter in Edinburgh had been collecting on his behalf. Half of it was to provide an income for his mother until her death, while part of it went to Bob, Katharine and Dora, the children of Alan Stevenson, Thomas's brother.

Fanny got the benefit of the literary properties – the royalties yet to come – plus manuscripts, furniture and personal effects. On her death, the royalties would pass to the Osbournes, who would also inherit Maggie's share of the British estate. The royalties were flooding in. Baxter heard about Louis's death while he was passing through the Suez Canal. He carried on and arrived in Samoa with the first copies of the Edinburgh Edition, and news of their great success, bringing in an immediate £5,000. Fanny also received a pension of sixty pounds, which she claimed as the widow of a Scottish advocate, the result of Louis's legal payments, all those years ago.

Maggie went home to Edinburgh after her son's death and lived with a sister, starting yet another life. 'Twice torn up by the roots,' she told friends. She learned to ride a bicycle while in her mid-sixties, and died of pneumonia in May 1897, aged sixty-eight. 'There is Louis, I must go,' were her last words, convinced she had seen him at the bottom of her bed. After her death, two books containing her letters from her travels in America and the Pacific were published.

Fanny, Belle and Lloyd lived for a year in California after Louis's death, then returned to Vailima, selling it after Maggie had died for the modest sum of £1,750 – modest when you consider that Louis had spent £4,000 on it and in theory it was a working plantation which should have been providing a proper income.

In 1896 Lloyd married Katharine Durham, a missionary teacher he had met in Honolulu, and they had two sons. At first, she and Fanny had got on well, both being very interested in the supernatural, convincing themselves they could talk to Louis in séances. Katharine called her second son Louis in his honour, but something had gone wrong between her and her mother-in-law, and Fanny refused to address him as such. By this time they were not speaking to each other anyway and Katharine and Lloyd were living apart. Katharine alleged that Fanny had married Louis for his money, her stories being accepted, then and now, by those who disliked Fanny anyway. According to Ellen Shaffer, none of Katharine's stories can be trusted. 'Katharine was real cooky. She even accused Belle and Lloyd of poisoning Fanny.'

Lloyd re-married, but went on to chase other women, including a Frenchwoman, by whom he had a child. He produced a few light novels but spent much of his time travelling and driving fast cars. He died in California in 1947.

Fanny also did a lot of travelling, especially in the company of a young gentleman called Salisbury Field, known as Ned, whom she met around 1905 when he was twenty-five and she was sixty-five. He was known for his gaiety, his quick wit, his flamboyant clothes, and became her secretary and then companion. Did she see him as a young Louis? Tongues wagged of course. Fanny survived the 1906 San Francisco earthquake and moved to Santa Barbara, where she died of a cerebral haemorrhage in 1914 at the age of seventy-four.

She left an estate worth £120,500, most of which went to Belle.

In the same year that Fanny died, Belle got married – to Ned Field. He was then in his mid-thirties, about the same age as her son Austin. More wagging tongues. Belle ended up rich, and very old, outliving her son Austin, who became a playwright, and her young husband Ned, who also wrote plays and film-scripts. Ned died in 1936, insisting in his will that he should be buried in a coloured shirt. 'He didn't want to depress anyone with solemnity, even in death.'

Belle died in 1953, aged ninety-five, the last survivor of the Vailima household.

So much for the personnel and the real estate. Now for the literary inheritance. One of Fanny's first tasks after Louis's death was to organise his official biography. Louis's original aim had been for Henley to do it, but this had changed after their row in 1888. There had been a vague rapprochement towards the end of Louis's life, when Henley's only child, a six-year-old girl, had died. Louis had written a letter of condolence, and Henley had written back to him, but their friendship had not been re-established. However, Louis had told Baxter he could pay Henley five pounds a month, which would keep him from starving: 'If I gave him more, it would only lead to him starting a gig and a Pomeranian dog.'

On Louis's death, as instructed, Lloyd opened a letter from Louis, written in 1888, the year of the row with Henley, which said he wanted his biography to be written by Colvin, just a modest book, using some of his verses and letters. He wanted it done fairly quickly, in order to provide some money for his family. Colvin started work, but not on the biography. Instead, he arranged the publication of the unfinished *Weir of Hermiston*, Louis's letters to him from Vailima and then two volumes of his collected letters. These were carefully expurgated – missing out the embarrassing letters to Mrs Sitwell (soon to be Colvin's wife) and also any references to Fanny's mental problems in Samoa.

Four years after Louis's death, there was still no sign of the official biography; by this time Fanny and Lloyd had taken against Colvin, thinking he was not the person to do it anyway, never having been in sympathy with the Samoan years. He pleaded that he had been busy with his British Museum job, but that he had started three chapters. There was then an unseemly argument between Lloyd and Colvin over money, and the result was that Colvin was relieved of the task of writing the biography. Fanny awarded the job instead to Graham Balfour, the young cousin who had been staying at Vailima at the end of Louis's life. He was actually a second cousin, educated at Oxford, a barrister who had never practised, who had devoted his time to travelling the world studying various arts, landing first on Louis in 1892 on the way back from Japan.

Balfour's *Life of Robert Louis Stevenson* appeared in 1901. Considering that it is official, and that the widow was still alive, it is surprisingly readable, but is naturally not very strong on warts and weaknesses. It is not total hagiography, giving a fair account of his dissolute, atheistic student days, but it does create the impression that Fanny and Louis had a fairy-tale romance, in which nothing ever went wrong. Balfour's son, Michael Balfour, wrote an account of his father's biography in 1981, saying the only indelicate fact which his father knowingly missed out was that Louis and Fanny slept together before their marriage.

One person who was greatly aggrieved by the biography was W.E. Henley. He wrote a slashing attack on it in the *Pall Mall Gazette* of December 1901, saying that it was 'an essay in make-believe' – adding that RLS had been a study in make-believe himself. Henley refused to recognise the portrait Balfour painted of RLS as 'an angel clean from heaven . . . this Seraph in chocolate, this barley sugar effigy of a real man'. The real RLS was 'riotous, scornful'. This is not the RLS that Henley knew.

In his review, which was over 5,000 words long, he suggests that he knows the truth, he can bring out the skeletons from the early days, promising that he will reveal all one day – which he never did. If only he had named a few names, told a few stories, which most people agree he knew, dating back to those Edinburgh days, his argument would have been much stronger. He probably also had, hidden away, some of Louis's semi-pornographic writings, which would have been interesting to read.

He alleges that RLS was vain, unable to pass a mirror without looking in it. He says Louis was hopeless at music and that he,

Henley, taught him all he knew, and even then his only tune for many years was 'Auld Lang Syne'. As for RLS always being ill, does that mean we should always praise him? 'That a man writes well at death's door is no sure reason for making him a hero.' Henley says a poor consumptive seamstress deserves as much fame as RLS. 'After all, there is as much virtue in making a shirt as there is in polishing a verse or completing a chapter of a novel.'

When he eventually comes to the works, one might have expected Henley, with his literary skills and experience, to have done a good destructive job, but he confines himself to attacking RLS's wit, style and talent, saying he does not like any of his books. 'If I want reading, I do not go for it in the Edinburgh Edition. If I crave the enchantment of romance, I go for bigger books than his – of *Esmond*, say, *Great Expectations*, *Redgauntlet*. If good writing be in my appetite, are there not always Hazlitt and Lamb.'

Behind the attack lie clear resentment and jealousy. He complains that he did so much for RLS, 'ministered to his artless and homely needs', but that he was never the same person after he went to America. This would appear to be a dig at Fanny, though she is not criticised directly.

One remark in the Balfour book which particularly offended him was the reference to Louis allowing him five pounds a week – but no more, or he would start a gig and a Pomeranian dog. This was, presumably, some sort of old joke between them. In the book, Henley's name is not used when this letter is quoted – he is referred to as Mr Z – but Henley recognised himself, and was furious. 'It scarce becomes the man who had several kennels of Pomeranians and kept gigs innumerable. . . .'

Henley did make one or two worthwhile points, but he ruined his case with petty gibes, trivia and personal abuse, unsupported by evidence. The public adulation of RLS was in danger of becoming over-romanticised and decidedly sickly. Naturally, Henley's review was dismissed by all RLS-lovers, and mostly still is, and yet, when the present wave of Fanny-demolition is over, I would not be surprised if some future biographer does not go back to this part of Henley's attack and build up a case to prove that RLS was a poseur, a performer who carefully created and nurtured his lovely, sugary, wholesome public image; that in real life he could be selfish, autocratic, vindictive and nasty; that it was he who gave Fanny a bad time.

There was a slackening of interest in RLS in the 1920s, co-inciding with a period of re-assessment which happens after the death of any Great Writer. Perhaps there was some disappointment in literary circles that he had not attained the stature of Dickens, which had once been expected of him, and that he had spread his talents too wide, and too thin. New literary heroes such as D.H. Lawrence and Shaw came along for the general public to follow and admire. True fans countered this with the formation in Edinburgh of the Robert Louis Stevenson Club.

Many writers in recent years have been influenced by him, from Graham Greene to Daphne du Maurier, and abroad he has been greatly admired by Borges, Calvino, Nabokov and others. His academic standing seems indeed to be higher abroad than in Britain where he is more often quoted than studied at universities. Academics like people who can be easily categorised, who stick to their last, who produce a body of work in a recognisable vein. RLS is a household name, but the man in the street would be hard put to name many of his books; *Treasure Island* and *Dr Jekyll and Mr Hyde* have passed into almost every language, but few people realise who created them. He is still sometimes confused with the Father of Railways, George Stephenson.

Over the years, countless adaptations of his books have been done on radio, television and film. In the cinema, *Dr Jekyll and Mr Hyde* leads the way with eleven versions so far, the first in 1908. Stars have included John Barrymore, Spencer Tracy, Christopher Lee and Kirk Douglas. Next comes *Treasure Island* with six, the first in 1920 and the latest in 1993, closely followed, surprisingly, by *The Suicide Club*, which has been filmed five times, first in 1909. *Kidnapped* has been done four times, *Ebb-Tide* three times, *The Wrong Box* twice. The following have been filmed once: *The Black Arrow*, *The Body Snatcher*, *The Master of Ballantrae*, *Pavilion on the Links*, *St Ives*, *The Sire de Maletroit's Door*, *The Treasure of Franchard*. Not all the film versions retained the original titles. The total is thirty-six films.

There has never been a film of his life on the big screen, though it has been done countless times on radio and television.

This seems strange, as it has so much colour, drama, adventure, love interest, not to mention semi-naked beauties. Perhaps the hundredth anniversary celebrations in 1994 will prompt some company to commission a film based on his life.

There are over a hundred events planned for the centenary year, so much so that a co-ordinator has been set up, based in the National Library of Scotland. They all sound very exciting, and include two major exhibitions in Edinburgh – at the National Library of Scotland and at the Royal Museum of Scotland – plus smaller ones in California. There will be a festival of *Jekyll and Hyde* films, at least three musicals, walks, talks, dinners, displays, television and radio documentaries, special editions of many of his books, the launch of a locomotive called Robert Louis Stevenson, and the issue of a banknote from the Royal Bank of Scotland with his head on. No commemorative postage stamps in Britain, alas. The RLS Club failed to swing that. Och well. The Samoa Post Office has already produced an RLS set, several years ago.

24

Last Letter

Dear Louis,

Just two final places I must tell you about – well, one place and one person, both of which I think might interest you.

Firstly, let's pop back to Edinburgh for a meeting of your club, being held this evening at the Church of St Andrew and St George in George Street – the club in honour of you, that is, not any of the clubs you yourself were a member of, such as the Savile and the Athenaeum. How strange, by the way, that the visiting cards you used in Samoa gave two addresses – Vailima and the Athenaeum, London. Did you think it was smarter than the Savile?

The Robert Louis Stevenson Club, founded in 1920, is one of the nation's leading literary societies, enjoying something of a boom these days. There were about seventy of my fellow members present, well-heeled, well-upholstered folk, mostly solid Edinburgh citizens, many of them successful lawyers, with a fair scattering of titles; decent people, who care about culture, literature and the arts. And they love you, you can do no wrong. They think only good of you, not wanting to hear any ill, any gossip, anything disagreeable.

We were in the undercroft, the coffee and biscuits already laid out for half-time, gentlemen busy with chairs, ladies busy with arrangements, discussing who will speak and when. Suddenly, the undercroft was flooded with the noise of hymns being sung, very loudly. Then prayers being called for. We stared at each other, narrowing eyes, cocking ears, looking around. Where on earth was it coming from? We had gathered to hear a lecture on

Samoa, not take part in some sort of religious séance. The sound was eventually tracked to a loudspeaker, connected to the church upstairs. Someone had left it on.

The lecture was to be given by a retired headteacher of an Edinburgh Primary School, Margaret Carnie, assisted by her twin sister. Both wore cardigans and at first I could not tell them apart, till they started good-humoured sisterly bickering, the one about to give the talk telling the other not to interrupt. She began with an apology. She had planned to show a video film of Samoa, taken specially on her recent visit by a gentleman friend, but alas, his video was stolen at the airport. Instead, her lecture would be a slide show, using her holiday snaps. She was sorry, but they were not meant for public consumption – as she herself appeared in almost all of them! We all smiled indulgently.

In the event, the slide show was most interesting. They hadn't gone into Vailima itself, but they showed the exterior of the house, before the Mormons' arrival, with a large Mercedes outside. The large Mercedes was there in every picture of the house. It hasn't got an engine, Miss Carnie explained. It was there for show.

After the lecture, we broke for coffee and I talked to various members. One woman gave me a postcard of RLS, produced for the society. Two others came up to me and said that they were Stevenson family, but they did not like to talk about it. One of them, who said her grandmother was one of your first cousins, gave me some good advice on Davos, but I had to admit I never managed to fit that in. The other said her great-grandfather was one of your uncles and she had some Stevenson family papers at home which I could see, but she did not care for publicity.

My friend Lady Dunpark of Heriot Row was there and she introduced me to Sir John Leslie, who was visiting her from Ireland. 'I'm proud to say I've shaken his hand – which means I've shaken the hand of a man who has shaken the hand of a man who has shaken the hand of RLS.' I didn't quite catch the exact connection. That's the problem of coming from a family where both your mother and father had masses of brothers and sisters. I think half of Edinburgh is now related to you.

In the second half, we were entertained by two members who gave a dramatised reading of *Thrawn Janet*, done in broad

Scots. I found it a bit hard to follow, but it was performed with great enthusiasm and emphasis.

Afterwards, I spoke to the club's secretary, Alistair Ferguson, Writer to the Signet. He 'inherited' the job in 1974 as the then junior partner of a firm of solicitors where Charles Guthrie, son of Lord Guthrie, your old Spec friend, was senior partner and first secretary of the club. Someone from the firm has traditionally been the club's secretary, thanks to Lord Guthrie's involvement in its foundation. Great literary names of their day, such as J.B. Priestley, Walter de la Mare and John Buchan, have addressed the annual dinner. Originally the club owned 8 Howard Place and ran it as a museum, but sold it in 1963 when the contents were transferred to the Lady Stair's House Museum. The official membership, when Alistair took over in 1974, was 200. 'But many of them were dead.'

Today, they have 300 active members and hold five events a year – outings and lectures. Half the members live in Edinburgh, a quarter elsewhere in Scotland, and the rest in England or abroad. In 1985 they launched a campaign to have an RLS memorial in Edinburgh, which brought in a lot of money. A simple memorial tablet was unveiled in Princes Street Gardens, but there were heated discussions about whether the rest of the money should go on a piece of sculpture. In the end, part was used to set up a medical fund, the 'RLS Memorial Trust for the alleviation of respiratory disease in children', of which I'm sure you would approve. But there is still no public statue of you in Edinburgh. Why should California have led the way all these years?

Now let's move to Hawaii. Everybody today has heard of Waikiki Beach, that unspoilt haven where you spent six months in 1889, and few want to go there. It's mass tourism gone mad, the most over-developed beach in the world. That's the usual image. But there was one good reason for stopping off in Hawaii, on my way home from Samoa. I wanted to meet someone called Robert Van Dyke, whose name I'd been given by the Mormons. I'd been told he was reclusive and slightly eccentric, but if I managed to see him I'd learn more from him about your life than from anyone else alive.

I arrived in the middle of the night by plane from Fiji. Even in the dark, I could see that Honolulu was just another big American city (population 350,000), with looming skyscrapers. I went straight to sleep in my hotel, the Halekulani, very palatial, right on Waikiki Beach. It was mid-morning when I awoke. All I could see from my bed was a magnificent seascape, with a few yachts and the fringes of a perfectly formed white beach. Had all the stories about Waikiki been unfair? Then I realised my blinds were only half-pulled. Once I opened them, I got the full horror. Standing on the beach, leaving only a few inches of sand, was a line-up of giant hotels, twenty to thirty storeys high. The proportions were all wrong, like a warship in a duck pond, a jumbo jet landing on a village green. All these massive hotels, fighting over one tiny strip of sand. I could understand why real estate in Waikiki was the most expensive in the USA.

I had breakfast in my room, then I rang a number I'd been given for Mr Robert E. Van Dyke. His mother answered, sounding ill, and I apologised for troubling her. She gave me another number, but there was no reply. I rang his mother again, more apologies, asking if Mr Van Dyke could ring me. Then I went for a walk on the beach.

It had looked appalling from above, viewed from my tenth-floor bedroom, a mass of bodies, but once I was down amongst them I was surprised how clean it was, no litter or rubbish, with showers at regular intervals, free for all to use, lots of life guards, and no signs of hustlers or beach-traders. Horrible, but organised, regulated horribleness.

I walked the full length, towards Diamond Head, then returned to the hotel and tried Mr Van Dyke again. No luck. I went down for a swim in the hotel pool, leaving instructions where I could be found. I didn't fancy the sea, as to reach it would mean stepping over a million bodies.

Mr Van Dyke rang me while I was swimming and I took his call at the pool-side. I told him about my book and asked if he could spare me some time. 'I am very busy today. I have been sent a clock belonging to Aunt Maggie and am trying to sell it for the owner.' You mean Mrs Stevenson, Louis's mother? 'Yes, if only you'd come yesterday.'

I kept him talking, asking about the clock, burbling on about where I'd been, what I knew, as it's vital to flash your knowledge, display your credentials, pass certain unspoken tests before any expert will open up. All right then, in one hour's time. He'd be at my hotel.

An hour passed. He arrived at my hotel by taxi, a rather hefty middle-aged man wearing a Hawaiian shirt. From the back of the taxi, he struggled to pull out a large shopping basket on wheels, the supermarket sort, loaded with plastic bags, brown paper carriers, old folders, things wrapped in faded bits of cloth and worn blankets. He explained the disarray, saying he'd gathered the stuff very rapidly from five locations where he kept his Stevenson collection. He wheeled it all across the reception hall and into the lift. At least no one would think of mugging him. His possessions looked too humdrum.

For the next seven hours, he talked about you, Louis. Firstly over lunch in the hotel, and then back in my room, where he eventually opened up his scruffy packages to reveal a treasure trove of unbelievable objects, things I never imagined still existed.

Robert is aged fifty-six, an American Hawaiian, cultivated, literary, reclusive, that much was clear. I picked up the impression he was a bachelor, as it came out he lived alone in a flat at one end of Waikiki, but also cared for his eighty-five-year-old mother, living at the other end of Waikiki. It seemed he had been married several times.

He also gave the impression he had never worked, saying he had private means, then another time he said he had once owned the largest old jewellery manufacturing firm in Honolulu. His family on his mother's side had lived in Hawaii a hundred years, descendants of Charles I, another branch had been among the first Americans, arriving in the *Mayflower* in 1620. His father's family had been Dutch aristocrats, arriving in 1638. His father had had a private income. He had gone to several colleges in the States, taking courses he wanted, leaving to return to Hawaii, with no desire for a degree. 'As I wasn't going to work in any firm, I saw no reason to bother with a degree.' After college, he travelled, round the States, round the world many times. Since then he has devoted himself to collecting. Some of his main themes have been Mark Twain, Jack London, Oscar Wilde, George Bernard Shaw and you.

He had grown up in a family of collectors and had been exposed to the wonderful world of Stevenson as a child of eight when he first met Lloyd Osbourne and his sister Belle. In the company of his mother and grandmother, they had called upon them in Santa Barbara. Lloyd was then seventy-eight and Belle eighty-eight. Before the family called again the next year, 1947, Lloyd had died and Belle was in the process of selling her large home, 'Serena'. 'Belle had given much of the Vailima furniture to the "Stevenson House" museum in Monterey, but the barn remained full of wonderful furniture and boxes of books from the library at Vailima. A great "Treasure Island" of a barn. We were encouraged to take what we wanted. I've always regretted we didn't take more.

'Yes, the gossip had been that Field, Belle's husband, had been Fanny's lover. One of the absurd legends that follows the Stevenson story. Field had been the son of Fanny's best friend, a girlhood friend of Indiana days. He became her travelling companion and helped her with editing a new set of Stevenson's works for Scribner's of New York. Field was independently wealthy, though twenty years separated them in age. From her marriage to Field in 1914, to his untimely death twenty years after, Belle spent the happiest days of her life.'

Robert got to know about the Vailima years at first hand from Belle and was given diaries, scrapbooks and letters about her life and Fanny's. Long after her death, he tracked down other people who had been given things by Belle. He looked in their attics and garden sheds, identified items from old photos. He acquired things from auctions and dealers, till today it would appear that he has the largest private collection of RLS material. He does not compare himself, though, to the great collections in the National Library of Scotland or Yale. His collection is different in that it is filled with many personal items of the entire Stevenson family.

He is not sure how many items he has, but the collection contains 173 of your letters. Of Fanny's letters, he recently acquired seventy-five new ones, bringing that total to 225. There is a great deal of furniture, seven tables, sixteen assorted chairs, cutlery, crystal, books, several trunks, including one filled with clothes which belonged to Fanny and Belle, and a strong box full of fabulous jewellery.

In 1983, Robert's mother sold the family home and alas most of the larger treasures were put into storage.

'I am a Belle and a Fanny fan. It always upsets me that Louis's old friends hated her so much, giving her titles such as an old witch, which was grossly unfair. Fanny's greatest fault was that she was a greatly independent woman, in a period of great clinging vines. Her worst fault in the male-dominated Victorian world was that she was an American. So the lies against her came into being and have been repeated generation unto generation. They went on about her dark skin, as if she were some kind of exotic native. Absurd. This woman worked in her garden constantly and wherever she lived she created a botanical wonder. Fanny was very different from the Victorian woman who barely saw the light of day out of her drawing-room. She was not powdered in ghastly porcelain-white.

'I do not believe either that she was mental in the last years in Samoa. She was simply, as we would understand it today, a woman undergoing menopause. Did you know that she had a baby at Vailima? She was fifty-one years old at the time. Not an impossibility with a woman who read all of the main medical journals of the day in an effort to keep her Louis alive. She refers to this event in a letter to her sister Cora which I have. It was a boy, stillborn at seven months. Buried in a tin box below the floor of the cellar. I have told the Mormons they should look for it. With the advanced techniques of DNA today we should have no trouble analysing that this is the child of Louis. We have many samples of Louis's hair as a baby, and at the time of his death.'

So they must have been sleeping together in Samoa? 'Well, why not . . . but not all the time. This was a man riddled with sickness who rose at all hours of the night. Of course they maintained separate bedrooms.'

I asked about the apparent lack of affection between them, the few moments of anything intimate in their diaries and letters.

'Anything of a sexual nature was omitted. You can see clearly where bits have been crossed out, great chunks of it in fact. All through the letters I have noted this. Louis was a world figure by the time Balfour did his biography and the family wished Fanny and Louis to be squeaky clean. Belle was always like this when we talked to her. She would have nothing bad ever said about Fanny.

'I like Fanny and Belle because they were so liberated, typical of many nineteenth-century women. They rolled their own cigarettes, like miners did. They were tough, yet soft and kind, and they were tough survivors out in a man's world. Much later women would crawl back into the closet.

'I have the original version of the cable which Fanny sent Louis. I do not wish to reveal the details, as I will probably publish it myself some day.' I suggested it might have something to do with her being ill, and he nodded. 'Belle was so furious with her mother when she sent the cable, that she went off on horseback and married Joe Strong.'

I asked how he knew that. He said it was in family letters and in Belle's diary in his possession. 'Sam gave Fanny and Louis $100 for their honeymoon. Did you know that? He sent her $100 a month while they were in Europe studying art. Her father in Indiana also gave her some $5,000 over the three years she was away. Sam, of course, was still supporting her when Louis arrived in California. Joe and Belle and their child Austin lived in Hawaii for some eight years, which is why Louis had come to stay here for six months in 1889. From the earliest days of his marriage Joe had had other women, long before Samoa. It was here though that the marriage began to break down. Austin went on to become a successful playwright, and Janet Gaynor as the heroine in his film *Seventh Heaven* won one of the earliest Academy Awards.

'I met Lloyd several times before his death, and even a child can realise something is wrong with an affected phoney British accent. By his marriage to Katharine, he had two sons, the second of which died in a Mexican brothel. Lloyd also fathered and acknowledged an illegitimate son named Sam Osbourne. . . .'

Robert in full flow was hard to stop. I did try to intervene several times, asking for his proof, but he was off on another anecdote. At last he started unwrapping the assorted bags and bundles, talking all the time and giving the history of every item. First came the jewellery, rolled up in a travelling jewel pouch made of cloth. He pulled out a bracelet made of your baby hair, cut when you were five. The front contained a miniature portrait of you, to the rear of this was a golden curl of your hair. Your mother had had the bracelet made on a trip to Paris. As you were an only child, she always feared you would die. Next came a locket worn by Fanny containing a baby curl and a lock snipped the night you died. The lettering reads 'RLS 1850' and on the reverse 'RLS 1894'. Then came a diamond lorgnette of Fanny's with a platinum chain of twenty-four one-carat diamonds.

'Fanny could finally afford expensive things as the royalties poured in. From six months' royalties on *Treasure Island*, she had enough to build a grand mansion in San Francisco at the corner of Hyde and Lombard, a magnificent building ninety years old.'

Again Robert dipped into the magic bag. Out came a handful of rings. The first was the topaz you were wearing the night you died. One of the three rings you bought in Sydney in 1893. Then came a large emerald and diamond ring cut from Fanny's hand the night she died; a toe ring worn by Belle in Samoa; an earring you gave to Fanny as her first present; and Fanny's wedding ring.

Each ring was produced with a flourish, held up for my inspection. I was allowed to try them on, if just on my pinkie. Robert explained the stones and the settings, detailing the provenance. Now and again if I queried whether a ring had been on Fanny's finger or on Belle's toe he would produce photographs from another bundle, some of which I recognised, if only from copies. With the aid of a small magnifying glass, he identified the exact ring on the exact digit.

One of the biggest pieces of jewellery was a pearl- and diamond-encrusted piece that could be worn either as a necklace or as a head band. It had a matching bracelet. The pearls had been found in the lagoons of Tahiti in the voyage of the *Casco* from 1888–9. There are several well-known pictures in which this necklace appears. One of the smallest items was the pair of gold cufflinks you were wearing the night you died.

'See this locket on this necklace,' Robert said, pulling something out of the bag and holding it up to the light. 'This used to contain cyanide. Fanny put it there at the time of the Samoan wars, just in case. The idea was that she and Belle would commit suicide rather than have their heads cut off. She always had a secret hideout in every house she ever lived in. This even goes back to childhood in Indiana, where she lived in great fear of the summer storms of lightning and thunder. She had her secret crawl space in Vailima, just a small cupboard. I've told the Mormons to be on the watch for that.'

Next came a bundle of books, wrapped in brown paper. There was your own copy of *A Child's Garden of Verses* containing sketches done by you. 'Nobody in the world knows this exists. I've first editions of all of Stevenson's works, both English and American editions. Nearly every one is signed by Stevenson to some member of the family. Including *Charity Bazaar*. Aunt Maggie sold her last five copies of it to an American book dealer in 1893 for one pound a piece and I have one of them.'

From another bundle came photographs, a great many of them unpublished. One of the Vailima photographs shows a telephone in the great hall, which I never knew existed. 'They were the first people to have one in Samoa. All it did was connect by dynamo the upstairs with downstairs. A curiosity, used with great show.' One very old photograph showed Mrs Stevenson, your mother, pregnant with you. There were also numerous paintings and sketches done by Fanny and Belle. Plus Fanny's own cookery book with her handwritten recipes.

'Do you know what this is?' Robert said, producing a small statue. 'This is Ko Ung, the Inca idol which a sea captain gave to Belle. The whole family made wishes to it for good luck and health. Don't you remember – Louis wrote a number of poems about it.'

We spent a long time going through one of Belle's scrapbooks, filled with cuttings, photographs and letters. Then there was her own copy of her book *This Life I've Loved*. This contains twice as many photographs as appeared in the published version. It also contains handwritten notes and additions. Robert hopes to republish Belle's book one day in its entirety, perhaps in a limited edition for collectors. I got him to take some snapshots of me with some of the items, such as Fanny's locket, the ring you were wearing when you died, proof when I got home that I hadn't imagined it all. Then I asked about his future plans for his collection. After all, he has no children.

'Nobody knows about me, or what I have, so all is pretty safe at present, but it is a problem. I do worry about fire and theft.

Keeping things in storage is very expensive. I did once in 1990 write to the RLS Club in Edinburgh, because I was travelling there on a holiday and offered to host a luncheon or a tea to show many of my treasures, but no one answered. Oh well. If they wanted anything for a 1994 exhibit I should probably have to say no. You know most of the furniture I have is Chippendale collected by Thomas Stevenson and there are today some very valuable pieces. The letters, papers and pictures I shall probably leave to Yale University. The personal material – who knows? As to its value, how the hell would I ever know? I am not trying to sell it and really don't care. I was a lucky little kid fifty years ago to have acquired all of this. I love it, because I love Fanny, Louis and Belle.'

Notes

Notes and further information on the present-day chapters which may help those desirous of following the RLS trail.

Chapter Two: Edinburgh
Birth House – 8 Howard Place. Not open to the public.
Colinton Manse, Colinton. House not open but church and graveyard are.

Chapter Four: Edinburgh
Simpson's House – at 52 Queen Street Gardens. Now owned by the Church of Scotland. 'Discovery Room' can be visited by appointment. Tel 031-225 1054.
17 Heriot Row – Lady Dunpark has now given the house to her son John Macfie and his family and is living elsewhere in Edinburgh. Not open to the public. Lord Dunpark died in 1993.
Lady Stair's House Museum, Lawnmarket, tel 031-225 2424.

Chapter Six: Edinburgh
National Library of Scotland, George IV Bridge, EH1 1EW. Tel 031-226 4531.
Other Edinburgh sites associated with RLS: Swanston Cottage, plaque outside; Hawes Inn, South Queensferry, tel 031-331 1990, used in *Kidnapped*.
Accommodation: Most splendid b. & b.s in Edinburgh are next door to each other in the New Town; Mrs Sibbet at 26 Northumberland St, EH3 6LF, tel 031-556 1078, and Mrs Smith at number 28, tel 031-557 8036. Booking vital. If you want to go at Festival time, ring one year ahead.

Chapter Eight: Cévennes
Donkey hire – André du Lac, Fugères, Saint-Martin 43150, Le Monastière-sur-Gazeille, tel 71 03 80 07.
Recommended hotel near Monastière: Hôtel de la Loire, 43490, Goudet, tel 71 57 16 83.

Recommended map, 32 francs – Sur Les Pas de Stevenson, FFRP,
8 Avenue Marceau, 75008, Paris, tel 723 62 32.
Tourist Information for Cévennes – Parc National des Cévennes,
BP 15, 48400 Florac, tel 66 45 01 75.
Monastery – Abbaye de Notre Dame des Neiges, 07590 Saint-Laurent-
les-Bains, tel 66 46 00 68.

Chapter Ten: Monterey
Stevenson's House is at 530 Houston St. Information on guided tours
from Monterey State Historic Park, 210 Olivier St, Monterey, CA 93940,
tel 408 373 2103.
Old Monterey Preservation Society – 525 Polk St, Monterey, CA 93940
Hotel – Merritt House, 386 Pacific St, Monterey, 93940, tel 408 646 9686.

Chapter Twelve: San Francisco and Silverado
RLS's digs in SF were at 608 Bush St. Plaque outside. Monument
in Portsmouth Square, San Francisco.
Handy Hotel, very posh – Ritz Carlton, SF, tel 415 296 7465.
Silverado Museum – 1490 Library Lane, St Helena, CA 94574, tel
707 963 3757.

Chapter Fourteen: Hyères
RLS's house, Villa La Solitude – 4 Rue Victor Basch, plaque outside,
not open to the public.
L'Office du Tourisme, Park Hotel, Hyères, tel 94 65 18 55.
Hotel: Hôtel du Soleil, Rue de Rempart, tel 94 65 16 26.

Chapter Sixteen: Bournemouth
Skerryvore – 61 Alum Chine Road. House gone, now a small memorial
garden, always open.
Reference library – the Lansdowne, Bournemouth, BH1 3DJ, tel
0202 292021.
Tourist Information – Westover Rd, Bournemouth, BH1 2BU, tel
0202 789789.

Chapter Eighteen: Samoa
Aggie Grey's Hotel, Box 67, Apia – tel (010 685) 22880.
Western Samoa Visitors' Bureau, PO Box 2272, Apia, tel 20180.
Recommended beach hotel – Coconut Beach Club, PO Box 3684,
Apia, tel 20071.

Chapter Twenty: Samoa
Honorary British Consul, Bob Barlow, Kruise, Va'ai and Barlow.
NPF Buildings, Beach Rd, Apia, PO Box 2029.

Chapter Twenty-Two: Samoa
RLS Museum/Preservation Foundation Inc, PO Box 21, Utah, USA
84603 or PO Box 67, Apia, Western Samoa.

Chapter Twenty-Three

RLS 100 Steering Committee – co-ordinator, Helen Lawson, National Library of Scotland, George IV Bridge, Edinburgh, EH1 1EW.

Chapter Twenty-Four

RLS Club – secretary, Alistair Forbes, WS, 5 Albyn Place, Edinburgh, EH2 4NJ.

Select Bibliography

Note: To save space, Robert Louis Stevenson is referred to as RLS throughout.

Letters
The bulk of the manuscripts are in two places:
Beinecke Collection, Yale University, USA.
National Library of Scotland, Edinburgh.

Published letters:
The Letters of RLS, edited by Sidney Colvin, four volumes, 1923.
The Letters of RLS, edited by Bradford A. Booth and Ernest Mehew, Yale University, 1994. (Vols I and II. Six more volumes to come.)
RLS's Letters to Charles Baxter, edited by Ferguson, DeLancey and Waingrow, OUP, 1956.
From Saranac to the Marquesas and Beyond, by Margaret Isabella Stevenson [Letters from RLS's mother to her sister], 1903.

Contemporary Biographies, Diaries and Memoirs
RLS's Edinburgh Days, by Eve Blantyre Simpson, Hodder, 1898.
The Life of RLS, by Graham Balfour [official biography], Methuen, 1901.
Memories of Vailima, by Isobel Strong and Lloyd Osbourne, Constable, 1903.
Recollections of RLS in the Pacific, by Arthur Johnstone, Chatto, 1905.
Cummy, by Lord Guthrie, Otto Schulze, Edinburgh, 1913.
RLS, The Man and His Work, Bookman extra number, Hodder, 1913.
The Cruise of the Janet Nichol [Fanny Stevenson's Diary], Scribners, 1914.
RLS, Some Personal Recollections, by Lord Guthrie, W. Green, Edinburgh, 1920.
The Life of Mrs RLS, by Nellie van de Grift Sanchez [Fanny's sister], Chatto, 1920.

RLS, his Work and Personality, edited by St John Adcock, Hodder, 1922.
I Can Remember RLS, edited by Rosaline Masson, Chambers, 1925.
RLS and his Sine Qua Non, by Adelaide Boodle, John Murray, 1926.
Cummy's Diary, edited by Robert T. Skinner, Chatto, 1926.
The Colvins and their Friends, by E.V. Lucas, Methuen, 1928.
This Life I've Loved, by Isobel Field, Michael Joseph, 1937.
Our Samoan Adventure [Fanny's Diary], edited by Charles Neider, Weidenfeld, 1956.

Later Biographies and Studies
Stevenson's Shrine, by Laura Stubbs, De La More Press, 1903.
The Faith of RLS, by John Kelman, London, 1903.
In the Track of Stevenson, by J.A. Hamerton, 1907.
On the Trail of RLS, by Clayton Hamilton, Hodder, 1915.
A Book of RLS, by George Brown, Methuen, 1919.
A Life of RLS, by Rosaline Masson, 1923.
RLS, Man and Writer, by J.A. Steuart, London, 1924.
RLS, by G.K. Chesterton, London, 1927.
RLS and the Scottish Highlands, David Morris, Eneas Mackay, 1929.
RLS at Davos, by W.G. Lockett, Hurst and Blackett, 1940.
The Strange Case of RLS, by Malcolm Elwin, 1950.
Voyage to Windward, by J.C. Furnas, Faber, 1952.
The Violent Friend, by Margaret Mackay [biography of Fanny Stevenson], Dent, 1968.
RLS and his World, by David Daiches, London, 1973.
RLS, by Paul Binding, Oxford, 1974.
RLS, by James Pope Hennessy, London, 1974.
The Cévennes Journal, edited by Gordon Golding, Mainstream, 1978.
The RLS Companion, edited by Jenni Calder, Paul Harris, 1980.
Stevenson and Victorian Scotland, edited by Jenni Calder, Edinburgh University Press, 1981.
The Prose Writings of RLS, by Roger Swearingen, Macmillan, 1980.
RLS, The Critical Heritage, edited by Paul Maixner, Routledge and Kegan Paul, 1981.
RLS and the Beach of Falesa, Barry Menikoff, Edinburgh University Press, 1984.
Footsteps, by Richard Holmes, Hodder, 1985.
RLS Treasury, by Alanna Knight, Shepheard-Walwyn, 1985.
RLS in the South Seas, by Alanna Knight, Mainstream, 1986.
RLS, A Life Study, by Jenni Calder, Hamish Hamilton, 1980.
Dead Man's Chest, by Nicholas Rankin, Faber, 1987.
Dreams of Exile, by Ian Bell, Mainstream, 1992.
RLS, by Frank McLynn, Hutchinson, 1993.

Works

Published works, in individual book form (as opposed to the collected editions, such as the Edinburgh or the Tusitala Editions), arranged in chronological order of appearance, with brief details and some personal comments to assist those who might wish to try some of the lesser-known works.

(*The Pentland Rising*, 1866, a small historical pamphlet, and *The Charity Bazaar*, a four-page sketch, are not included as they were private publications, though they do appear in the Collected Editions.)

Stars: My personal ratings on whether a book is a pleasure to read. *Treasure Island*, *Kidnapped*, *Dr Jekyll*, *Travels with a Donkey* and *A Child's Garden of Verses* hardly need recommending, but there are others which have been overlooked and are underrated.

 ★★★ Should not be missed.
 ★★ Highly recommended.
 ★ Interesting.

1. *An Inland Voyage*, 1878, Kegan Paul. Travel. Account of a canoe trip taken on the Belgium–France borders with Walter Simpson. Frontispiece by Walter Crane. Nothing much happens, but very charming, amusing, some good descriptions of people and conversations, nicely reflective on the human condition. ★★★
2. *Edinburgh, Picturesque Notes*, 1879, Seeley, Jackson and Halliday, London. Portrait of Edinburgh life and legends, originally appeared as a series of magazine essays. Scathing, racy, colourful, anti-Edinburgh lawyers, weather, hypocrisy. Loved by everyone in Glasgow. ★★
3. *Travels with a Donkey in the Cévennes*, 1879, Kegan Paul. Travel. Frontispiece by Crane. Journey with Modestine from Monastier to, rather than in, the Cévennes. Highly praised, right from the beginning. More serious, more historical than *Inland Voyage*, but not as light and charming. Written at a fairly unhappy time in his life, because Fanny had flown. Signs of padding. Not much fun, but loved by schoolteachers as a classic

of fine travel writing. ★★

4. *Virginibus Puerisque*, 1881, Kegan Paul. Collected essays, written in his mid-twenties, most of which had appeared in the *Cornhill Magazine*. Sold slowly as a book, but interesting for RLS fans to see his youthful views on Marriage ('man becomes slack, selfish, fatty'), on Hope, Love, Truth, Death, etc. Some wise observations, some clever remarks, but a lot of word-spinning. A bit stodgy for today's tastes. ★

5. *Familiar Studies of Men and Books*, 1882, Chatto and Windus. More collected essays, but literary and learned this time – on Victor Hugo, Burns, Pepys, John Knox. Shows the breadth of his reading, but not much of his wit.

6. *New Arabian Nights*, 1882, Chatto and Windus. Short stories, so some fiction at last. The best is *The Suicide Club*, which has a brilliant plot. Also good is *The Rajah's Diamonds* and *The Pavilion on the Links*. Great fun, even when melodramatic and implausible. ★★

7. *Treasure Island*, 1883, Cassell. Novel. Originally called *The Sea Cook*. Published in episodes in *Young Folks*, author 'Capt George North'. Written to amuse his young stepson Lloyd while on a rainy holiday in Braemar, taking all the clichés from boys' adventure stories of the time, but making it literary, polished and exciting. Quiet start amongst young readers, but the book version made him famous with adults. Gladstone loved it. Endlessly reprinted and filmed. A true classic. Long John Silver, Ben Gunn now part of our heritage. ★★★

8. *Silverado Squatters*, 1883, Chatto and Windus. Journal of his honeymoon, spent in a disused silver mine in the Napa Valley, California, 1880. Very personal, unlike *Travels with a Donkey*, thus fascinating for anyone interested in his life, or the period. Good character sketches, topographical descriptions, cleanly, briskly written. ★★★

9. *Prince Otto*, 1885, Chatto and Windus. Novel, set in an imaginary German principality. Second attempt at long fiction, totally different from *Treasure Island*. He saw it as a romantic comedy and tried very hard to get it right, writing some chapters six times, but it is a failure. Sentimental, dreary, silly, unless of course it was meant as a fable and we have all missed the point.

10. *A Child's Garden of Verses*, 1885, Longmans. Originally *Penny Whistles – for Small Whistlers*. Memories of his own childhood in Edinburgh, dedicated to his old nurse, Cummy. Charming without being cute, witty without being winsome, wise without being world-weary. Classic childhood poems, for all ages. ★★★

11. *More Arabian Nights*, 1885, Longmans. Also called *The Dynamiter*. The only book he wrote in collaboration with his wife Fanny, thank goodness. Long, mostly very silly sequence of connected stories which start with some Irish bombers. Interesting introduction, added later by Fanny, which explains how it was written in France as an amusement when RLS was very ill. ★

12. *The Strange Case of Dr Jekyll and Mr Hyde*, 1885, Longmans.

Long short story. 'I was dreaming a fine bogey tale,' said RLS when Fanny woke him from a nightmare one morning in Bournemouth. Wrote it in three days, Fanny did not think it worked, so he burned it and wrote it again. Overnight sensation. Quoted in London pulpits, loved in New York. Now passed into almost every language. ★★★

13. *Kidnapped*, 1886, Cassell. Novel. Unlike *Treasure Island*, it was based on a real historical incident, the Appin murder of 1752 in the Scottish Highlands. Combines historical romance with a thumping good adventure. Another children's classic. ★★★

14. *The Merry Men*, 1887, Chatto and Windus. Collection of short stories. Title story preposterous, but book worth reading for *Markheim*, first-class murder story cum morality tale, *Will o' the Mill* and *The Treasure of Franchard*. *Thrawn Janet* is in Scots dialect. ★★

15. *Memories and Portraits*, 1887, Chatto and Windus. Collected essays. The best are the part-biographical ones – *The Foreigner at Home* (about being Scottish), *Thomas Stevenson* (his father), *A College Magazine* (student days), *A Penny Plain and Tuppence Coloured* (childhood games). Fascinating for true RLS fans. ★★

16. *Underwoods*, 1887, Chatto and Windus. Poems – first collection for adults. Contains his 'Requiem' ('Home is the sailor'), but mostly sickly and dreary. Dedicated to his doctors. Presumably they were pleased.

17. *Memoir of Fleeming Jenkin*, 1888, Longmans. RLS's only biography, though he did start others. Jenkin was the distinguished Professor of Engineering at Edinburgh, friend and mentor to RLS. Interesting for the light it throws on RLS's student days. ★

18. *The Black Arrow*, 1888, Cassell. Successor to *Treasure Island*, also a serial in *Young Folks*, set in rural England during the Wars of the Roses. Young readers loved it, more than *Treasure Island*, but RLS himself dismissed it as 'tushery'. He was right.

19. *The Wrong Box*, 1889, Longman. Novel, co-written with his stepson Lloyd Osbourne. Meant as a black farce. 'So silly, so gay, so absurd,' said RLS correctly. Yet it has twice been turned into a film, so it must have something.

20. *The Master of Ballantrae*, 1889, Cassell. Novel – longest one so far. Starts in Jacobite Scotland and ends in the USA. Ambitious tale of family downfall, which RLS found difficult to write, stopping and starting, but never quite succeeding. ★

21. *Ballads*, 1890, Chatto and Windus. Poetry. Folk legends, written in verse. A failure with the public, who preferred RLS in prose or writing for children.

22. *Across the Plains*, 1892, Chatto and Windus. Travel. Stage two in RLS's journey to California in 1879. First stage was by sea (*Amateur Emigrant*) – this is the train journey across the USA (plus some other essays). Thin and lacking in incident, but he was tired and ill. ★

23. *The Wrecker*, 1892, Cassell. Novel, longest so far, written in collaboration with Lloyd Osbourne, never a good sign. Meant to be a

mystery thriller, with confidence men and crooks, using locations RLS knew well, such as Paris, San Francisco, Edinburgh, the South Seas. Some snappy dialogue, but mainly tedious.

24. *Three Plays*, 1892, David Nutt. All written with W.E. Henley. Their first play, *Deacon Brodie*, an Edinburgh melodrama, has a good plot and was performed once in the West End in 1884, convincing Henley that they were about to make their fortune. *Beau Austin*, a stylish comedy of manners, was also performed in London, with Beerbohm Tree in the lead. *Admiral Guinea*, a slave-trader drama which includes the character of Blind Pew, was not performed till after RLS's death. They wrote a fourth and final play, *Macaire*, a supposedly literary farce, which again was not produced in RLS's lifetime. In the end, playwriting was a mistake, a waste of time and talent. They are unlikely to be performed again, and are not worth reading, alas, not even as mistakes.

25. *A Footnote to History*, 1892, Cassell, 1892. The history of Samoa from 1883 to 1891, not a riveting subject, even at the time. Readers in London and New York ignored it in droves, yet RLS put so much into it. More misdirected energies.

26. *Island Nights' Entertainments*, 1893, Cassell. Fiction – three long stories set in the South Seas, one of which, *The Beach of Falesa*, is considered a minor masterpiece, full of sex and violence. *The Bottle Imp* and *The Isle of Voices* are not quite as strong. ★★

27. *Catriona*, 1893, Cassell. Novel – the sequel to *Kidnapped*, again with David Balfour, written after an interval of six years, by popular demand. More historical, more legal than *Kidnapped*, with less excitement, but it does have a love interest. RLS himself thought highly of it, the sort of fiction he wanted to write. His public loved it. Now seems too involved. ★

28. *The Ebb-Tide*, 1894, Heinemann. Novel – Pacific melodrama about nasty people. First draft written with Lloyd Osbourne, then RLS finished it off, with a struggle. The public did not like it much.

29. *The Amateur Emigrant*, first appeared in Edinburgh Edition of 1895, now usually in one volume with *Across the Plains*. First stage of his Atlantic journey. His father hated it, thinking it disgusting, mixing with such low-class people, and withdrew it from publication. A social documentary, brilliantly written. ★★★

30. *Weir of Hermiston*, 1896, Chatto and Windus. Unfinished novel he was working on when he died in 1894 – which looked like being his masterpiece. Feels like it, with dramatic father-son relationship, two excellent women characters, great narrative drive. Probably would have been three times longer, but still enough there to admire and enjoy. ★★★

31. *St Ives*, 1897, Heinemann. Novel, also unfinished, but he was on the last chapters, so it is almost all there, though Quiller-Couch kindly finished it off. Romantic adventure of French aristocrat held in Edinburgh Castle. RLS knew it was a potboiler.

32. *Songs of Travel*, 1896, Chatto and Windus. Poetry. Posthumous collection of verses, mainly written on his Pacific cruises.

33. *In the South Seas*, 1900, Chatto and Windus. Travel. Account of his first Pacific cruises, on the *Casco* and the *Equator*, before they ended up on Samoa. Good descriptions of people met and places visited, not so gripping on native legends, which was what Fanny warned him against, but a fascinating read. ★★

34. *Tales and Fantasies*, 1905, Chatto and Windus. Three strong stories which had appeared earlier in magazine form. *The Misadventures of John Nicholson* is interesting for the father-son relationship. *The Story of a Lie* is a good tale but with a poor ending. Best is *The Body Snatcher*. ★★

35. *The Art of Writing*, 1905, Chatto and Windus. Collected essays – best is on how he came to write *Treasure Island*. ★

36. *Lay Morals*, 1911, Chatto and Windus. Yet more collected essays. Most interesting is the Father Damien letter. ★

37. *Records of a Family of Engineers*, 1912, Chatto and Windus. Biographical fragments of his family history, unfinished on his death.

Index